THE COMPLETE CENTRE-FORWARD

THE AUTHORISED BIOGRAPHY OF
TOMMY LAWTON

BY
DAVID McVAY
&
ANDY SMITH

SPORTSBOOKS

First published in Great Britain by
SportsBooks Limited
24 St George's Square
Worcester
WR1 1HX

© David McVay & Andy Smith 2000
First Published 2000

Front cover from a painting in the Tom Lawton collection of
his father playing for England against Switzerland.

A catologue record for this book is available from
the British Library

ISBN 1 899807 09 8

Printed and bound in England by
Redwood Books Ltd.,
Trowbridge, Wiltshire.

This book is dedicated to Tommy Lawton, Wilf Mannion,
Frank Swift and Sir Stanley Matthews, without whom...

Acknowledgements

A whole host of people generously gave up their time to talk to us about
Tommy Lawton including Wilf Mannion, Sir Stanley Matthews and Don
Mosey, all three, unfortunately, are no longer with us. Many others also
contributed to this project in many different ways Our grateful thanks to
you all.

Tommy Asher, Mike Bondy (MJB Research), David Bull, Bryon Butler, Mike
Carey, Bert Collins (Collins Sports, Northampton), David Collins, Chris
Cowdrey , Lord Cowdrey of Tonbridge, Gareth Davies, Ian Davies, George
Edwards, Sir Tom Finney, Ian Garland, Emma Gilkes (Hulton Getty), Cyril
Griffen, Angela Hall (Liverpool Daily Post & Echo), Emma Harris (PA
News), Gerry Harrison, Don Haworth, Lynne Hill (Associated Press),
Chris Hilton, Duncan Holley, John Holmes, John Hughes, Billy Ivory,
Edgar Jessop Oswaldtwistle), T G Jones, Steve Kirby (Eskay Books), Tim
Lawton Jnr, Steve Lewis (Sports Bookshop, Cardiff), Dave Luxton
(Sportspages), Arthur Milton, Trevor Mitchell, Cliff Morgan, John Motson,
Randall Northam (SportsBooks), Nottingham Evening Post Library , Guy
Oliver, Gerald Phillips, Sabrina Phipps (Solo), Jackie Sewell, Richard
Shepherd, Ray Spiller (Assocn Football Statisticians, Ceri Stennett, Nick
Syrett, Derek Tapscott , Gordon Watson , Jack Wheeler , Barrie Williams,
Tommy Wilson, Daniel Valla
Photography, Haverfordwest

CONTENTS

INTRODUCTION
ANDY SMITH

Whenever I went back to Nottingham, I would call in and see him. Thin and fragile in later years, he walked slowly, occasionally using his stick, but his back was straight and his head was held high with that famous Lawton nose jutting proudly at the world.

One Saturday in October 1996 (after Sports Report *of course) I knocked at his door. He seemed smaller than usual, frailer. "I've got something for you," I said and handed him a copy of Cliff Morgan's autobiography. Tommy peered at the message which Cliff had carefully inscribed on the title page – 'To my great friend and hero, in appreciation of your class and style.' Tommy's eyes immediately filled with tears. Recognition from one sporting legend to another.*

He was tired, I could see that. I showed him the Notts County book I had bought second-hand a few days earlier. He autographed it, the hand a little more spidery than before, but the 'T' and the 'L' retained that characteristic flourish.

"What's happening at Notts these days, Tom? They need you back, obviously." Tommy did not joke about these things – "They're a waste of time." The judgement of Lawton.

I did not realise how little time he had left. Within a week his housekeeper, Irene, phoned to tell me. Pneumonia had set in, he had no appetite and was growing weaker.

It was inevitable.

Some months earlier, sitting in his room talking of Shearer and Shack, Seaman and Big Swifty, Tommy mused, "There were three of us, you know, three who played for England before and after the war – Sir Stan, Raich and me. And there were three who played in Cup Finals before and after the war – Raich, Willie Fagan and someone else. Who was it?" I did not know and combed the record books but could find no trace of a third. I enlisted the help of John Motson and neither could he.

"There are only two, Tom," I told him, but he did not believe me.

So, I bet when when he arrived at the gates of football's Valhalla, he would have made straight for his old pal and asked Big Swifty "Who was that third man?" And they would begin reminiscing and Big Swifty would bring out the pack of cards and the two of them, I can see them now, would start to laugh and Sir Stan and Wilf, smiling Joe and the great Dixie would gather round and it would be, "Do you remember when..."

CHAPTER ONE
STAR QUALITY

Aged 70 and more, he would eye visitors to his room coolly as if to say "I know why you're here. You're here because I'm Tommy Lawton." The interview, or photo-session, would then be conducted on his terms, in his time. He gave little away to those he did not know and nothing to those he did not trust. The desperate days of the sixties and seventies had, if anything, made him a much more private person.

From his first entry into professional football, his life had been recorded in headlines. He was a star. In their book *Masters of Soccer* Delaney and Edelston put it so well "His name was mispronounced with awe in every country in the world." Alex James, the great Arsenal and Scotland inside forward who played with some of the best centre-forwards of his era (like Hughie Gallacher) and against the others (like Bill Dean), insisted that Lawton was "the lightest mover of any big man who ever played football." It was Lawton's size, coupled with his easy, loping stride that gave him such an aura on the field. That, and his appearance – "his long, intent, sharp-eyed face, with the commanding nose and the sleek, black shining hair."

Whenever he ran onto a pitch the crowd would nod to each other and point at the handsome figure in the number nine shirt. He had a real presence.

The power in his legs that produced such speed also gave him his astonishing ability to outjump defenders. For so many of his generation, Lawton climbing head and shoulders above his markers in the penalty area to head for goal or down to his inside forwards was a thrilling, unforgettable sight. His ability to 'hang' in the air, waiting for the ball to come across, was likened, 40 years on, to Michael Jordan's aerobatics in the NBA. He had always been able to leap prodigious heights and developed the art further when he joined Everton in 1937. "I used to watch Dixie Dean training at Goodison; how he jumped for the ball, how he moved into position to shoot or to head. People have said that he 'taught' me everything. Well he didn't. Dixie was not what you would call a great teacher. I learned mostly from him by watching. The abilities he had couldn't be taught because they were part of the uncanny instinct he had for the game. His power to jump at the right time, the way he pinpointed the ball with his head or with either foot was, to me, nothing short of genius. Just by being with him, you could learn something. The one thing he did tell me, soon after I arrived at Goodison, was about moving my feet to get into position to head the ball. We were training one day and he just strolled over and said 'You think you can head the ball, don't you, son?' I said, 'Well, I'm not bad!' And he just came back with 'You'll be no bloody good 'til you move your feet more!' So I watched him for a bit and whereas I was waiting and then jumping, he was moving all the time, so that he was in the right position every time to take off and head it. It was good advice." Tommy was always disparaging about formal coaching. Watching and learning was preferable to "all that blackboard stuff" and simply by spending so much time on the training pitch and underneath the stands at Goodison with Dean, Tommy gleaned a mass of football knowledge. Dean was renowned as a generous man, but allowing Tommy to observe him at close quarters and so improve his own game was, according to Tommy,' quite amazing because he knew that I'd been bought to replace him." Lawton always maintained that Dean was the best header of a ball he ever saw – "he was better than me in the air. You couldn't say that Dixie was a complete centre-forward, he was a goal scoring machine, the best ever but I would say that Di Stefano and George Camsell were better all round players." Tommy obviously changed his mind about Dixie over the years. In *My Twenty Years of Soccer* he wrote that Dean's great shooting ability with his head and his feet, allied to his "incredible positional sense made him just about the most complete centre-forward you could possibly wish to meet." That was in 1955. By 1973, Di Stefano had been on the scene and Tommy had also remembered the virtues of Camsell.

Yet, it is difficult, if not impossible, to compare Di Stefano and Dean, ages apart, performing different functions in their teams. Di Stefano was widely recognised as a brilliant play-maker and goal scorer, the Argentine who led Real Madrid in their great years and who, along with Gento and later Ferenc Puskas, made them such an attraction world wide.

Camsell scored 59 goals in Division Two for Middlesbrough in 1926-27, only to be eclipsed a season later when Dean scored 60 for Everton in Division One. Camsell's goalscoring ability was uncanny (18 goals in nine games for England, yet still not certain of a place because of the claims of Dean, Pongo Waring and Ted Drake). He was a ruthless, accurate striker.

Still, the comparison between Dean at his peak and Lawton some ten years later is irresistible. Lawton said of Dean that he "timed his leaps to the split second and he could hit a ball as hard with his head as most men can with their feet." Denis Compton, meanwhile, after he had played on the left wing for England against Scotland in a 1943 war-time international at Maine Road thought that Lawton was the best centre-forward he had ever seen.(Lawton had scored four in England's 8-0 win that day). "Believe it or not," said Compton, "but Tom can actually 'steer' a ball with his head, and when you send over a cross that you feel is worthy of a goal, it is more than likely, if it is any good, that Lawton will nod it in the back of the net." Ron Greenwood, the former England manager, was a friend and great admirer of Tommy's. Greenwood was centre-half at Brentford when Lawton joined from Notts County. In his book, *Soccer Choice*, Greenwood recalled a match at Griffin Park in September 1952 between Brentford and

Blackburn Rovers. "The ball came in the air down the inside-left channel to him (Lawton). His outside-left (Les Smith) moved into position but as Tommy went up he saw Ron Suart coming across to intercept and, with the ball still coming, Tommy seemed to hang, adjust, let the ball go just a little bit further – and then nod it inside Suart for our winger to run onto. He made his decision and adjustment after he'd jumped!" All too often Lawton has been described along the lines of one of the "rugged attacking heroes of legend."

Yet Tommy was not the archetypal English centre-forward in the manner of Nat Lofthouse, Tommy Taylor and Bobby Smith or, later, Mick Jones, Malcolm Macdonald and Alan Shearer. He was the consummate all-rounder, seemingly without a weakness. Tall, strong, extremely lithe and athletic, with great control, he moved rapidly over any kind of surface and could have played an integral role in any system devised today. Strangely his former Everton team-mate T G Jones doubted whether his own abilities could be utilised in the modern game "Don't get me wrong, I'd like to play today, but I have no idea what position I'd play."

Tommy himself had no doubts "I'd play in exactly the same way – scoring goals and laying 'em on too! All the great players of my day, Matthews, Doherty, Carter, Mannion, they'd have no trouble in today's game. A great player will fit into any system." Compton thought that Lawton's greatness stemmed from "perfect balance – as in cricket – anticipation and above any and everything else, patient practice. No man could hope to become as talented as he without putting in a good deal of hard work." Lawton had certainly worked hard and the ethics of his first professional coach, Ray Bennion at Burnley and his Turf Moor drill, definitely paid off. As an amateur at Burnley, Bennion would have Lawton dribbling round the pitch and shooting at the 'B's' in the beer advertise-ments on the hoardings. Greenwood also thought that the intense practice of Lawton's early days at Burnley was invaluable. "It meant he had to keep the ball low and strike it very precisely (to hit the letters on the hoardings). This is one of the reasons why he very rarely lifted his shots into the crowd. He was a beautiful striker of the ball, hard, accurate and always with that flat trajectory."

Four days after turning professional at Burnley, Lawton scored a hat-trick against Tottenham that demonstrated his supreme ability and self confidence. The second goal was a header – the sort of goal that became a Lawton trademark in the subsequent 20 years. Even though he had just turned 17, he had the timing to outjump opponents, had developed the knack of being able to hang in the air at the top of his jump and direct the ball wherever he wanted.

That was October 1936. Turn the clock forwards to November 1947 when Lawton made his debut for Notts County in the Third Division (South) at Northampton Town. Once again he scored with a brilliant header as Notts won away for the first time that season. The Northampton centre-half given the onerous task of marking the then current England centre-forward was Bob Dennison who had played pre-war with Newcastle, Nottingham Forest and Fulham. "I just couldn't believe it," he said after the match. "I just couldn't believe that anyone could jump that high; not and head it in too!" Lawton was to leave many other Third Division defenders similarly bemused by the time Notts gained promotion three years later. Greenwood, who played with and against Lawton, said "I know from hard experience that he was a difficult man to stay with. It was no good trying to climb above him in the air, a hopeless exercise, so I always attempted to stay goalside of him, never more than a yard or two away, and do my best to intercept." Nijinsky – the prince of ballet dancers – was once asked how he performed 'the grand leap.' Apparently he replied "Well, you jump and at the top of the jump – you wait a little." Tommy was no ballet dancer, quickstep possibly, but that describes him perfectly in the action of heading a ball.

Maurice Edelston knew Tommy well. They played together in war-time internationals and in services games. Later they were in opposition when Edelston was at Reading and Lawton at Notts. "His climbing and sense of time and distance are as nearly perfect as possible,." wrote Edelston in 1949, a year after Tommy had been dropped by England. "Leaving the ground at exactly the right moment he appears to hover in the air at the height of his 'climb'... Any cross from the wings is directed goalwards as though jet propelled."

Tommy insisted that his style of game changed after his move to Notts County. He soon discovered that Third Division defenders moved slower than those in the top flight, but that the pass came through slower from colleagues too. He reasoned that if he stayed upfield in an orthodox centre-forward's role, he would see little of the ball so he adopted a deeper lying position – "more of a scheming inside-forward." Hours of practice with Jackie Sewell paid off, "the understanding between us became like mental telepathy." During the three seasons that Lawton and Sewell played together at County, Sewell scored 78 goals, Lawton 88 and he was main provider too! He once compared his position at Notts County to that which Sandor Hidegkuti played for Hungary in their great side of the fifties and Don Revie's acclaimed deep lying centre-forward role for Manchester City in 1954-55. "Judging by the publicity that Hidegkuti received you would have thought his was a new method of centre-forward play, but it was used before either Hidegkuti or Revie were even born! Alex James did it for Arsenal before the war, wearing number ten rather than number nine, but the game he played was no different from the game I played at Notts, Hidegkuti played for Hungary or Revie for the City. It's an excellent system, provided that you have the men to to make it work. Hidegkuti had Kocsis and Puskas to score the goals, Revie had Hart and Hayes, at Notts we had Sewell and Evans." (Evans was Billy Evans, with Notts from 1949 to 1952 but not primarily renowned as a goalscorer, only seven in Notts'

1950 promotion season, but this is probably simply a case of typical modesty from Tommy, who deep-lying or not, still top-scored for Notts that season with 31). At the start of his Everton career, Lawton capitalised on openings provided by Dixie Dean who had earlier been making goals for Jimmy Dunn.

Coming towards the end of his playing days, Lawton was helping Sewell become the most expensive player in British football and then, later still, at Arsenal, according to Edelston and Delaney: "the line swung on him like a compass on a pin. He scored relatively few goals, but the short accurate flicks from his forehead to either side made goals for Lishman and Tapscott and his majestically swept, low forward passes opened wide pathways for the wingers." Dean's craft of the '20s and '30s, learned by Lawton, was passed on to players of the '50s and '60s. Even later, when Tommy was manager at Notts County, he helped a couple of young centre-forwards learn their trade – Jeff Astle and Tony Hateley. The time-honoured method of producing good players has always been through experience, passed on from one generation to the next. Tommy's story begins in the early part of the last century, progresses through the War Years and the so-called Golden Age and into modern times. There will never be a satisfactory answer to the question of who was the best ever centre-forward. But wherever that little matter is discussed, Tommy Lawton deserves a mention.

CHAPTER TWO
SIMPLY THE BEST

Edelston and Delaney were certain of Tommy's position in the hierarchy of British centre-forwards. "We have seen many incomplete centre-forwards who were first class players and some of them played for England. Some could run and shoot like Milburn, who liked the ball on the ground; some could plan like Revie, from behind the line; some, like Drake, were powerful and could shake off punishment; some were bold and dangerous like Trevor Ford; some were cool, accomplished dribblers like Finney; delicate and accurate like Allen; some were big and strong and found the open spaces, like Kevan; Some could beat a man on the ground, some in the air, some could shoot on the turn, some could snap onto a through pass; some could marshall the line, some inspire it. Lawton could do it all."

Tom Finney had no hesitation in naming Lawton as the man who would lead his ideal forward line, though "under considerable pressure from Stanley Mortensen, Nat Lofthouse, Tommy Taylor, Jackie Milburn and Gary Lineker." The great Preston and England winger thought that "Lawton was the best of the bunch. The greatest header of the ball – his headers had the power of shots... there has never been a better all round number nine than Tommy Lawton."

Finney has always insisted that the display of the inside forwards against Wales at Maine Road in October 1946 was the best of its type he ever saw. The trio inside the two wingers, Finney and Bobby Langton of Blackburn, were Carter, Lawton and Mannion. "Every move they made was planned, every plan carried danger." Tommy did not recall the game with any great clarity or with the enthusiasm of Finney. He was, however, always delighted to score against his old Everton pal, T G Jones – 'Yanto.' – the Welsh centre-half.

At his home in Bangor, North Wales, as he approached his 80th birthday, T G reflected on the merits of the two great Everton centre-forwards he played with and against – Dixie Dean and Lawton. "Today, Tom Lawton would have been another Shearer," says T G. "Maybe even better. He was big, strong and accurate. He was a great header of the ball – some of the goals he scored just simply amazed me. Dixie was completely different. Tom was better on the ground than Dixie but not so good in the air. I don't think anyone was as good in the air as Dixie.

"Speed was about equal; in shooting and control, Tommy was the better of the two but they were both good in different ways. They were different types of people too. Dixie spent a good many years at Everton – he was adored and could do almost anything he wanted. Tom was young – only

13

17 when he arrived at Goodison and he had to behave himself. If he stepped out of line he would have been stamped on. He was quieter. Dixie was the boss."

As for Tommy, he always acknowledged that Dean was his idol and he never let it be suggested that he was a better player than Bill Dean. Journalists who saw both players at their peak generally agree that it was impossible to determine who was the best, but Charles Buchan, despite regarding the England team that beat Italy in 1948 as the finest he had ever seen did not pick one of the eleven in his *Manager's dream of a perfect team'*(1950). He went for Dean at centre-forward – "a wizard with his head and accurate with his feet... always in the right place at the right time," left out even Matthews and Swift as he chose players predominately of his own vintage, all pre-World War II and some pre-World War I. Perhaps a case of looking back a little too fondly and ignoring immediate evidence?

Once Lawton won his place in the England side in October 1938 he became a permanent fixture, not missing an official international until his last appearance in September 1948. As he played in an era when England were the strongest team in the world, the title "Best centre-forward in the world" was naturally applied to him.

Yet, like Buchan, not everyone agreed that he was the best of all time and some even disputed that he was the best of his own era. Stanley Matthews for example regarded Freddie Steele of Stoke City as being quicker than Lawton and thought that Steele, had it not been for injury, could have been the best centre-forward ever for England. Matthews cited Steele's "pace and change of pace" and his shooting with either foot to give him the edge over Lawton, who, nevertheless, was unrivalled in the air and the only player he could think of liable to match Steele.

This time, maybe, a little home town and club bias entering the equation here? Steele, like Matthews, was born in Hanley. Steele was a year younger than the great winger and their careers at Stoke City initially coincided. Between 1936 and 1937, Steele appeared six times for England and scored eight goals. Yet only once did he team up with Matthews in the England side – against Scotland at Hampden in April 1937, Steele scored but England lost 3-1, despite a brilliant display from Matthews on his recall to the team.

Providing centres from the left in five of Steele's six internationals was Joe Johnson, also of Stoke. Walter Winterbottom, during his days as Manchester United's centre-half, thought that Steele was pacy and difficult to mark but not in Lawton's class. He once summed up Steele as "a good all round centre-forward... a quick, elegant footballer, good with his head" adding by way of comparison "a little like Alan Gilzean." Now Gilzean, the Scottish international who was at Tottenham in the '60s and early '70s was a fine player, but more of a target man and provider than a goalscorer as his record of 93 in 343 league games indicates. Gilzean was not on a par with Lawton and, it has to be suspected, neither was Freddie Steele.

Like Matthews, Stan Mortensen, who played often enough with Tommy to appreciate his talents, also put him a close second in his catalogue of ideal centre-forwards. Not this time to Freddie Steele, but to Ted Drake. Mortensen appeared to suggest that Drake was more of a team man than Lawton when he wrote in *Football Is My Game* that Drake "never eased up and was completely unselfish, always on the look out for an opening for the inside fowards. He never gave a thought to the idea of conserving his energies with a view to playing just a little longer." He did admit that Lawton "at his very best was only a fraction behind Drake... with his tremendous shooting power and wonderful knack of heading a ball from a high centre..." Drake, according to Matthews was "as strong as a horse... give him a through ball and he ploughed through anything."

Drake was injured in a war-time match at Reading in 1945, effectively ending his career. Pre-war he had scored 124 goals in 168 league games for Arsenal and won five England caps between 1934 and 1938, scoring six goals. After Steele's run of caps, England tried a number of centre-forwards including Joe Payne, the ten goal man from Luton; George Mills of Chelsea; Mickey Fenton from Middlesbrough and Frank Broome of Aston Villa. Drake's form in Arsenal's championship season of 1938 earned him an England recall against France in May and he scored twice in the 4-2 win in Paris, but by the following October his place had gone to the precocious Lawton, who then played 23 consecutive full internationals either side of the war. Drake was a fine player, idolised at Highbury, but he failed to hold down an England place in the days when selectors met to vote on every position in the team. He was certainly worth more than five caps – but was he better than Lawton?

Another centre-forward to shoot to prominence was Albert Stubbins who had first played for Newcastle United in 1937. Through the war years he scored 245 goals in 199 appearances including 15 in five consecutive matches in 1941. In September 1946, he was bought by Liverpool for £12,500 and for them scored 75 goals in 161 league games before he retired in 1953.

In a war-time international against Wales in 1945, he had replaced Lawton as England's centre-forward. It was scant reward for a fine player. His supporters included the Newcastle manager, Stan Seymour who thought that "The only advantage Lawton might have over Stubbins is with his heading. Stubbins is cleverer on the ball." Even Tommy's great friend Frank Swift, the man he roomed with on England trips, his partner in playing all kinds of practical jokes and in impromptu comedy shows, hedged his bets when asked to name his best centre-forward. He went for Lawton or Hughie Gallacher. He explained his choice *in Football in the Goalmouth* – "Tommy is fast moving, beautifully balanced and, for a big fellow, a brilliant ball player; but Gallacher, like Matthews was uncanny... it was literally true that the only way to dispossess him was to kick him off the ball." Swift then declared "if you like your centre-forwards tall, then

Lawton is the best; if you go for the little man, then take Hughie Gallacher."

Gallacher, who played for 20 years in the Scottish and English Leagues, was at his peak between 1925 and 1935 when he was in the First Division with Newcastle United, Chelsea and Derby County. His record of 387 goals in 541 Scottish and English League matches, plus 24 in 20 full internationals, is outstanding. A pocket dynamo of a player, five feet four inches tall, he was a genius on the pitch and a rascal off it. He also happened to be a favourite of Tommy's.

In December 1934, Tommy was taken by Grandad Riley to see Gallacher play one of his first games for Derby County against Blackburn Rovers at Ewood Park. The little Scot had been signed from Chelsea for £2,750 just a month earlier. He was in dazzling form that day, scoring all five Derby goals in their 5-2 win. Afterwards, the 15-year-old would-be centre-forward met the 32-year-old real thing. "Young man," said Gallacher in the manner of Brian Clough many years later, "keep your nose clean and you'll do all right in this game." It was not the last meeting between the embryonic international and the battle-hardened veteran. Less than a year later, Lawton was playing for Burnley Reserves against Derby's second string at Turf Moor. Lawton had been blotted out of the first half by Ralph Hann, an uncompromising professional who had joined Derby from the north east. Lawton trooped off disconsolately at half-time thinking that he had failed miserably and would never make a footballer.

Suddenly, there was an arm around his shoulders and Gallacher telling the lachrymose Lawton "learn to cover the ball with your body. If you're being tackled from the right then keep the ball on your left. If they're coming in from the left then keep it on your right and they've got to come across you." Tommy could barely stammer out his thanks to 'Mr Gallacher,' overwhelmed at the kindly gesture from one of the game's great players.

Lawton and Gallacher had little in common in size or temperament. The diminutive Gallacher was constantly in trouble on the field because of his fiery nature. Once he was sent off for suggesting to a referee who asked for his name that if he did not know who he was then " he shouldn't be reffing the match." Tommy, six feet tall, always appeared to be coolly in control. Despite intense provocation, he was never booked.

Off the field, both men's private lives were frequently in turmoil – disputes with directors, failed marriages – but Tommy was never the big drinker that Gallacher was claimed to be. Like Gallacher, Tommy was always immaculately dressed, a stickler for being properly attired at all times; a collar and tie with a handkerchief in the top pocket. Like Lawton after the war, Gallacher played for both Chelsea and Notts County, ironically being replaced at Meadow Lane by Bill Dean, who had lost his place at Goodison to Lawton.

Both Gallacher and Lawton experienced hardship and poverty. Lawton confessing that he was often depressed enough to contemplate suicide.

Gallacher did kill himself – on a railway line at Low Fell in June 1957. Two players to whom he had offered advice were united in grief. The great Newcastle United and England centre-forward Jackie Milburn said "I could never understand how a man who had been idolised by thousands could feel so alone." At the time Tommy had just taken Kettering to the championship of the Southern League and accepted a lucrative offer to manage Notts County. He looked to be on his way in the management game. Like Milburn, he could not understand the reason for Gallacher's suicide but later, somewhat poignantly considering his own misfortunes, wrote that Gallacher had experienced a "fairly traumatic time off the field and in many ways he was a misunderstood man. Certainly nowhere near as black as people liked to paint him." By the time he wrote that in the *Hughie Gallacher Story* in 1989, Tommy knew the price of living in the goldfish bowl of fame.

CHAPTER THREE

1919-35 BOLTON
FORMATIVE YEARS

On October 6th 1919, Thomas Lawton was born at 43 MacDonald Street in Farnworth, a suburb of Bolton. He was named after his father, a signalman on the Lancashire and Yorkshire Railway at the nearby Moses Gate Junction. His mother, Elizabeth, was a weaver at the Harrowby Mill.

Considering the near endemic problems of the times, the unemployment and general poverty, the Lawtons were well off compared with other families in their district and the big, healthy baby was loved and well cared for, his mother having given up work. He was just 18 months old when his parents split up. Baby Tommy went with his mother to live in the house of James Hugh Riley, his grandfather, just off the Folds Road, closer to the centre of Bolton.

Grandad Jim was football mad. Before the war he had been an amateur with Turton Rovers, a club with a history going back further than Bolton Wanderers and a major influence on the game in the area. Riley encouraged his four sons, Jack, Fred, Harold and Jim to play and there was little doubt that his Grandad's influence would ensure that young Tommy would grow up with football an intrinsic part of the fabric of his life. Tommy always called his grandfather 'Dad.'

The Rileys were a mining family but in the '20s the Lancashire coalfield was not the place to be. Production had peaked there in 1913 and with seams becoming more difficult and uneconomic to mine, plus the slump in 1921 and the General Strike of 1926, pits closed down and men were laid off, the Rileys amongst them. In the mining communities, poverty was rife.

However, around Bolton, the cotton industry still employed about 58,000 in the 200 spinning mills, weaving sheds, finishing works and ancillary industries such as bleaching and dyeing. Production was in full swing and Tommy's mother, a skilled weaver, was employed full-time at the Denvale Mill, just off the Tonge Moor Road. She produced the only regular wage in a household of eight. The men were rarely offered more than one day's work a week. Home was a small terraced house in a street of 22 similar dwellings – communal lavatories in the yard outside; inside, two rooms and a scullery downstairs, two bedrooms upstairs.

Overcrowded, certainly, with seven adults and a baby packed in, but Tommy only remembered that "it was a good home, full of warmth and contentment. We never had money to spare but we never went hungry." If the men had been at work during the day, they washed in cold water in the tiny kitchen. Hot water was only ever a weekend occurrence, when a fire was lit, and, of course, on Mondays when it was used to wash the family's clothes.

Monday in childhood was a distinct memory for Tommy – "the house full of steam with clothes hanging on the 'maiden' (clothes horse) in front of the fire. On fine days, the washing would be hung out across the street. There were lines put up from our house to the Kyte's opposite. I remember my mother going mad once because someone had let the coalman drive his cart down the road and the clothes were all covered in smuts."

Generally, he saw little of his mother who worked a 12-hour day in the weaving sheds, so, consequently, he was always out and about with his uncles, especially Harold, Fred and Jack, "There were no playing fields around, so we'd go 'on the bottom' as we called it – just a strip of wasteland at the end of our street by the railway arches. We made goalposts with coats and jackets and we'd just play any time of day. On Sunday mornings, after church, there was usually a game organised against a team from another part of Bolton with sidestakes.

"My uncles would play and they'd get a tanner (6d=2p) a man if they were on the winning side. One day, I was about 10, they were short so Uncle Jack said to me, 'Go and get your boots you're playing.' So I played on the wing against grown men and big lads. I got clogged and I just sat down and cried but my Uncle Fred came over and said 'Get up. What are you crying for? Come on, we're on a tanner a man! You'll only get threepence if you keep going on like that.'

"So I just had to get up and carry on playing. A tanner, you see, paid for their Saturday night out, a couple of pints and a packet of fags." It was good initiation for Tommy. Using his nippy skills, he soon learned how to avoid trouble.

His was a childhood punctuated by sounds so different from today's world. No cars on the cobbled street, only the clip-clop of horses pulling the carts of the coalman, milkman and occasionally a farmer from out of town selling vegetables. Greengrocers came round twice a day. Their carts had lights for the afternoon delivery in winter. No electric doorbells, but the tap-tap-tap of the door knocker. No telephones. So neighbours and friends from miles away walked round and called in. One end of the street led down to 'The Bottom.' At the other end, the Tonge Moor Road saw a few cars, but mainly trams and buses, horses and carts.

Tommy became steeped in football. Conversations at meal times over the long-stewed 'lobby' or 'scouse' at home were inevitably about little else. Bolton Wanderers won the FA Cup in 1923, 1926 and 1929, were usually to be found somewhere near the top of the First Division and their teams were studded with star players. More than 50 years later, Tommy could still reel off their names – Harry Nuttall and Jimmy Seddon "played together in England's defence against Scotland in 1929;" Fred Kean, like Seddon an England centre-half, "I think they signed him from Sheffield

Wednesday;" Bill Butler, "winger, played for England, a local lad, he had been a miner at Atherton;" Dick Pym, a goalkeeper capped three times for England, "he was a fisherman from Devon, but everyone regarded him as being one of us, a 'Lanky'; Teddy Vizard, the Welsh international winger 'played well into his forties, Joe Smith was his inside-left. They said Joe had the hardest shot in football, he scored in that first Wembley final."

It was no wonder that with Wembley and the FA Cup occupying so much of the conversation of his formative years that Tommy's ambition to play in a Wembley final should assume such importance to him. Meanwhile, few meal times passed without a mention of one David Bone Nightingale Jack.

Jack was Bolton born and bred. His father, Bob, had been a trainer at Burnden Park and his two brothers, Rollo and Donald, had played for the Wanderers. With Vizard and Smith on Jack's left, Bolton had a most potent forward line. Between them Jack and Smith scored more than 300 league and cup goals in eight seasons, Jack scoring 144 in league matches alone and gaining the distinction of being the first player ever to score in an FA Cup final at Wembley. In October 1928 he was signed by Arsenal for a then world record, £10,890, in excess of the previous record by more than £3,000.

Arsenal, who had signed Jack to replace the veteran England centre-forward Charlie Buchan, regarded the fee as a bargain for the tall, elegant goal scorer but the fans in Bolton were distraught at losing their outstanding player, the epitome of great style. "It was the first time I remember being aware of Arsenal," recalled Tommy. "I was about nine at the time and had heard of Arsenal of course but I had no idea of who, what or where they were. For some time after that, like everyone else in Bolton, I hated them."

Tommy's first experience of formal education was at Tonge Moor, a local council school, just off Thickett Road. The original building dates from mid-Victorian days. Initially, there was just one large schoolroom where children from the age of four to eight were taught writing, reading, arithmetic and religion. "We sang a lot of hymns – 'Fight the Good Fight', 'To Be A Pilgrim' stuff like that. Singing and looking out of the window to see if it was raining. If it wasn't, we'd be allowed out onto the field at the back."

For football, Tommy was trained and coached by the sports master 'Bunny' Lee. "I had never been able to kick a ball with my left foot, but every afternoon at four o'clock after school, he took me across to the field and we practised shooting and passing with a plimsoll on my right foot and a boot on my left. He would kick the ball across to me and I had to shoot from whatever angle.

"Using the right foot soon became pretty painful! In the two years at Tonge Moor, I practised like that almost every day and in the end I was as good with my left as with my right."

The school, is still there, extended now, with the playing field adjoining. It was a time, in later life particularly, that obviously fascinated Tommy, probably because it all had changed so quickly. Even in his seventies he was as enthusiastic about his schooldays as he was about his triumphs with England. "We've all done it haven't we? You know, put down our coats and ganzies, sweaters and all as goal posts, then begun a game of 'kicking in.' Then, before you know it there are ten or a dozen lads all ready to join in. Well, as a lad in Bolton, I'd be playing on the way to school, dinner time, on the way home, whenever. We'd all imagine ourselves as top players, my pals and I."

For Tommy, any one of his boyhood friends could pretend to be David Jack, since his interest by then had been captured by Dixie Dean. "I had to be Dixie didn't I? I'd say to them all 'You be who you like, but I'm Dixie." The impromptu game would take place, sometimes just five boys, occasionally as many as 15, the gang of lads swarming after the ball "usually an old tennis ball, sometimes a battered football that we'd stuffed with newspaper when it was too old to blow up again. We'd play in all weathers so by the time we got home we were filthy, covered in mud or dust depending on the time of year."

The rules and etiquette of the games were handed down from generation to generation. No offsides, the pitch was as wide as 'the bottom' itself, so no throw ins and no corners. Tommy was dismayed to see these types of games dying out in more modern times when children preferred to watch TV or play computer games. In his sixties, he watched a group of schoolkids playing on Woodthorpe Park in Nottingham. "One young lad was quite good and I went over to tell him that if he practised hard he could make a fine player. But he wasn't interested. He said he was going home to watch something on TV."

Fifty years earlier nothing would have prevented the young Lawton from kicking a ball about. "It was the year (1928) that Dixie scored 60 goals in the league. He must have scored about 80 in all games, but, I tell you, 'Little Dixie' scored, oh, it must have been about ten times as many.

"All those games in the school yard or on 'the bottom' were great but, you know, I never realised the value of them until a couple of years ago (about 1990). I was listening on the radio to Bill Walsh (coach of the San Francisco 49ers). He was asked about his quarterback, Joe Montana. They said 'How does this chap win all these games when there's no time left? He's so cool.' And this coach said 'Well, it's probably because he knows all about how to handle himself when time's running out because he played as a lad in the streets in Pennsylvania or somewhere and when you're playing in the street every game's a big one in your imagination isn't it? You know, in your mind, how many times did you score the winner at Wembley in the last minute?

"So when this Montana had been playing in the street he'd won every game like that, so it was all in his mind. He'd been doing it all his life, he'd got used to it. I thought, 'That American is dead right!' It reminded me of one of my first games for Everton, a Cup replay at Tottenham. (White Hart

Lane 1937). There were all sorts of things going on. I scored one. Dixie got two, but we lost 4-3. A great match! I can say that now but I wasn't very happy when we came out of the dressing room. There were all these press men there and they wanted to know what was it like for me as a kid of 17 to play alongside Dixie. I just had to laugh, I mean, in my mind, I'd been playing with Dixie nearly all my life!"

At the age of nine, Tommy changed schools when Castle Hill was opened, which was nearer to his home. Brand new, it was state-of-the-art for the 1930s but Tommy moved with some trepidation, he could not believe there was anywhere like Tonge Moor and nobody like Mr Lee so he was pleasantly surprised when the headmaster, Fred Milner, turned out to be a sports fanatic. Castle Hill School is also still in use. A typical building of its day, a one storey structure, with folding wood and glass classroom doors that open out onto a schoolyard with a playing field beyond, all set at the back of a row of terraced houses running down Tonge Moor Road.

Tommy was soon in the school team, playing regularly against boys three or four years his senior, but his experiences 'on the bottom' had prepared him for anything he was likely to encounter in school football. Eight years later, Nat Lofthouse, also Bolton born, started at the school and was picked for the team. As Dixie Dean was Tommy's idol, so Lawton was the hero of Lofthouse. "Just think," young Nat told his brother Tom as they walked home after being chosen for the school for the first time, "I'm going to fill Tommy Lawton's position!" An enviable record for Castle Hill School, two England centre-forwards of such pedigree – Lawton and Lofthouse.

Big for his age and impressive at schoolboy level, Tommy was selected for Bolton Town Schools in 1930. In the meantime, Tommy had surprised himself and delighted his mother, by winning a scholarship to Folds Road Central School. So, another move and more dread that football would not be a priority. However, a week before the Bolton Town Schools game, the Folds Road Central head, F P Lever, asked Tommy if he played football. Young Lawton suddenly came to life and assured the headmaster that he was "quite a good player."

Mr Lever promised him a trial for the school team "saying I might be lucky enough to play if I showed up well. I did, so they picked me and a day later I turned out for the Bolton representative team!"

After Tommy's grandmother died in 1930, grandad Jim spent all his time overseeing Tommy's progress. "He was my staunchest admirer and pal, he nursed and advised me. He was one of the main reasons why I was able to get such a great start in football." Wherever Tommy went, his grandfather was with him, watching every match he played in his early days, cajoling, protecting, reassuring. They had no money for the tram or bus fare. They walked to each game, Jim Riley carrying the youngster's kit. "We had nothing to spend at all on what you might call 'luxuries.' When the studs on my boots wore out, grandad made new ones, because we couldn't afford to buy any."

As well as the extra training he received from his various sports masters, he would be taken to the top end of Bolton, 'Scotchman's Stump' at Belmont, for more training by his grandfather every Friday night. 'Scotchman's Stump' marked the spot where, in the 1840s, George Henderson, a Scottish pedlar, was murdered. In 1912, a group of Bolton's working men made it a permanent, solid memorial, while at the same time, preserving the open space of the moorland for recreational pursuits. Away from the smoke and noise of the town, Tommy would sprint and exercise, then it was back home. "The old tin tub would be brought downstairs, a hot bath, 'pobbies' (warm milk and bread) and bed.

"We were poor," recalled Tommy, "but I can't remember being anything other than warm and well fed. Sometimes I'd be sent down to the corner shop to get enough for the family dinner 'on tick.' Usually, it was my mother who had to pay when she got her wages at the end of the week, but the shopkeepers were alright about it. They knew they'd get their money eventually."

At school, Mr Lever, soon to be known as 'Pop,' was just as great an influence as Grandad Riley and, a rarity in those times, he "spared the rod." According to Tommy, "he could detect a lie just by looking at you. He loved teaching, he loved football."

In the yard, the boys would play with a tennis ball, a goal chalked on the wall. Pop would watch from the window of his study and, on occasions, coach. When wayward shots disappeared into the grounds of the Church Army hall next door, retrieving the ball became a major hazard because of the guard dog there, Pop paid for wire fencing to be installed on top of the playground wall.

The games master at Folds Road was Nobby Foster, a man whose enthusiasm for sport, and football in particular, was infectious. The school had no playing field attached so the boys had to run two miles to the nearest recreation ground. "That made no odds to us. We'd do anything for a game. Lessons were an intrusion."

W H Horrocks succeeded Pop Lever as headmaster. He was just as keen to harness Lawton's potential. Under him, the Folds Road team won everything they entered and their centre-forward scored a phenomenal number of goals. By his own estimate, 570 in three seasons for his school and for Hayes Athletic, the local Bolton League side he played for on Saturday afternoons. After playing for Hayes, if he was within running distance, he would dash to Burnden Park to see the last few minutes of Bolton's league game for free, the gates by then being open before the final whistle. Among the players he admired were Ray Westwood, Bolton's left-winger, who played six times for England, his last international app-earance being only two years before Lawton's first, and the captain and half-back Harry Goslin, signed by Bolton from Boots Athletic in Nottingham. Tommy spent many hours gazing through the window of Goslin's cycle shop in Bolton as much in awe of the professional footballer as the bicycle he had no hope of possessing. Tragically, Goslin was killed in action in the Second World War in Italy.

Success for Bolton Town Schools was followed by a call-up for Lancashire Schools, Lawton winning his Red Rose badge at the age of 13. In 1933 and 1934 he played in every game for Lancashire in the schools' county championship, including the 'crunch' matches against Yorkshire at Bradford and Nelson. He was first reserve for the England Schools' International Trial at Dewsbury in 1933 and disappointed not to get a game.

Meanwhile, Tommy was not the only 'star' in the Riley household. His mother, working at the Denvale Mill, was an extra in the Gracie Fields film *Sing As You Go*, shot at the Mill and around Tonge Moor Road in 1933.

At Goodison Park in March 1933, Bolton played Liverpool Schools in the final of the Lancashire Schools Cup. Astonishingly, by the standards of these days, the attendance was more than 22,000. Lining up for Liverpool that afternoon was George Burnett (Everton's goalkeeper post-war). In the last five minutes, Burnett parried a drive from Lawton that prevented him from scoring a hat-trick and Bolton from equalising as they went down to a 3-2 defeat. 1933-34 was Tommy's last season at school and this time he was picked to play in the England Schools' trial match, for the North against the South, at Broughton in Manchester. Right-half in the North team was Harry Johnston from Droylesden, later captain of Blackpool and Footballer of the Year in 1951. After the war, he was to play twice for England with Lawton. At Broughton, the two met for the first time and became life long friends. Lawton scored a hat-trick as the North won 7-0. It was not enough to convince the selectors. He played in two more trial matches at Durham and Rotherham, again scoring goals, but even then, was left out of the team. Tommy was still annoyed some 50 years on when he recalled: "a chap called Whittle was picked as centre-forward for England and he was the centre-half who was marking me in the trial! I never was capped at schoolboy level. I can't understand why not. It was one of the biggest disappointments of my life." (Tommy was, undoubtedly, disappointed but Billy Whittle had nothing to do with him not being awarded a schoolboy cap. Whittle, from Bolton, played for England in 1931).

The rise to prominence of young Lawton had attracted the attention of his local league club, not surprisingly, since one of his teachers at Folds Road was the Bolton amateur, Alf Thompson. Walter Rowley, then one of the coaches at Bolton, invited Tommy along for training at Burnden Park each Tuesday and Thursday under Jimmy Seddon, the man who, only a couple of years earlier, had been one of the prime subjects of meal-time conversations in the Riley household. At 14, professional football seemed incredibly glamorous to Tommy, as it undoubtedly was considering the alternative lines of employment that were on offer in Bolton at the time. It was only natural that he saw his future at Bolton Wanderers. The immediate problem to solve, however, was how to ensure that Tommy earned a living until he could turn professional at the age of 17.

Grandad Riley was not about to see any club take advantage of his young talent. Tommy was ineligible to make money from the game, but the family had been making sacrifices for too long. Whichever club signed Tommy Lawton was not about to get him for nothing. Bolton's manager, Charlie Foweraker, was very keen to take Lawton on amateur forms and the club made a somewhat premature announcement that they had indeed signed the star of local schools football. Had it been left up to the youngster – "I would have signed there and then," admitted Tommy. "But my grandad, Pop Lever and Bill Horrocks had other ideas.

"We went along to Burnden Park to see Mr Foweraker and he said the club would find me a job until I was old enough to sign professionally at 17. My grandfather said, 'What sort of job can you offer him?' And Mr Foweraker replied, casually, 'Oh! We'll get him a job in a butcher's shop.' My grandad wasn't very impressed by that.

"He said 'As a delivery boy, riding a bike? How much is that going to pay?' Well, when he was told about 7/6d (37p) a week, he just got up and said 'I can find him a job like that anytime. Good morning, you'll never see us again!' And we walked out." Improbable as it now sounds, other clubs were strangely reluctant to sign him. Lancashire being the cradle of professional football, there appeared enough clubs in the vicinity to suggest that at least one would take a chance on a young lad with a knack for scoring goals, but there was not even a flicker of interest from the likes of Manchester City or United, Preston North End or even Accrington Stanley! Bill Horrocks, who lived up in the Rossendale Valley, decided that, in the meantime, Tommy had to move up a class in non-league football. It was farewell to Hayes Athletic, hello Rossendale United in the Lancashire Combination. In his first game for them against Bacup he scored a hat-trick in a 9-1 win. Rossendale played in blue, Everton blue, while Bacup were in black and amber stripes, though after half-an-hour on a quagmire of a pitch it was difficult to tell the difference. One player however stood out. Mick Tollman, Rossendale's manager, took Jim Riley to one side "Look," he said, "this lad is good, but I can't sign him at 15, it's not fair to him. If he was 17, then I would take him and I'd make thousands out of the transfer!'"Apparently, that only confirmed what Riley already knew, Tommy Lawton was the business.

Liverpool invited the young Lawton, grandad Riley and Bill Horrocks to Anfield to watch a game against West Bromwich Albion. Discussions were held afterwards but nothing came of it. Bury were supposedly keen, but never pursued their interest, In the meantime, Tommy went to work at Walker's Tannery in Bolton polishing the heads of golf clubs.

The next club to invite Lawton to their ground was Blackburn Rovers. In December 1934, Tommy and Grandad Riley travelled to Ewood Park on the day the great Hughie Gallacher was playing one his first games for Derby County. The rest of the visit was "a complete waste of time" as Blackburn did not make take the matter any further.

Eventually, Sheffield Wednesday were the only club to make Tommy an offer. Their manager, Billy Walker, told Jim Riley that he was willing to provide Lawton with free digs and 10/-(50p) a week pocket money to sign as an amateur, with the promise of a job later. Tommy was very tempted, his Grandad less so, probably because there was nothing on the table for him. Ostensibly, it would have been a good move, Wednesday were rebuilding effectively into a side capable of challenging for the First Division title (finishing third and winning the FA Cup that season). If it had been Tommy's decision alone, he would have gone to Hillsborough. Bill Horrocks, though, read of Wednesday's intentions in the local paper and arrived at the Tannery demanding to know if Tommy had signed anything yet. Tommy said "No, but I'd like to go there." The Lawton 'sponsors' took the matter up and a deal was all but settled when Tommy's mother stepped in. Sheffield, 40 miles away, was too far from home – "He's too young to go away on his own," she said and that was the end of it.

Ten days later, on March 8th 1935, Tommy Lawton signed amateur forms for Second Division Burnley. Burnley were hardly a better proposition for an ambitious youngster than Sheffield Wednesday but the terms of the agreement were more than interesting. Bill Horrocks had tipped off an old friend, Wilf Hopkinson, a Burnley director, about the availability of Tommy Lawton. Hopkinson was surprised. He, and his colleagues, had assumed that Lawton was certain to sign for a top club. Made aware of the 'extras' that were being demanded, Hopkinson smoothed the way. Tommy Lawton was taken on as an amateur and given a job in the club offices as assistant secretary to Alf Boland at a salary of £2/10/0 (£2,50) a week; Grandad Riley was appointed assistant groundsman, earning £3/10/0 (£3.50) a week: and, eventually, the Riley family was given a rent free house in Brunshaw Road just up the hill from the Burnley ground at Turf Moor.

"Second Division or not, I forgot about Liverpool, Sheffield Wednesday, even Bolton," said Tommy. "It was my big chance and I was determined to take it."

Messrs Lee, Milner, Lever, Horrocks and Riley are among those responsible for having developed excellent footballers in Bolton over the years. including some prime goalscorers like Jack, Lawton himself, Nat Lofthouse and Bill Holden who played for Burnley after the war. The dynasty continued into the '60s and '70s through England centre-forwards Frank Wignall and Paul Mariner.

Even at 15, Tommy was a big lad – five feet 11 inches tall and weighing 12 stone 2lbs. The mainly carbohydrate diet was obviously to his liking. Every meal was served with potatoes of some description and bread. Potato pie arrived on the table at least once a week. Tripe and onions, sausage and mash were among the usual fare. Anything left from one meal appeared at the next. There were few delicacies – an egg perhaps, maybe jam occasionally.

Tommy, who knew no different, just wolfed down the lot and grew up happy and healthy. After a game, he would sit by the fire, if lit, as his grandfather analysed his performance. Tommy would listen and learn, usually while eating a piece of his favourite bread and dripping. "I suppose they'd say today that it wasn't the proper diet for a growing lad. But it didn't do me any harm. Wherever I played, you'd hear the men in the crowd say 'That number nine's a big 'un!' Something must have been right."

CHAPTER FOUR
1935 – BURNLEY
LEARNING THE TRADE

For the first three months, Tommy and Grandad Jim made the bus trip from Bolton to Burnley daily, a round trip of about 40 miles. Initially, most of the route was familiar, across to Ramsbottom then a wait before moving on to Rawtensall, the closest town to where Rossendale United played, then on again to Burnley. From leaving home to arriving at Turf Moor took two hours. In the morning Tommy would work in the club offices, while Jim was employed on the 'A' team ground. In the afternoon, Tommy would train with the other youngsters on the groundstaff and he soon became a regular in the 'A' team.

As a town, Burnley was very different to Bolton. Tommy had been used to Bolton's long, dark terraced streets. Burnley was smaller, built along the Calder Valley and apparently surrounded by hills, with Ingleborough and Pen-Y-Ghent in the far distance. The town's buildings were black and sooty but the outlook was lighter and less claustrophobic than Bolton.

In 1929, Burnley was the biggest cotton weaving town in the world and when Tommy moved there in 1935, the main feature of the place was the cluster of mill chimneys jutting up and over the Calder Valley and only mill owners, never footballers, had made their names and fortunes there. The club found the family a rent-free house on Brunshaw Road at the top of the hill from the Turf Moor ground. Tommy was then able to put in extra training in the evenings and he quickly settled into life at a league club, loving the whole exciting atmosphere of the place, even though Burnley were struggling in the Second Division. One of the reasons he enjoyed life so much was the influence of Ray Bennion.

Throughout his early life, Tommy was fortunate to be guided by a succession of individuals who had his best interests at heart – his Grandad, Pop Lever and Bill Horrocks at school, Ray Bennion at his first club. Bennion had retired the previous season after a career spanning 14 years, 12 with Manchester United where he was a tough, uncompromising half-back, good enough to win ten caps for Wales. As club coach at Turf Moor, he soon spotted Lawton's potential.

During his first summer at Burnley, Tommy worked with Bennion every day. With the coach in goal, Tommy was encouraged to shoot from every angle "Hard as you like, into the corners." When Bennion needed a break from picking the ball out of the back of the net, he would chalk a spot on the wall of the stand and Lawton had to hit it nine times out of ten, while Bennion sat close by keeping count. His most famous scheme to improve Lawton's skills was to send him dribbling round the touchline. Every time he arrived at an advertising hoarding announcing "Burnley's Beer Is Best" he was to swivel and shoot to hit the capital 'B's on the sign. Failure meant starting all over again. More than anything, Tommy thought, it was this training routine that produced his deadly accurate shot.

Tommy had also discovered a new hero. George Brown. Brown had played nine times for England, seven times as inside-forward to Dixie Dean, which to Tommy only increased his aura. He was in the Huddersfield Town team that won a hat-trick of championships under Herbert Chapman between 1924 and 1926. At Aston Villa, he was capped again before he moved to Burnley. Aged 33 he was nearing the veteran stage though he was far from finished.

Young Lawton immediately admired and liked him. "He was a charming chap, wonderful company. He showed me many of the skills that had taken him to the top. I hung on his every word and attempted to develop my game along the same lines." At the start of the 1935/36 season, Lawton was still in the 'A' team but scoring goals. Bennion's advice to him "Whenever you see the white line of the penalty box – hit it" was paying off. In September 1935, just before his 16th birthday, Burnley's manager, Tom Bromilow, decided Lawton was ready to make his debut for the Reserves at Maine Road against Manchester City. Tommy was unhappy with his performance. "I didn't do very well at the start in the reserves. It was a big step up for a lad of only 15, but I went back to the 'A' team, practised and trained even harder and I got another chance." For the 'A' team, Lawton scored 25 goals, at an average of about a goal a game.

Tommy acknowledged the help he received from the senior professionals at Burnley during that time. Captain Alick Robinson and goalkeeper Tommy Hetherington were particular influences. Ronnie Hornby and centre-half Bob 'Reo' Johnson were also always ready to give him a tip and a word of advice. Lawton kept his place in the second team, despite, for the first time in his life, finding goalscoring was not easy – just three in 13 appearances – but his all-round play regularly impressed. Meanwhile, Burnley were struggling for survival in the Second Division. In the seven matches after beating Bradford City 3-0 on February 1st, Burnley scored just three goals and picked up only five points out of a possible 14.

George Brown had by now moved on to First Division Leeds United; Welshman Ces Smith was at centre-forward but had not scored for eight games. Ray Bennion suggested to chairman Tom Clegg that Lawton should be given a chance with a comment along the lines of "He can't do any worse and a taste of league football would be good experience for him."

So Lawton became the youngest centre-forward ever to play league football at 16 years 174 days. The first man to congratulate him on his selection was Ces Smith, the man he had displaced. Alongside him, Bob

Brocklebank, recently signed from Aston Villa, was to make his home debut and Ernie Hancock was moved from right wing to inside-right. Other players, before and since have made their league debuts at an earlier age. Albert Geldard, later to play alongside Lawton at Everton first appeared on the wing for Bradford Park Avenue in 1929 aged 15 years and 158 days, but to entrust the coveted number nine shirt to a lad of 16 was unheard of. The *Burnley Express and News* trumpeted 'Burnley's Boy Leader' and surmised that no more than one centre-forward ('Sportsman' suggested 'Boy' Browell of Hull City) had made his league debut at an earlier age.

Immediately, Lawton was a crowd puller. An above average 12,350 where there at Turf Moor to see his debut, but the 1-1 was a disappointment. The *Express and News* described the performance as "puerile, the season's worst – Burnley get a point they did not deserve." Tommy saw little of the ball, though the crowd roared encouragement whenever he did. His one shot at goal went narrowly wide and he completely mis-kicked in a crowded penalty area when a Hancock corner reached him ten yards from goal. 'Sportsman' thought Lawton "keen and fearless" but pointed out that Bycroft, the Doncaster centre-half, had him permanently under control as he "kept him on the blind-side, or the young centre-forward found himself faced with the task of trying to scramble the ball past a trio of defenders. He might have improved his role had he left the centre-of the field more and so drawn Bycroft, who stuck to him closer than a brother, out of position."

Many years later Tommy recalled the game and "big, burly" Syd Bycroft – "I'll never forget that experience. I've still got the bruises from what he did that day!" Bycroft was playing his first game at centre-half for Doncaster "He wasn't there to be belittled by a callow youth, he gave me no quarter and taught me there's a world of difference between a good amateur and a good professional." Burnley earned a point from the game with a late penalty.

Tommy was downcast having failed to do what he had been selected for – score a goal. "I didn't play very well. I was overawed. I thought I'd let everyone down. I cried myself to sleep that night and thought I'd be better off giving up the game, there was no future for me." Fortunately, the Burnley directors, selectors too in those days, had seen enough to think he deserved another chance. There were eight matches to go in the season, relegation was a distinct possibility as they were fourth from the bottom of Division Two, a point ahead of Barnsley and Port Vale, and had scored only 38 goals, one fewer even than Hull City, marooned nine points adrift at the bottom of the table.

The next match was away at the Vetch Field against Swansea Town. The near 500 mile round trip was, at that time, the longest journey Lawton had made in his life. "It started on Friday morning when we caught a train at Burnley station for Manchester. Changed onto another for Shrewsbury and then another for Swansea and the real journey began! We just went on for hours through Wales calling at all sorts of out of the way places before we reached Swansea just as it was getting dark."

The next day, young Tommy Lawton truly arrived in league football as he scored two Burnley goals in a 3-1 win. Midway through the first half, Ronnie Hornby crossed from the left. High above everyone else in the area, Lawton's head made contact with the ball and it bulleted past goalkeeper Stan Moore into the back of the net. His first goal in the Football League that became a trademark for so many of his next 230. "I was mesmerised. Alick Robinson raced across to hug me. Together we dashed over to Ronnie Hornby. I was overjoyed." In the second half, Robinson, from left-half, produced the perfect through pass that Lawton ran onto and, right footed, hit powerfully past the goalkeeper for his second. Naturally, Lawton was pleased with himself. "I went back into the dressing room with a head the size of Birkenhead. Full of beans, dancing about. The other lads said 'You might think you're the cat's whiskers now y'know but you won't do that every week.' I paid no attention to them, but then Billy Dougall, the trainer shouted 'Just 'cos you've got two goals, don't start thinking you're a great player, now sit down and be quiet.'"

At Swansea Victoria station, Lawton tried to buy an *Evening Post* to see the match report. Alick Robinson saw what he was about to do and strode across to stop him. On the way home, the Burnley captain told the still excited youngster "Don't think too much of yourself. You've a long way to go and a lot to learn." The team returned to Burnley in the early hours of Sunday morning. Tommy was still on a 'high.' "Billy Dougall took me home and said to my grandad – 'He's not to see the papers. Take out the sports page and throw it on the fire.' At the time I was really cheesed off about it, but it was the beginning of me keeping my nut down. A good thing."

Even in the morning when Tommy ran downstairs to see the Sunday paper, his grandfather had beaten him to it. The sports pages were burning in the fire. "I wanted to go down to the ground y'know and show off – 'Look at me, I'm the greatest!' but my Grandad wouldn't let me. He made me stay in all day."

The following weekend was Easter. Tommy was looking forward to playing three games in four days, two against Manchester United. On Good Friday he lined up against them in front of the biggest crowd at Turf Moor that season, 27,245. United were in contention for the championship of Division Two, which, eventually, they achieved, though narrowly, ahead of Charlton Athletic. Wing-half Jimmy Brown, who had moved to United from Burnley in June 1935 was back at Turf Moor for the first time, while in United's forward line, George Mutch was their top goalscorer, signed the previous season from Aberdeen for £800. A year later, Mutch was on his way to Preston for £5,000 earning instant fame when he scored the winning penalty in the 1938 FA Cup Final at Wembley in the last moments of extra-time against Huddersfield.

"We really wanted to win that game, as much for Ray Bennion, who'd played at United for years, as for the club, because we were still in relegation trouble. In the end we got a draw, 2-2. Tommy Bamford, a Welsh international, scored their two. He wasn't a big fella, but he was quick. He could play anywhere, centre-forward or out on the wing. I couldn't do anything against their centre-half, George Vose. He was a Lancashire lad, a great player, not just a stopper, he could really play." Vose was from St Helen's. United had spotted him playing for his local team, Peasley Cross. Tall, fair haired and good-looking, he had played in an England trial game that season, but was never capped. On Good Friday 1936, Lawton admitted he made little impression on Vose. "He was too good for me. Whatever I tried, he had covered. That's how football is though. Two goals against Swansea, then nothing against United. Up and down." *The Daily Dispatch* confirmed Lawton's view : "Lawton, 16-years-old but strong and plucky, had few decent passes and was practically blotted out by Vose, who was at his best for this important game." Before the end of the game, Tommy pulled up sharply and suffered a groin strain. He was sent home to rest and told to forget about playing in the other two games over the Easter weekend. "Ces Smith came back in for the games against Norwich and the return with United." By then Vose was injured and could not play for United. but it made no difference, Burnley still crashed to a 4-0 defeat. Tommy played in the remaining four games that season for Burnley, scoring three more goals, including two at Bury – "just to show 'em what they'd missed by not signing me!" Burnley avoided relegation, though 15th place in Division Two probably flattered them overall.

CHAPTER FIVE

1935 – BURNLEY TURF MOOR STAR

Most of the summer Tommy spent at Turf Moor – either training with Ray Bennion, or on the cricket ground, where he played in the Lancashire League as an opening batsman. It was during this period that he learned more of the art of heading. Bennion would hang a ball by its lace to one of the stand's beams and instruct Lawton to jump and head it. "Get up and over the ball and you can send it anyway you like. Get underneath it and it'll only go up." It was the same advice that almost 20 years later, Lawton was passing on to Derek Tapscott at Arsenal.

Tommy loved his cricket but his mind was full of football. He played with and against the likes of the West Indians Learie Constantine and Manny Martindale, the pro at Burnley. "They were the first black men we'd ever seen. The kids in the street would cheek Learie off. They'd call out 'Hey, Darkie, you been down the pit?'" Significantly, Lawton noted how they were able to move the ball in flight. "I thought if they could do it with their hands then maybe I could do it with my head."

At Bennion's training sessions he practised hard but without much success. "I did learn how to do it, eventually. In the end I had such control over the ball that I could put top spin or back spin on it. When it came off in a match and ended up in the net, there were centre-halves who said 'You jammy so and so!' But I worked at it, it wasn't luck, it was timing."

The Burnley cricket ground is next door to Turf Moor. Tommy had played a few Lancashire League games in 1935, but produced his best season in the summer of 1936. "It was a very high standard of cricket. Every side had a top class pro – there was George Headley over from Jamaica at Haslingden, he was the best batsman in the world, as good as Bradman. Amar Singh, the Indian all-rounder, was at Colne. Against us, he hit a century in no time. Syd Hird from Australia, a leg-spinner, played for Ramsbottom. Rishton had a fast bowler – Bob Rae, a local lad and Enfield had Jim Bailey, a left-hander who made a lot of runs for Hampshire after the war.

"Then there was me! Sixteen years old playing against these fellows. I remember Manny coaching me before the game with Nelson and showing me how to spot Conny's slower ball. When I went in, the first ball he sent down was his slower one and I hit it over the football stand for six! Next ball was his 'special' – he was quick – but I hit that for six too!" Tommy finished 30 not out as Burnley won the derby game.

Tommy was obviously no mean cricketer. Billy Cook, who had been on the Lancashire staff, thought he would have made it in county cricket and encouraged him to play as often as possible. Cook was another all rounder, having played football for Preston North End and Oldham Athletic before the First World War.

A couple of innings in the Worsley Cup, the Lancashire League's knock-out competition were quite memorable. Against Enfield, he opened with Martindale and they knocked off 113 to win inside the hour remaining. Off the last over, to be bowled by Jim Bailey, Burnley wanted six, Lawton was 81 not out. He failed to score off the first five, then crashed the last ball of the match over the sight screen. The club presented him with the ball, mounted on a silver stand. A memento that he kept to the end of his life.

In the next round against Colne, Lawton hit 50 in half-an-hour, reaching his half-century with a straight six off Amar Singh, the Indian test fast bowler. "They were such sports in those days. Conny grinned from ear to ear when I hit him for six and Amar Singh was clapping my 50 before the ball had reached the boundary! They got their own back later though!" Except that in the Cup against Colne, Lawton went onto 91 not out. The hat went round the crowd and he received about £20 in copper, mainly halfpennies and farthings. That season, Lawton topped the Burnley batting averages with 369 runs at an average of 24.60.

He missed the last few matches of the cricket season because he started the 1936/37 Football League season as first choice centre-forward for Burnley and scored twice in the 3-0 home win over Nottingham Forest in the opening day fixture. Prior to the game, Tommy, in company with many of the 11,498 spectators, had watched the cricket on the ground next door.

Don Haworth, the journalist, author and playwright, lived in Burnley in the '30s and vividly recalled the atmosphere of 'match day' in the town. "Burnley didn't often attract much of a crowd in the Second Division but there was still a special feeling about a Saturday afternoon. The shift in the mills finished at one o'clock and soon afterwards the town centre-would be empty. Then people would come out of their houses, the atmosphere would be one of liberation! At the bus station there would be half a dozen of the green Todmorden buses, usually the most you saw at any one time would be two. Off these buses would spill dozens of men who'd come in from places like Todmorden and Bacup. They wore tweed overcoats and cloth caps, it was like a uniform. They all smoked, pipes or cigarettes, so the top decks of these buses were like mobile gas chambers."

The nearer the ground, the more intense the crush and the noise. Don Howarth heard "the shouts of the programme sellers, the clatter of police horses and the clicking of many turnstiles. There was a distinctive sound to football at Turf Moor. The rumble of feet on the wooden stand floor at the cricket field end of the ground. And it was dark. Throughout the game, with most of the spectators smokers, you'd see matches flickering like fireflies all around. It was difficult to see through the murk to the opposite end of the ground, the Spion Kop. The Kop was just an artificial mound of ash and cinders. There was no terracing as such and hardly any seating. Only the rich, the bourgeoisie, actually sat in the stand. The doctor would arrive in his car at five to three and sweep through the main door and up to his seat. The rest of us would walk to the ground, filling the whole width of Brunshaw Road." Tommy missed five games in September through injury but was back for the away draw at Southampton on October 3rd, three days before his 17th birthday.

The Burnley secretary-manager Alf Boland told him that, as soon as he turned 17, there would be a professional contract for him to sign. Tommy dutifully reported the news to his grandfather and was upset to hear him mutter "We'll have to see about that."

On his birthday, Tommy, accompanied by Grandad Jim and Mick Tollman from Rossendale United, went into Alf Bowland's office. Three of the Burnley directors were there too, Tom Clegg, Wilf Hopkinson and George Tate. The forms were already made out, awaiting only the formal signatures but Jim Riley had other ideas. "He's not signing unless he gets 500 quid."

It was a totally outrageous and illegal demand, but he later told Tommy that he had his interests at heart. "As soon as they've signed you, they'll be looking to transfer you for a few thousand. You'll see nowt of that, all you'll get is your accrued share of benefit, which won't be much." It was Mick Tollman who had put Riley up to it by telling him to demand the under the counter payment and that "it was done all over the place."

While employed in the office, Tommy had been on his starting wage – £2/10/0 (£2.50) – without a rise or a bonus for the goals he scored. His grandfather told him to carry on working as usual. Two days later, Tommy and Jim Riley were called back into the secretary's office. This time, Charles Sutcliffe, secretary of the Football League was there too. He spelt out the position. "We could suspend you *sine die* for these demands." Riley countered with: "I can keep him an amateur all his life, there's nowt you can do about that." Sutcliffe was unmoved. "If he signs for a club other than Burnley, I'll go through their books and if there's any discrepancy I'll suspend the club and the lad too." Riley realised he had no option but to back down and so Tommy Lawton signed professionally with Burnley, earning £7 a week, with bonuses of £2 for a win and £1 for a draw.

The following day, Tottenham Hotspur were the visitors to Turf Moor. The Lawton story was already intriguing most of Burnley, now it assumed fairy-tale proportions. Tottenham, even in the Second Division, had a crowd-pulling, star-studded team including the Welsh international winger Willie Evans, plus a quartet of England caps – George Hunt at centre-forward, Wally Alsford, the left-half, inside-left Willie Hall and Arthur Rowe, the centre-half. For one reason or another four of these internationals were absent for the game at Turf Moor, but Rowe did play, marking Lawton, while out on the left wing for Spurs was a man destined to make his name for England but at another sport – Bill Edrich, the Middlesex cricketer. Later, Rowe was one of the game's master strategists, initiating the famous Spurs 'push and run' side when he became their manager after the war but on October 10th 1936, he was given the run around by the teenage Lawton.

The crowd – 19,260 – was at that time Burnley's best of the season, Lawton admitting afterwards that his mood before the game swung variously between "totally self-confident and utterly riddled with doubt." Thirty seconds after the kick-off all doubts had been vanquished. The ball was worked out to the right wing by Robinson, Gastall centred, Lawton nodded down for Stein, continued his run into space, collected the return without breaking his loping stride and fired powerfully into the net. A goal after half a minute of his professional debut, dramatic indeed but so much more was to come. His second goal was a header at the far post from a Gastall corner as he outjumped everyone else in the penalty area and he should have completed his hat-trick before half-time but missed an easy chance. Three minutes after the break, he latched on to another pass from Gastall, left Rowe trailing and thumped in an unstoppable shot for number three. Even then he could have had more. Outpacing Rowe and homing in on goal he shot over the top, then went round goalkeper Hooper only to roll his shot wide of the post.

"Sportsman' reported in the *Express and News* that "Rowe could not hold him... it was a triumph well merited."

Tottenham pulled a consolation goal back – through John Morrison, a player destined to feature again in the Lawton story. It was a highly impressive start to a professional career, though his grandfather and Ray Bennion appeared more concerned with the chances he missed rather than the goals he scored. Unfortunately, it was not the start of a good run for Burnley. The following week about 10,000 Burnley fans, inspired by their new young tyro, made the short trip over to Blackpool by train and charabanc. There was no repeat showing. Burnley lost 2-0. "The old pros at Burnley – Bob Brocklebank, Alick Robinson, Dusty Miller were really good to me. I was a big lad, growing all the time at Burnley, I was nearly six foot tall and about 13 stone, but I wasn't able to think like a man. I didn't have their speed of thought so they were always helping me. Shouting and encouraging me, never giving the ball unless it was 60-40 in my favour. I'd be upset at missing chances, because I just loved scoring goals. I was hungry for goals. Bob Brocklebank would say to me 'Don't worry about missing if you're having a go. If you score one in every three chances you get, you'll have 30 goals a season.' He was right. I always remembered that and passed it on to some of the lads coming up after me – like Jackie Sewell, Derek Tapscott, Tony Hateley and Jeff Astle. All good goalscorers because they had a go. If you're going to score 'em, you'll also miss 'em!"

Inevitably, Tommy discovered there was more to life than football. Being in the local spotlight, he attracted the attention of the young female population of Burnley. Ron Greenwood, later England manager, was born in the town and, after his family moved south, he would return for his annual holidays to a village on the outskirts – Worsthorne. Tommy, two years older than Greenwood, was already a hero of his and to Greenwood's delight, began courting a local girl who lived opposite the Bay Horse pub in the village. "When Tommy was at her house we'd be outside, trying to catch a glimpse of him. When we did – Utopia! Peeping Toms and happy to admit it!"

Tommy enjoyed being a young local celebrity in Burnley. In 1991 he recalled "It gave me a good feeling, you know, to walk down the street and the people would be looking and saying 'That's Tommy Lawton.' It gave you a lift to know that someone had recognised you. I suppose I became a little big headed, but then there was always my grandfather and the other players around to knock it out of me. Players like Arthur Woodruff. He'd known hard times. He'd walked from Bradford to Burnley, across the Pennines, just to get a trial at Turf Moor. We earned a good wage compared with the average working man who got about £4 a week in those days or about one pound ten (£1.50) on the dole."

The pitch at Turf Moor was usually heavy. The ground had been built close to the town centre and drainage was poor. Consequently, the old fashioned leather ball soon became caked with mud and extremely weighty. Tommy's strength and power was invaluable, it was an industrial task to heave the ball from one end of the field to the other.

Even so, there was still an aura about being a professional footballer – even a reserve at Burnley at the time. Don Howarth related how his friend's house became "a centre of glamour. Norman Clee's cousin lived there, a beautiful girl who was an attendant at the Pentridge cinema. She was being called for by a young Burnley player – Billy Jeavons. She was deliciously scented from the spray she would pump into the air between houses to kill the germs and smells audiences left behind. He wore a sports coat and flannel trousers. To us, these two represented the height of glamour, all the more because they were so modest. He changed the subject if you talked about Saturday's match. She said she didn't know Buck Jones but we still assumed she had more to do with the silver screen than simply sell tickets and ice cream." Tommy made a big impression at Burnley in a very short time. The crowds admired him as he was clearly in a different category to the other players. "If there was anything about me in the papers, the family would try to make sure I didn't see it. Of course, I saw some of what they said about me but it was nothing like the stuff that's written about Paul Gascoigne. There's a good player, but if I was his manager I'd be worried about his off-the-field activities. There's so much temptation around these days. It's easy to say, 'Nobody can touch me, I'm the greatest!' The most I had to worry about when I was at Burnley was that the newspapers were always saying 'Lawton to sign for Wolves, or Manchester City' or whoever! I was quite happy at Turf Moor, didn't give a thought to moving on and, anyway, I was always being told by my dad (James Riley) not to believe what they were saying in the papers." He was forced to believe it on the morning of November 16th 1936. Two days earlier, Lawton had scored both Burnley goals in a 2-0 win at West Ham United. Eight goals in nine appearances had made all the First Division clubs take notice of the young talent and several top clubs had sent scouts to watch him. On that Monday morning, Tommy answered the telephone in the club office at Turf Moor. On the other end of the line was George Allison, the manager of Arsenal. Allison wanted to speak to the Burnley secretary, Alf Boland. Tommy told Allison that Boland was not there but that he could take a message as he was the assistant-secretary. Allison said "I want to make an offer for the transfer of Lawton. Tell Mr Boland I shall phone again." Seven other clubs also called, among them Wolves, Newcastle United, Manchester City and Everton.

"I was in a daze. I couldn't make a choice, though Arsenal were the glamour club that every pro wanted to play for and, secretly, I did too." For a while, there was no progress on the transfer front until shortly after Christmas when it became apparent that Arsenal were no longer in the running but Everton most certainly were.

In the late afternoon of New Year's Eve 1936, Tommy was called into the Burnley boardroom. Two Everton directors, Will Cuff and Tom Percy were there, along with the secretary-manager Theo Kelly and the Burnley chairman, Tom Clegg, who explained that Everton wanted to sign him. Tommy insisted on talking first to his grandfather. Called into the boardroom, James Riley stipulated that if "Our Tom's going to Everton, then I'd better go too, to look after the lad." It was agreed, Riley was offered a job as deputy groundsman at Goodison. Unfortunately, ill-health prevented him taking up the post.

It dawned on Tommy that the left wing partnership of Jimmy Stein and Dusty Miller had arrived at Burnley from Goodison on free transfers in October, immediately before he had signed professional forms. He suspected that a deal had long been agreed with Everton. The fee was £6,500 – an astonishing figure – a record for a lad of 17 who had played just 25 league games (while delightedly scoring 16 goals). Saying farewell to his friends and colleagues at Turf Moor was a wrench for a teenager. He never forgot the help and advice he was given by Tom Clegg, Billy Dougall and Ray Bennion in particular. "Without their help, the cocky boy footballer would never have found the right road."

CHAPTER SIX
1937 – EVERTON
HEADING FOR THE TOP

Tommy was fond of recalling the chronicle of events surrounding his move to Goodison. "I signed on New Year's Eve in 1936. The fee was £6,500 – a bloody fortune! But I didn't see any of it – it was a record for a teenager at the time and I'd only been a professional since my 17th birthday. Anyway, the next day, New Year's Day, I had to report to Everton. Well, it wasn't a Bank Holiday like these days, it was a normal working day and people were all over the place on their way to work. I caught the train, eight minutes past nine from Burnley to Liverpool Exchange. I was really nervous because I'd never been that far on my own before – it sounds stupid now, but even though I was 17, I'd been everywhere with my grandad or my mother or with the team, you know.

"There was nobody to meet me at the station either so I asked this porter 'How do you get to Goodison Park?' He told me to catch a number four tram from down on Dale Street and the conductor just nodded like when I asked him if he went to Goodison. Then when I was waiting to hop off, he was looking at me and I just looked away but he said 'Hey, you're that young Lawton aren't you? And I said 'Yes.' He just stared at me for a bit and then he said 'You'll never be as good as our Dixie!' So I just said 'Oh! Thank you very much.' And I got off feeling very small.'

The tram-conductor's comment could not have dented Lawton's confidence to any great extent because "at the ground, I knocked on the dressing room door and waited and then the door burst open and there was Joe Mercer with that wide grin of his and he says 'It's young Lawton isn't it? My you're a big lad!' And before I knew it I'd said 'Yes and I can play a bit too!' He just laughed and introduced me to all the first team players, all getting ready to play Preston. There was Jackie Coulter and Ted Sagar, Charlie Gee and Billy Cook – all good players but there was only one that I really wanted to meet and I said to Joe 'Where's Dixie, then?' And that moment the door flew wide open almost knocking me over and in he came. 'I'm here' he said and grabbed my hand. He looked a sight as if he'd only just tumbled out of bed. His hair needed a comb through it and he hadn't shaved; he'd a little stubbly beard and he had a pair of old slippers on his feet.

"He put his arm round my shoulders and took me on one side. He said 'I know you've come here to take my place' and he was looking straight into my eyes and I started to say 'Oh no...' but he shook his head and said

'Anything I can do to help you I will. I promise, anything at all.' Well, what could I say? I just stood there and said 'Thank you, Dixie.' For a moment he just looked me up and down and then he said 'My name is not Dixie.' I didn't know what he meant 'til he said 'My name is William Dean, but you can call me Billy.'"

Dean hated his nickname, given because of his dark skin, but in common with almost everybody else, Tommy referred to him always as Dixie. Dean had realised what the Everton fans and other players had ignored – that, at the age of 30, there were few years left for him at the top, marked as closely as he was, with the ever present possibility of injury. Dean had suffered half a dozen serious injuries including cartilage trouble twice, normally enough to end any player's career in those days, yet he appeared in 36 league matches and scored 24 goals in that 1936/37 season. Lawton had to bide his time.

On January 2nd 1937, Tommy played in Everton's colours for the first time. It was a reserve match at Goodison Park against, ironically, Burnley. "I went into the Burnley dressing room before the game and they gave me some stick. 'All that money and you're back with us; they must think a lot of you here then.' It was all good natured stuff, but Reo Johnson, the centre-half, was marking me that day and he called over 'I bet you five bob, you don't score, Tom.' Well, I couldn't refuse that bet could I? I made him pay up too, because I scored and we won 2-0."

Gordon Watson remembers Lawton walking through the dressing room door at Goodison for the first time. "We'd heard of him, of course we had, he'd been in the papers a lot because of all the goals he'd scored at Burnley, but we were surprised when he came in. He was only 17, but he was a big, strong, strapping lad, very fit. And we just couldn't believe the fee. Most of us had cost nothing like that, I mean, Everton paid Blyth Spartans just a few hundred quid for me! But £6,500 for a 17-year-old!"

Sensational as the transfer of the teenage Lawton to Everton undoubtedly was, it was overshadowed in the national news by the constitutional crisis surrounding the abdication of King Edward VIII. Tommy himself read the newspapers but failed to grasp the significance of events in London. "I was far too taken up with what was going on at Everton." The Rileys had moved back from Burnley to Bolton. Tommy spent Sundays with his family, returning to Liverpool on Monday mornings, now unaccompanied by Jim Riley who was suffering with asthma. In his place, Dixie Dean virtually adopted the youngster and, for his first few weeks at Everton, there were occasions when Lawton would arrive at Exchange Station on a Monday to find the big man in his little Morris waiting for him. Dean had been impressed with Lawton from their first meeting and they would drive to the ground for training, talking about anything and everything to do with the game.

Dean said of Lawton, "He was just the right build for a centre-forward. I told him he was joining a great club. Often, after training, he and I used to play head tennis, which I like to think helped him to perfect his headwork for scoring goals." Watson remembers that Lawton and Dean worked together under the main stand, Dean throwing up a large cased ball, "stuffed with wet paper to make it as heavy as a medicine ball" and Lawton had to head it at squares marked 'A' and 'B' on the wall. Tommy was living in digs close to Goodison Park until Everton rented him a club house in Fazackerly. His grandfather and mother moved in too. The accrued share of benefit that Lawton received after his transfer from Burnley amounted to £175 and it came in useful. With Grandad Riley now unable to work, the family was dependent on Tommy's £7 weekly wage. As he was in the reserve side in the early days, they were without the bonuses enjoyed at Burnley.

Six weeks after joining Everton, Lawton was brought into the first team for the match at Wolverhampton Wanderers as Dixie was rested prior to the fifth round FA Cup tie with Tottenham. On February 13th 1937, in front of 35,000 spectators, Lawton trotted out onto a boggy Molineux proudly wearing Everton's number nine shirt. As news of his debut became known, he received a bagful of letters and telegrams from his friends wishing him well. It was a mammoth task for Everton who were without two other first team regulars, Charlie Gee and Alex Stevenson, apart from Dean. Wolves were in good form, having just beaten third in the table Brentford in midweek 4-0.

Wolves tore into Everton, who struggled in the cloying conditions. Faster, nippier and more powerful, by half-time, Wolves were 4-1 up, J G T Clayton had scored the first hat-trick of his career, George Ashall on the left wing had tormented the acting captain Billy Cook with his pace, while Lawton found it impossible to find space away from Stan Cullis, though 'Bee' (the nom de plume of Ernest Edwards) in the *Liverpool Echo* applauded him for his "never-ending endeavour" and thought he was unlucky not to score when his shot deflected off a defender past the goalkeeper Gold, only for 'Bunny' Bell to be ruled offside. With 15 minutes to go, Wolves were 5-1 up and coasting when Coulter prompted a rare Everton raid. Bell, one on one with the goalkeeper was brought down, suffering a severe leg injury. With the penalty area ankle deep in mud, Cook reckoned that Cliff Britton would not have the power to score from the spot so gave Lawton the chance to "have a go at it." According to 'Bee' – "Lawton took the kick like an old man of the game and thus gained his first goal in a series that will grow very large in due course."

For a Merseyside reporter he heaped lavish praise on Wolves for their 7-2 victory – "They nearly approached the Newcastle team of its glorious days than any other side seen in modern football." (Newcastle had won the title in 1905, 1907 and 1909). 'Bee' also compared Ashall with Billy Meredith, the Manchester United star of pre-Great War days. He also felt obliged to point out that Everton were guilty of dirty play – "Cunliffe damaging Gardiner in an incident that left a nasty taste," and Cook was in trouble for persistently arguing with the officials. It was not an auspicious start in the First Division for Tommy. He did not forget it, but rarely recalled the game, preferring to describe the first time he teamed up with Dixie in a match he regarded as one of the most extraordinary he ever played in.

A week after his debut Tommy was back in the reserve side for a match at Bury. In the dressing room at Gigg Lane, he was already showered and changed when news came through that the first team had salvaged a draw in the Cup game with Tottenham at Goodison. Coulter had scored a last minute goal after Dean had missed a penalty. When Tommy arrived back at Goodison later that Saturday evening, the talk was all about the Cup match being a near brawl and the Everton directors (and team selectors) insisting that changes had to be made for the replay.

After a meeting on the Sunday evening, word was sent round to Tommy at home to report to the ground early the following morning for the trip to London. At Goodison, Lawton made straight for the notice board outside the dressing room. Sure enough, on the team sheet he was included at inside-left, with Dixie at centre-forward. The directors had left out Coulter (despite his goal) and Stevenson (because of 'flu) and brought back Torry Gillick on the left-wing and Albert Geldard on the right. Geldard had been dropped from the team after being barracked three weeks earlier by the home fans at Goodison and had all but joined Huddersfield. Now, he was determined to impress and after two minutes, beat the Tottenham left half, Grice, and crossed to the near post, where full back Whatley half cleared. 'Bee' was again reporting for the *Echo* – "At this stage up stepped Master Lawton to crack a shot so hot and fast, so rushing, that goalkeeper Hall saw nothing of it. It was a crackerjack shot and taken with Lawton's well-known first-time fury of pace." Tommy was thrilled by: "My first 'real' goal for Everton" and Dean was quick to congratulate him. "Here was the boy who cost £6,500 making his mark in Cup history, yet a year ago he was but an amateur for Burnley" – 'Bee's' comments in his 'runner,' his commentary on the game dictated down the 'phone while the match was in progress. It was a goal that made history, though not for the reasons 'Bee' was intimating. As the ball beat the goalkeeper, Dixie turned to Joe Mercer and said "Well, that's it then. That's the swan song. That's the end of it." He had seen his successor.

After 20 minutes, Everton were two up. Geldard provided the centre-for Dean to crash first-time into the top right hand corner of the net. Lawton might have made it three as Dean dummied another Geldard cross, but it was Spurs who scored when Morrison (one of the instigators of the Goodison brawl) beat Sagar superbly from 20 yards. Midway through the second half with Everton 2-1 ahead, Gillick was tripped in the area and the referee – Mr Mee from Mansfield – gave the penalty. Tommy saw Dixie pick up the ball and place it on the spot. "I knew instinctively that this was a penalty he just couldn't afford to miss." Meanwhile the

Spurs players were pleading with the referee to consult a linesman.

To Everton's amazement, the referee changed his decision about the penalty and awarded Spurs a throw in. Apparently the Everton throw-in which had re-started the game prior to Gillick's run had, according to the linesman been a foul throw. With half-an-hour to go, Morrison headed past Sagar, but was given offside. At the other end, a Lawton shot was on target until diverted wide off Vic Buckingham. After 66 minutes, Lawton collected a pass from Mercer and fired in a 25-yard effort that hit Dean in the middle of the back. Ten yards from goal, Dean spun onto the ball and volleyed it past Hall to make it 3-1 to Everton. Strangely that goal only served to lift the White Hart Lane crowd rather than subdue them.

"They started to roar their team into action," said Tommy. "For a club game I don't think I've heard anything like it. It was like a miniature Hampden Roar." After two minutes of raucous support from the fans, McCormick's cross from the right was met with a solid header from Morrison that left Sagar groping. Everton were convinced Morrison was offside, but no linesman flagged and the referee awarded the goal. 3-2 to Everton with 22 minutes left. Everton were still the better team. Geldard was unstoppable on the right but both Dean and Lawton were kept out by great saves from Hall. Four minutes from time with the crowd still at full throttle, Meek equalised from close range. Extra time loomed.

"Two minutes before, it seemed as though we could have run all day," said Tommy. "Now we were dog-tired. It was like a machine that had been running at full power had suddenly been switched off." Spurs were now in charge. Miller set off down the left, tracked by Cook who tried to tackle him but failed. Sensing the danger, the full-back came back for another hack at Miller but missed completely and the winger centred. The ball clipped Gee on the shoulder and, fortuitously, looped back to Miller who pumped it across again. This time the ball eluded everyone including Sagar but not Morrison who nodded into the unguarded net.

"Losing my first cup-tie hit me harder than the others," said Tommy. "I was nearly weeping with disappointment and frustration. The crowd surged onto the pitch but nobody noticed us trudging off." One effect of that defeat at Tottenham was that Lawton now felt a real part of the Everton set-up. The circumstances of being knocked out of the Cup drew the team together and, for Tommy, there was the constant encouragement of Dixie Dean to help him through. Everton's full-time training was starting to pay off. The big lad was turning into a muscled man. His speed off the mark was improving and, following Dean's example, he was timing his headers perfectly. Three of the experienced players in particular, Dean, Britton and Sagar, were constantly on the training ground practising with Tommy.

Three defeats in four games was hardly likely to impress the Everton fans and even the prospect of 30-year-old Dean and the 17-year-old Lawton teaming up for the first time at Goodison Park failed to attract a big crowd for the Wednesday afternoon visit of Leeds United on March 3rd 1937. Only

17,064, well below average, turned up, even though it was an important game for Merseyside. If Everton won, Liverpool's relegation worries would have been eased and Leeds would have sunk deeper into trouble.

Leeds introduced a new full back, Ken Gadsby and their latest signing from Aston Villa, the former Liverpool inside-right, Gordon Hodgson. Hodgson, an England international, immediately threatened Ted Sagar's goal with a close range header from an early Leeds corner. In the heavy conditions though, it was Everton who posed most problems as Dean charged through to shoot narrowly wide before Lawton cut in from the right and brought a good save from Albert McInroy in the Leeds goal. In the Leeds penalty area, the mud and sand mixture proved a real handicap to the slow-turning defence while Everton had obviously learned from their Molineux experience the month before. A spectacular shot by Dean from 25 yards made it 1-0. Lawton scored the second when he trapped a Gillick corner and shot on the turn into the bottom left of McInroy's net.

From then on, Leeds were simply overrun. All five Everton forwards scored, Dean and Stevenson claimed two each. Lawton had made a big impression in the 7-1 win with his speed, apparently gliding over the top of the mud, and the power of his shooting. With Dean brilliant in the air, it appeared to be the beginning of a new great strike partnership, but Dean's comment at White Hart Lane proved fact. The pair played together in only seven games in that 1936/37 season and just twice in 1937/38. A glance at the records shows that, astoundingly, only once in those seven matches were they on the winning side – that Wednesday against Leeds in March 1937.

At the end of that 1936/37 season, Dean had scored 24 goals in his 36 league games, Lawton had three in ten, enough to earn him a close season trip to Denmark, where Everton were due to play three matches, his first journey abroad at the age of 17.

Tommy enjoyed every moment of the tour, including, remarkably, the sea crossing from Harwich to Esbjerg. With the North Sea unusually calm, he even was able to eat meals on board, something which he found impossible later in life. It was not an especially demanding trip. With time to spare and relax, the players went sight-seeing and shopping and frequented an open-air bar in the city centre-to savour the atmosphere of the Jubilee celebrations of King Christian. Tommy was no linguist and was dismayed to order two lagers and be presented with a plate of sausages. He played in the three games on the tour, replacing Dean at centre-forward in the second match in Copenhagen against a Representative side, where he was surprised to find the opposition making as many as six substitutions at half-time.

For the final match, against the Danish national team, Dean returned and Tommy moved back to inside-right. All three games had been played in summer heat, but in this one, the players suffered excessively and did well to earn a goalless draw to finish unbeaten on tour. Tommy diplomatically said that he was impressed by the football of the Danish players, though he thought England had nothing to worry about from that direction at the time. A disturbing incident on the ferry home upset Tommy. A Lascar (East Indian) seaman stabbed a Danish clergyman in the arm and jumped overboard. The ferry stopped, sent out a boat to pick up the apparently crazy individual, then had to turn back to hand him over to the police in Esbjerg. Tommy did not enjoy the return journey and for the rest of his life was a bad traveller.

CHAPTER SEVEN

1938 – EVERTON SCHOOL OF SCIENCE

Gordon Watson was 20-years-old and already on the staff at Goodison when Tommy arrived. The ex-miner from Seghill in Northumberland had been signed by Everton from the famous amateur side Blyth Spartans four years earlier. He had impressed as a young centre-half, but opportunities there were limited with T G Jones and Tommy White around. Instead, he soon developed himself into a fine all-round utility player, capable of filling virtually any position. The Everton club trainer Harry Cooke regarded him as "one of the best passers of a ball in the country, second only to Matt Busby." Now in his eighties, Gordon lives not far from Goodison, the memories of those great days in the late thirties undimmed. "On the morning of every away match, Harry Cooke would come into your hotel room with some Andrews Liver Salts. 'I don't need those' I'd tell him – 'I eat my own cabbages!'" One of the local newspaper's profile pieces on Watson when he first broke into the team described him as 'a keen alotmenteer.' It is difficult to imagine any modern day Premier League player owning up to working his own vegetable patch.

The team spirit within the Everton camp was usually extremely high. "There were no splits or rows or arguments, we were a very happy family. Everybody was friends with everyone else. You used to look forward to training because we just loved going to the club. I lived in Huyton, next door to Billy Higgins, in a club house. We couldn't afford a car so when there was a bus strike in 1938, we just set off to walk to training, five miles there and five back. Did our training and thought nothing of it. We just loved playing and training. We were paid £8 a week but nobody moaned, we didn't know any better. When they put a contract in front of us, we just signed it. Never read it, we were just happy to be playing." Watson told how Lawton teamed up with T G Jones, slightly older than Tommy, but coming from a similar working class and almost sheltered background. "They were room-mates wherever we went. They always dressed smartly. When they went out, it looked as though they were going to church! They were very nice lads, hardly ever swore and never drank. Some of the team liked a beer or two – Dixie especially. One Friday night before a game with Chelsea, he went out with Jack Elliott, one of the trainers, and they got a bit the worse for wear and slept the night at Goodison on the St John Ambulance stretchers! Chelsea had signed this new centre-half called Peter O'Dowd who'd boasted that Dixie wouldn't get a kick in the game. Well,

Dixie woke up, drank a pot of hot coffee, had a bath and went out and scored five!"

That was in November 1931, Everton won 7-2, four of Dean's goals were headers. O'Dowd, later to play for England, was outclassed along with the rest of the Chelsea side that included two of Scotland's 1928 'Wembley Wizards' – Hughie Gallacher and Alec Jackson. According to Watson, "Billy Cook and 'Golden' Miller were another two who enjoyed a beer, but never round by the ground, they always went out to a country pub. The two Tommys though, they'd go out to see a show. Tommy Lawton loved music halls and the pictures."

In August 1937, 30 professionals reported for pre-season training at Goodison. Watson remembers:"'They would divide us into two groups. The younger lads would be sent out on a long run, road work. Andy Tucker, Harry Cooke's assistant would follow us on his 'bike. At the ground, Harry would be in charge of the experienced men, like Dixie and Jock Thomson." *The Evening Express* reported that "a warm welcome was given to Jack Davies, the only newcomer to the side from Chester. He is a wiry lad of the greyhound type and is nicely moulded."

Nicely moulded or not, Davies appeared only once in the Everton first team – in a war-time league match against Liverpool in 1939, when he scored! After the tour of Denmark, Tommy had spent the rest of the summer working off the remains of puppy fat through a strict regime of lapping Goodison, sprinting and ball work, plus cricket, golf and swimming. He began the season in the Central League side while, for the first team, things started badly. With Dean at centre-forward, they lost 4-1 at home to Arsenal and then 2-0 away at Manchester City. For the third game of the season at Bloomfield Road, Lawton was drafted in at inside-right to support Dean at centre-forward. Jimmy Cunliffe, and the Irish international left wing pair of Jackie Coulter and Alex Stevenson were the three players dropped as the directors called up Lawton, plus the Scot, Peter Dougal, an inside-left signed during the summer from Arsenal. and left winger Doug Trentham. The changes had no great effect. Everton lost 1-0 and sank to the bottom of the table.

Dean's influence was on the wane, his battles with Theo Kelly were beginning to have an effect. When he was an integral part of the team, Everton's tactical talks had been limited. Once, famously, to a mere "We lost because you buggers can't play" after Everton had gone down to their first defeat of the season in September 1931 at home to, of all clubs, Port Vale. Everton, relegated from Division One a season earlier had started well in their quest for promotion, but Dean was injured for the Vale match and watched from the sidelines. Hence his insight into the team's short-comings.

Theo Kelly had taken over as secretary at Goodison in 1936 after the death of Tom McIntosh. McIntosh was the man who had signed Dean for Everton from Tranmere in 1925. Dixie admired him and Kelly was never likely to be able, in Dean's view, to replace him. However, in 1938 he was made Everton's first official manager. In trying to impose his authority on the players, first he had to negate the influence of Dean. T G Jones said that "Dixie was the boss. Young players at Everton had to keep in order otherwise they were pretty soon stepped on. When I first went to Everton you almost bowed in awe and respect to Dixie. He was the big name in football. Virtually every Everton player was an international, but it was Dixie, along with a couple of England centre-halves, Charlie Gee and Tommy White who ran the show. Occasionally they'd call a meeting and they'd be telling the youngsters what to do. It was the best method of coaching I ever experienced.'

Tommy Lawton agreed. "All they ever said was 'Make sure you pass it to a man in the same shirt.' That was as close as we ever got to talking tactics. We just listened to what Dixie had to say and then went out and did it." As club captain, Dean met with Kelly to discuss team affairs. As the disagreements between them became more frequent, Dean admitted that both he and Tommy White, in separate incidents, struck the secretary when arguments raged. Dean was convinced that Kelly's policy was to oust the more experienced players from the side so that he could assume greater power. The friction ruined the family atmosphere around Goodison. T G Jones did not think much of Kelly – "He wasn't a manager, he was a secretary. He couldn't tell Dixie what to do on the field." But he could prevent him getting onto it and for the return against the defending champions, Manchester City, on Wednesday September 8th 1937, the unthinkable happened. Dixie Dean was dropped by Everton.

Lawton remembers the players looking in disbelief as the team list was pinned up outside the dressing room. "A sort of depression set in. I didn't know what to think. I was at centre-forward in place of the great Dixie. I mean! Well, I was delighted, surprised, but sad too." Everton had lost their three opening league fixtures and had scored only one goal. At last, Kelly had the excuse he needed to leave Dean out. He played just two more league games for Everton, at Grimsby in October and against Birmingham in mid-December. There was no sentiment where Dean was concerned from the Everton officials. Had there been, he would surely have been given the chance of making a 400th league appearance for the club. As it is, he is still there in the record books – 399 appearances for Everton and 349 goals. "That says it all," wrote Lawton once "the end of a great career and the beginning of one that could not hope to be as great." Later, Tommy admitted that on the day Dean was dropped he hurried home to the house in Fazackerley the club had found for him "Just to tell Grandad 'I'm not going to give him a chance of getting back.' Why not? He'd had a better run than most. I was still friends with Bill, but now it was my turn."

Dean was right about Kelly. For the rest of the 1937/38 season, Everton were preparing to play with a remarkably young side, Joe Mercer was one of the 'seniors' – aged just 23. Lawton had yet to celebrate his 18th birthday but his career as the first choice Everton centre-forward started well. He scored the opening goal in the 4-1 win over City although he was being marked by Bobby Marshall, playing his 495th league game (this was Lawton's 12th for Everton) and in goal for City was Frank Swift. "It was the first time that I'd set eyes on 'Big Swifty.' He looked like a giant! After the whistle he came into our dressing room and grabbed hold of my hand in his great big mitt. He said 'Keep going, son, you'll soon be better than all the rest!' Well, I didn't know what to say. I just mumbled something and he cuffed me across the ear and laughed." Later the pair became great friends and Tommy, along with Harry Johnston, spent many hours during summer months with the Swift family helping with their boat giving pleasure and fishing trips off Blackpool sands. Tommy, though, rarely ventured aboard.

"Swifty was one of the biggest men I ever met, in size and personality. He was over six feet tall and about 15 stone but he was quick, even to the ball that was coming hard and low. He could make amazing saves from shots that you thought were heading inside the post. But he had this amazing reach. Abnormal. From the tip of his thumb, to the top of his little finger, was almost a foot. A foot! I'm not exaggerating. It was about eleven-and-three-quarter-inches."

Ten days later, Lawton was back home again in Bolton for the game against the Wanderers at Burnden Park. "It was a real thrill. Playing First Division football in my hometown. Friends and relatives in the crowd all wanting me to do well and delighted for me when I scored the first goal." An extra incentive was that playing against the young, exuberant Lawton that day were two men he'd admired for years – Ray Westwood and Harry Goslin. Tommy stayed in Bolton that evening and, as became the habit of a lifetime, studied the local paper at length and discovered his was the first goal scored against Bolton in a first half that season and that he was the first man to beat both Swift brothers in 1937/38! (Frank's elder brother, Fred, was in goal for Bolton). He never, ever understood why football reporters took so much delight in imparting such trivia. "It's just a cover-up. It just covers up what they don't know about the game."

Tommy Lawton's first experience of a Liverpool derby came on October 2nd 1937 at Anfield. "We hadn't won there for years and though Liverpool had some grand players like Matt Busby, Jack Balmer and Barry Nieuwenhuys, we'd got some too! I mean, Dixie, Ted Sagar, Albert Geldard, great players! It seemed that they couldn't win at Goodison and we couldn't win at their place. All week round the ground, the fans were saying to us 'You've got to beat 'em this time' and others were sort of whispering 'Not without Dixie we won't.'" That derby game at Anfield remained Tommy's most vivid memory of his first full Division One season. Liverpool had not started well either, they were just a point ahead of Everton in the league, but Everton had not won at Anfield since Dean had scored a hat-trick in 1931. In between, Liverpool had thrashed Dean, Sagar, Geldard and all, 7-4 in 1933 and 6-0 in 1935.

"The atmosphere was electric. The two teams walked out side by side, the only league fixture in those days where that happened." For opposition players, the famous Spion Kop was an intimidating sight. "They made a tremendous noise. No captain, if he won the toss, ever allowed Liverpool to attack the Kop in the first half. They always played better going that way. So, just imagine it, my first derby, I scored a penalty at the Kop End and Everton won 2-1!" There was always intense rivalry between Everton and Liverpool, yet lasting friendships built up between the players, due, in some part, to the admirable custom in the '30s of inviting the opposing team for a social evening after the match. If the derby was at Anfield, the players met at Goodison and vice versa."

This was the first time that I met Tom Cooper, the Liverpool full-back. He didn't play in that first game, but he was there for a drink afterwards and we got on really well. He was a grand chap and a fine player, a beautiful passer and a rarity in those days, a full-back who loved to attack. It was a terrible shock when he died in 1940, early in the war." (Cooper joined the Military Police on the outbreak of war and was killed in a motorcycle accident in Suffolk in June 1940).

'The School of Science' grew up on away trips. The players, forbidden to walk around the town, even for a spot of leisurely shopping, would relax in the lounge of their hotel and talk about the game. The most effective way to learn. Lawton's promising start to the 1937/38 campaign – four goals in six matches since replacing Dean – certainly made the Everton crowd take notice. On the afternoon of Wednesday October 13th, Lawton was himself an interested observer of the England trial match, Probables against Possibles at Goodison. "Dixie said 'you'd better come along, you might learn something.' So Yanto and I sat in the stand with Dixie, mainly, I think, because Dixie wanted to give Albert Geldard some support. He was playing on the wing for one of the sides. I wanted to look at the centre-forwards." With one exception, the Probables side was the same team that had played for the Football League against the Irish League at Blackpool the previous week and won 3-0. The one change was Bobby Gurney of Sunderland for Chelsea's George Mills. The other number nine was Ginger Richardson of West Brom. It was the nearest the two triallists had been to England selection in over two years. "I'd not seen Bobby Gurney before, though I'd heard about him, he was a legend at Sunderland. They were both good players, but I thought they weren't as good as Dixie and he wasn't even in our first team! A couple of weeks before, we'd been beaten by Huddersfield and Alf Young, straw-coloured hair, big man, had no problem with me and he gave Ginger a hard time in the trial. At the other end, Stan Cullis and Wilf Copping kept Gurney quiet. I don't know what the selectors saw in that match, but I saw nothing which said ' Tom Lawton – you'll never get to the top in this game.'"

Lawton's cockiness had not gone unnoticed in the Everton dressing room. His fifth goal in eight matches came in the 1-1 draw with Leeds at

Goodison. By this time, Jim Riley's health was failing quickly and he was no longer an influential figure in Tommy's life. Unfortunately, the young centre-forward was beginning to believe his own publicity, forgetting the lessons drilled into him at Burnley by Billy Dougall and Alick Robinson.

On the Monday after the Leeds game, he walked into Goodison Park, whistling, smiling and feeling very pleased with himself. "I called out, 'Morning boys!' to the rest of them as they were getting changed and there was no answer – just silence, nobody even looked at me. I said 'What have I done then?' Still no answer till Dixie pipes up 'Who the hell do you think you are, with your 'Morning Boys?' Who're you calling boys?' And then he asked all the internationals in the room to stand up and there weren't many left sitting down. Dixie went round – 'Stevie's got 15 caps, Ted's 12, Billy 14, I've got 16 and how many have you got?' I felt about an inch tall. Next morning, I went in early and said nowt, kept my head down and then Dixie starts again 'Not good enough for you today then?' I just exploded. 'What the hell do you want me to do?' And I told them all where to get off and leave me alone. Next, they'd grabbed me and thrown me up in the air. My behind hit the ceiling, I came down in about four feet of cold water in the bath. I soon learned what I could say and what I couldn't, to have respect for the top players in the game and not to fancy myself too much."

Meanwhile, one of Lawton's biggest fans back in Bolton was following in his footsteps. Nat Lofthouse took every opportunity to see his hero play for Everton while becoming a regular in the Bolton Schools side and, in 1938, being awarded a trial for Lancashire Schools. On the way home from the trial match, Lofthouse and his schoolmaster-coach, Bert Cole, arrived at Moor Lane Bus Station. Waiting at the stop was Tommy Lawton, en route to Liverpool after visiting his family in Bolton. Tommy recognised Cole from his days at Castle Hill and the teacher introduced him to young Nat, six years his junior. Lofthouse recalled that first meeting years later. "I was tongue tied and could only nod like a dim-wit." Tommy's words of advice to the young lad? "Always try to bang in one or two, Nat. It's goals that count." Hardly great insight, borrowed from Bob Brocklebank, but impressive enough for the youngster and it was not the last time that Lawton offered Lofthouse advice. When the Bolton centre-forward was first picked for England (against Yugoslavia at Highbury in 1950) a telegram arrived from Tommy – "Go out and give them all you've got, Nat." The two goals he scored in that match were the first of 'The Lion of Vienna's' glorious international career.

CHAPTER EIGHT
1938 – EVERTON DROPPING THE PILOT

Dean spent most of the remainder of his time at Goodison in the Everton reserve side. By the end of the season they had won the Central League title by the considerable margin of ten points from Preston North End. The bulk of their 109 goals was scored by Dean and Bunny Bell, like Dixie a product of Everton's Merseyside neighbours – Tranmere Rovers. Dean was dropped from the first team in early September, but recalled for one game in October at Grimsby Town with Lawton reverting to inside-right. Everton lost 2-1 and Dean did not see first team action again until December. Everton had travelled to Aldershot to play an Army XI – for Tommy a first glimpse of the town where he was to spend so much of his war years. Early in the game (which Everton won 10-0) Lawton twisted an ankle and was carried off. On Saturday December 11th 1937, Dean replaced the injured Lawton for the 1-1 draw against Birmingham City at Goodison Park, the last time he wore the club's number nine shirt in a first team match. Tommy's second appearance in the FA Cup came at Stamford Bridge against Chelsea on January 8th 1938. The third round hurdle was successfully negotiated, Everton winning 1-0 with a goal from Alec Stevenson in the first half. The following Monday, the fourth round draw was broadcast on the radio for the first time ever. Everton drew the holders, Sunderland, at Goodison. "The excitement was intense," remembered Tommy. "Almost before the draw was completed there were orders for tickets being telegraphed in from all over the country."

It was hardly surprising. Everton and Sunderland had a history. In 1934, the two clubs had met twice over Christmas, Everton winning 6-2 at Goodison on Christmas Day, then losing 7-0 away on Boxing Day. Less than a month later, they produced an epic fourth round clash. 1-1 at Roker Park set up a replay at Goodison on January 31st 1935, one of the finest games ever played, Everton winning 6-4 after extra time in front of 59,213, with a hat-trick from Jackie Coulter, two from Albert Geldard and another from Alec Stevenson. One of those matches that the fans, even those who were not there, never stopped talking about.

Giving the 1938 occasion extra flavour was the fact that Sunderland had lifted the trophy the previous May, beating Preston 3-1. They turned up at Goodison with the side that had won at Wembley apart from Feenan for Gorman at full-back. Raich Carter captained the side from inside-forward. 68,158 packed Goodison that day, January 22nd 1938. Having studied

Bobby Gurney during the England trial three months earlier, Tommy now saw him at first hand. It was Gurney who scored a first half goal for Sunderland and with their 20-year-old goalkeeper John Mapson and Carter in inspired form, they controlled the game. "Our left back, Jack Jones, was injured and could only limp around on the left wing in the second half. Our defence did well to keep Sunderland out, especially with Raich at his brilliant best. Every time we tried anything Mapson was equal to it. He was a fine goalie, a couple of years older than me, so he was only about 19 when he won the Cup with Sunderland and he'd played in their championship side the year before! I remember that Sunderland signed him from Reading about the time I made my debut for Burnley. He'd only played once or twice for Reading, but Sunderland were desperate because Jimmy Thorpe, their regular goalkeeper, had died a couple of days after having a rough time against Chelsea. He'd taken a real battering and he never recovered. They changed the rules after that and so nobody could put his foot up against the goalkeeper when he had the ball in his hands and only barge him shoulder to shoulder." (Jimmy Thorpe was apparently diabetic. Raich Carter in his book commented that Thorpe was not well in his last season and required insulin injections). "Mapson would have played for England, except that Vic Woodley was around before the war and then 'Swifty' afterwards." (Mapson did make one war-time appearance for England in 1941, and played for Sunderland until 1952).

Three days after the Cup disappointment, Everton were on the road again, this time to London to meet the First Division leaders Brentford at Griffin Park. "Brentford had a good side in those days and they were in top form. They'd just beaten Portsmouth in the Cup and big Dave McCulloch was scoring a lot of goals. We looked a poor side that day and lost easily." In fact the 3-0 defeat seemed to signal another struggle against relegation for Everton. After two home defeats in succession (3-1 by Liverpool and 1-0 to Wolves), the board decided to take action. In modern times, that would mean the sack for the manager. Will Cuff, the Everton chairman, decided the team needed a change of scenery. "We were told to report to Exchange station on the Sunday night. Yanto said, as a joke, that we were going on holiday to the seaside! Well, it wasn't the seaside and it wasn't a holiday, but it did us a power of good. We went to Harrogate for a week." Under trainer Harry Cooke, the players were drilled, sent on long runs, sprints and practised incessantly, shooting in and heading. They also, for the first time, played six-a-side games. "This was ideal preparation for us, no dribbling, just one-touch fast football. I'm convinced that all that special training, which later became a regular thing, laid the foundations of our title winning side the following season." There was leisure time too. Tommy took up golf and at the local club met three Yorkshire cricketing heroes – Maurice Leyland, Hedley Verity and Frank Smailes. He liked Verity in particular, "a gentleman, very thoughtful. I was so upset when I heard that he'd been killed in Italy during the war. We went to see his grave when we were over there. We lost a great man when he died." The intensive training, especially the six-a-sides paid off. The team stayed in the north for the game at Elland Road against Leeds United. 'We made a brilliant start. Cliff Britton to Alec Stevenson, 'Stevie' to Jimmy Cunliffe, on to me, back to Jimmy and he scored – a move that was so fast that Leeds didn't know where we were coming from." Two goals for Cunliffe in that game, two for Lawton but only one point for Everton. Centre-forward Gordon Hodgson was in a run of prime form for Leeds and, as if to eclipse the memory of the previous season's thrashing at Goodison, scored four all of his own. According to Charles Buchan, Hodgson was "a forceful player with a strong shot, equal to anything in the country." He had toured England with a South African Amateur International side in 1924/5, stayed on and signed for Liverpool, playing for England three times in 1930/31. At 33, his best days were behind him. At least, some of them. Everton, evidently, also thought similarly about Dean, at 31. Everton had a new youthful look.

On March 11th 1938, Dean was transferred to Notts County, but not without acrimony. He always insisted that the only Everton official present when he signed for Notts was Theo Kelly and that the secretary said nothing while the formalities were completed, "not even 'goodbye.'" Dean was also upset that no Everton player took the trouble to see him before he left. Yet, like the public, the players had not been informed of the possibility of Dean leaving. Only 24 hours before the deal was signed, Everton had insisted that Dean would finish his career at Goodison. Tommy was sad to see him go. "He helped me a lot when I first joined the club. He had his faults, he was a boisterous character, but everyone liked him. He was often black and blue from the harsh treatment handed out by unscrupulous defenders, but he used to take it and never complained."

Dean lived around the corner from the ground in Goodison Avenue. "He would come walking in wearing old flannel trousers and, if it wasn't raining, bedroom slippers! In those days there'd be hundreds of people outside the ground before a match. Some of them couldn't afford to get in, so they just stood around and waited for the gates to be opened after half-time. I've seen chaps go up to Dixie and ask him for a ticket and he'd go to the office and get one of his 'frees' (complimentary tickets) or he'd buy one if he'd run out and give it to the man outside – 'Go and enjoy yourself, Dad!' he'd say. I saw that many times."

Gordon Watson remembers Dixie signing autographs endlessly. "There might be a thousand kids waiting but he'd sign for the lot of them. Dixie would give anybody anything." In Joe Mercer's opinion, there was little to choose between the two great centre-forwards. "Tommy was, technically, a better all-round player perhaps, but Dixie was better in the air." For Watson, Dixie, even at that advanced stage of his career, was "a little better than Tommy. Tommy was nearly as good even though he was only 17. Even then he was over six foot and about 13 stone." For most of the Everton fans, Dean was irreplaceable but Tommy grew up quickly. "He was soon so good that he couldn't be left out," said Watson. "He always did what he was told, he was never big headed. He turned into a great man."

Dean and Tommy remained friends until Dean's death in March 1980 at an Everton-Liverpool derby. In 1946, Dean took over a Chester public house – 'The Dublin Packet.' When Tommy left Everton for Chelsea in November 1946, the deal was completed in Dean's back room at the pub.

By the Easter of 1938, as many as 11 clubs were in danger of relegation from Division One, Everton among them. It was not until they beat Portsmouth 5-2 in the penultimate match of the season that they were certain of staying up. They finished 14th, but without the compensation of being above Liverpool who were 11th. Even so, it was a better effort than Manchester City, who, champions the previous season thanks to the great efforts of Lawton's 'mate' Frank Swift, were relegated, with West Bromwich Albion, to Division Two, an unbelievable change of fortunes. Swift was in goal all season, they scored more goals (80) than anyone else and still went down.

Meanwhile, Tommy ended the season with a flourish. Seven goals in eleven games including "two beauties against West Brom when we beat them 5-3. They had a fellow called Eddie Sandford playing centre-half, marking me, which was a bit odd because he was really an inside-left!" With 28 goals in 39 league games Lawton was the top scorer in the First Division and anxiously awaited news of the England squad to play Germany, Switzerland and France on tour during the summer. "the general impression was that I was worth a place and I'll admit it – I was big headed enough to think so too." The selectors decided to leave the 18-year-old Lawton at home and went for more familiar options. "I suppose they were right. It might have killed my ambitions and hopes if I'd have played and not been ready. Also, you have to remember, there were some fine centre-forwards around like George Mills, Ted Drake and even Frank Broome. All were experienced players compared with me."

It was Drake and Broome who went on tour with England. Drake had scored 17 goals in 27 league games as Arsenal pipped Wolves for the championship. Broome's 20 goals in 38 matches for Aston Villa came in a season where he had appeared more frequently on the right wing. Mills, England's first choice before Christmas was injured playing for Chelsea in February. Mickey Fenton, of Middlesbrough, won his only cap when he played centre-forward for England against Scotland in April and Bobby Gurney, who had played in the trial game at Goodison, saw little league action in the second half of the season at Sunderland. It was the last time any of them was considered for England at centre-forward.

It was no immediate consolation for Lawton that Everton were scheduled to play in an end of season tournament to mark the Glasgow Empire Exhibition at Ibrox Park. Later though, he regarded the Scottish interlude as a valuable precursor for Everton's championship season. The party stayed at the Skelmorlie Hydro on Wemyss Bay. Tommy fell in love with the area immediately and was a frequent visitor from then on. Three years later, he spent his honeymoon there.

Three other English clubs took part – Chelsea, Brentford and Sunderland and four Scottish clubs – Rangers, Celtic, Aberdeen and Hearts. The draw pointed to a Rangers-Celtic final, but Everton ruined any hope of that when they knocked out Rangers 2-0 in the first match. Lawton scoring one of the goals. "We were lucky," remembered Tommy. "They had to play the second half with ten men after their goalie, Johnny Dawson was carried off." In the semi-final, Lawton scored the winner as Aberdeen were beaten 3-2 to set up a final against Celtic at Ibrox. It was a classic Anglo-Scottish battle, played on a balmy June evening in front of a massive 82,000 crowd. "Nat Cunliffe was injured early on, so we played with effectively only ten men, but we held out and it went into extra time. Then their little Scottish international winger Jimmy Crum jigged his way through to put them in the lead. We had a 'goal' from Alex Stevenson disallowed for offside, but that was the best we could do." It was a great game, unlike the sterile pre or post-season, made-for-TV encounters of today. The huge, enthusiastic crowd playing a major role. "They were terrifying, waving flags and banners in the Celtic colours. They shouted and screamed and sang all match. I'd never seen anything like it." Off the field, even Lawton was persuaded to make a couple of trips by steamer to Arran and Dunoon and his golf improved further with regular practice. A variety night at Barrfield's Pavilion in Largs proved to the liking of Lawton and T G Jones. "On the bill was this stunning young dancer and singer, aged about 17. Well, Yanto and I were soon under her spell, even though she was wearing a red blouse and a white skirt that made her look like a Liverpool supporter!" The young lady, taking her first steps in show business, was Pat Kirkwood. Later in her career, Kenneth Tynan described her legs as the "eighth wonder of the world."

The two Tommys obviously had an eye for talent! "We clapped and whistled and gave her a great ovation, hoping she might notice us, but no luck. I tried to find out more about her and was told that she came from Manchester, a Lancashire lass, couldn't be better!" All attempts to introduce themselves at the stage door foundered. The way through to the young star's dressing room was guarded by her formidable mother.

CHAPTER NINE
1939 – EVERTON LEADING THE CHAMPIONS' LINE

For the 1938/39 season, Everton were unfancied to improve on their mediocre showing of the previous campaign. Bill Dean and Albert Geldard had gone. Geldard had been sold during the close season to Bolton for £4,500. Tommy was disappointed to see him leave – "He was the fastest thing on two legs over ten yards. We had other wingers like Torry Gillick, Wally Boyes and Jimmy Caskie, but Albert had played for England only the season before, when he'd kept Stan Matthews out of the team. I thought we'd miss him."

Cliff Britton was now a reserve team player and becoming more and more involved with coaching and training, though his playing career was to enjoy a renaissance during the war. 'Jock' Thomson was captain and left-half with Joe Mercer at right-half. When Gordon Watson replaced the injured Thomson, the average age of the team was only about 25. "We were a young side and the only thing we were bothered about was playing football and winning! It was a grand life, we just couldn't believe that we were getting paid for doing exactly what we wanted to do. Other lads of our age were working shifts down the pits or in factories. We got up every morning and it was football, football, football."

Yet there were other things going on in the world, not just the start of a new season. Hitler claimed the Sudetanland in Czechoslovakia was part of Germany. War was imminent. At Goodison Park, war did not enter the thinking at the 'School of Science.' T G Jones recalled that "Before the war, there was a kind of admiration for Hitler, for the way that he was rebuilding Germany. We never considered that war was coming and never thought that we would be involved in it. It wasn't until afterwards that we learned of all the terrible things he and the Nazis got up to." As Neville Chamberlain and his Foreign Office ministers tried to ensure "peace in our time," Everton began the season with a flourish.

The first match was away at Blackpool – duly won 2-0, Lawton scoring one of the goals and Everton, reportedly, playing like a side "ripe in the peak season. The forwards switched in and out and wandered with studied skill... Blackpool's defence was dazed, beaten and bewildered." There was a light hearted atmosphere around the ground among the 29,647 spectators, most of whom were Evertonians making a weekend of the trip to Britain's most popular holiday resort. On the field though, Everton had been clincial and ruthless. Lawton renewed acquaintance with Harry Johnston, who was now making a name for himself at Bloomfield Road. "After the game we had a drink and Harry said 'What's happened here, Tom?' He couldn't believe that we'd improved so much since the last season. It was just the confidence of youth, we didn't know any different." Four days later, Everton beat Grimsby at Goodison 3-0, two for Lawton in a three-minute spell, both goals from net busting shots "two of the hardest shots I think I have ever brought out of the bag. Alec Stevenson laid both of them on, rolling the ball across to me like we were playing on a billiard table."

The following Saturday, another home match, against Brentford, Lawton scoring both Everton goals in a 2-1 win. "They said in the papers that we were lucky because Brentford had most of the second half. But we had so much team spirit and ability, we thought, 'No-one can stop us!' We had all these little fellows up front who were so quick, Torry Gillick, Alec Stevenson, Wally Boyes, all under five foot four. Then Jimmy Caskie came in and he was no bigger. They had to be good ball players because they couldn't throw their weight about." Next up, another midweek game, Aston Villa at Villa Park. "

Villa had just come up from the Second Division and they were supposed to be really strong at home. Not many teams went there and won. But we did! We whipped 'em!" Lawton scored his fifth of the season, Stevenson added two more and Everton were at the top of the Division One table with a 100% record. Then came Everton's biggest test yet – Arsenal, the defending champions, away at Highbury. If there was a 'Team of the Thirties' it was Arsenal. Five times champions, once runners-up, they had won the FA Cup twice and been finalists as well, Virtually every schoolboy in the land could recite their team off pat: – "Swindin; Male, Hapgood; Crayston, Joy, Copping; Kirchen, Leslie Jones, Drake, Bryn Jones, Bastin."

Arsenal had not made the best of starts to the new season – a win against Portsmouth at Highbury, a draw at Huddersfield and a 1-0 defeat at Brentford. They had scored just three goals, two of them from their record signing Brynmor Jones, bought from Wolves for £14,500 that August. The fee was a sensation at the time, breaking the previous record paid by Arsenal for David Jack of Bolton back in 1928 by about £4,000. Tommy had played against Bryn Jones before. "I didn't know him very well. He was a quiet, shy type. That was surprising because, the story was, that one of the reasons Wolves sold him was because he was always ready to stand up for himself against Major Buckley. He had great ball control, good positional sense but he probably didn't score as many goals as he should have done. Although, I remember seeing him score a goal for Wolves, a couple of years before he was transferred to Arsenal, when he just hit it on the volley from about eight yards outside the penalty box and it just rose like a well-hit golf ball and flashed into the net just inside the angle of the right-hand post and cross bar. The 'keeper didn't move." Jones was in the mould of '30s inside forwards. Five feet six and 10 stone 5lb, but the tag "world's most expensive footballer" did not sit easily with him. The Arsenal manager George Allison later became so concerned about Jones wilting under the spotlight that he dropped him to the Combination side for a couple of games, only for a record crowd of 33,000 to turn up at Highbury to see him play in the reserves! "After the war, Tom Whittaker told me that signing Bryn Jones had been an expensive mistake," said Tommy. "He thought that Arsenal had enough good young players coming through that they didn't need to spend all that money. It might have different had the war not intervened, but he only really played for Arsenal that one season."

If being the world's most expensive player was hard enough to live up to, Jones also suffered because he was ostensibly the replacement for Alex James. "Alex could sell any kind of dummy, any time. Bryn didn't have the tricks of James, but he could open the game with one pass. He was quick and he could pass a ball accurately over 50 or 60 yards. He would swing long, hard low balls across field from one wing to the other, changing the point of the attack. He was a master of the cross-field pass." T G Jones remembers that: "Arsenal were the top dogs in those days. The champions, every player was a household name, virtually every one an international. We, on the other hand, were a team of youngsters. I think the oldest player on our side was Ted Sagar, the goalie, and he carried on longer than any of us!" Everton's preparations were thorough. On the Thursday before the game they travelled south by train from Lime Street to Euston. The LMS provided Everton's usual special carriage – first class accommodation, next to the restaurant car. Emblazoned down the side of the coach on a headboard just above the windows was 'Everton Football Club' with the club's emblem at either end. The carriage was used only by the team and officials when travelling away. In between times it was stabled in the sidings at Edge Hill.

"We stayed at Bushey and spent most of the time walking and playing golf. When we trained, it was mainly six-a-side matches," said Jones. These were fiercely competitive. "Harry Cooke had developed this idea to help our high speed passing game." On the coach from Bushey to Highbury the team was in high spirits. "Our theme song was 'McNamara's Band.' We were singing away when we came into London and the streets around the ground were packed with people. It wasn't like today when the fans are all in team shirts and hats. There were a few red and white scarves and rattles but mostly they were in overcoats. You see everybody worked on a Saturday morning in those days, most of them were coming straight from work. A quick pint in the local and then down to the match. They were mostly good natured. When they saw us they just shouted 'Up the Arsenal!' There was never any trouble in grounds in those days."

MATCH OF THE DAY

Division One
Arsenal v Everton at Highbury
September 10th 1938
Arsenal: Swindin; Male, Hapgood; Crayston, Joy, Copping; Nelson, Leslie Jones,
Carr, Bryn Jones and Bastin
Everton: Sagar; Cook, Greenhalgh; Mercer, T G Jones, Thomson; Gillick, Bentham,
Lawton, Stevenson, Boyes
Attendance 64,555

Highbury was packed that day to see the champions against the young pretenders.
Everton, going for a record fifth successive win at the start of a Division One
season, were unchanged – for the fifth time. Tommy had played at Highbury before,
but this time he took everything in as he sat in the palatial dressing room,
impressed with the underfloor heating and the spaciousness of the surroundings.
"It had everything. A treatment room with every kind of modern device, a players'
lounge. I loved playing there." The Arsenal team was announced. "Their forward
line looked a little strange, then 'Stevie' pointed out that Ted Drake wasn't playing.
And neither was Alf Kirchen who should have been on the wing." The rest of the
team was pretty familiar.

Everton were on top throughout the first half, so completely that sections of the
crowd, according to one reporter, "were inclined to wax facetious at Arsenal's
expense." Tommy started brilliantly. He drifted out to the left, picked up a pass
from Wally Boyes, 20 yards from goal and suddenly unleashed a shot that had
Swindin groping as it flashed wide.

With a quarter of an hour gone, Billy Cook rolled a free-kick to Joe Mercer.
Mercer made ground through the middle before clipping a perfect pass out to the
right wing where Torry Gillick killed it and pushed it through to Stan Bentham
mid-way inside the Arsenal half in the inside-right channel. Bentham slickly laid
off to Lawton who drifted out right. Male, Joy and Hapgood all closed in on the
young centre-forward. In the Sunday Pictorial, *George Casey suggested that*
Arsenal thought Lawton would "make a dash down the middle. But he didn't. The
18-year-old they say will lead England this season hoodwinked the defence."
Lawton shielded the ball, then released it to Alex Stevenson who left Hapgood and
Joy floundering, lured Swindin off his line and nonchalantly tucked it low into the
net For the rest of the first half it was an exhibition display by Everton, though it
was not until seven minutes before half-time that they scored a second – "another
wonder goal." according to Casey. "Again it was Lawton. Stevenson had a hand
in it too. He set Gillick going on the right wing. Gillick transferred to Lawton, who
it seemed, could not possibly score with the middle once again blocked by that
Arsenal barrier. But Lawton had a brainwave. He started to career to the left wing
and with his body at right angles to the goal swung his left boot round the ball to
completely deceive Swindin and everybody on the ground. Goal! And brilliant one
though it was, nobody shouted. It came too unexpectedly!"

Tommy explained "I did try to hit the ball with my right but the way was blocked, so I forced my way across goal and with Swindin moving across to the right post, sold him the dummy and hit it with my left foot and it went in just inside the left hand post. I was proud of that one!"

Charles Buchan in the News Chronicle put Everton's first half dominance down to the "quick interchanging of their attack." he also noted that Lawton "had a lot to do with the success. He beat Joy for the ball in the air, kept the wings moving and was ever dangerous in front of goal." Everton coasted through the second half, relying on defence and allowing Arsenal to swarm around their penalty area. Nelson, Crayston and Bastin each hit a post until eventually Bryn Jones drove in from almost 30 yards. It was a goal that impressed Tommy "It was a great shot. Deadly. A terrific volley from outside the box and the ball went into the top corner at supersonic speed. When he was at Highbury, he never struck true form because of that big fee . But he was a great inside-forward. He was so quick and he could find his wingers no matter where he was on the field. And he could score goals – as we found out."

Arsenal had been made to look second rate in the first half but they were the more impressive side in the second. Even so, Tommy thought "I don't think we played better all season." Thomas Wood in the Sunday Express reckoned that "Everton managed to give the impression that their record was a bit of a responsibility and they wouldn't mind getting rid of it." But for John McAdam of the Daily Express, Everton were exemplary – "the ball was handled like a weakly child – wheedled, guided, fed and occasionally belted." Not the kind of politically correct comment we have come to expect in the pages of the daily press nowadays.

Lawton was injured in a clash with Copping. "We collided once when we went for a ball and Wilf said 'Tha's jumping too high , Tom. I'll have to bring you down to my level.' Sure enough the next time we both went for a cross, I end up on the ground with blood streaming from my nose. Wilf was looking down at me and he said 'Ah told thee, Tom. Tha's jumping too high!' My nose was broken. When Arsenal came to Everton, Copping broke my nose again! He was hard, Wilf. You always had something to remember him by when you played against him." Most correspondents were lavish in praise of Lawton. "Lawton is more than a rusher and a finisher. He is a clever footballer, bringing his wing men into the game with shrewd flicks and widely flung and accurate passes. He is dangerous because he shoots from anywhere and for an 18-year-old really is an extraordinary footballer." Roland Allen in the Evening Standard was obviously convinced of his qualities and so too was Wood in the Sunday Express – "the secret of Lawton's goalscoring was that he never did the obvious and all the time was working extremely hard." On the train home to Liverpool, the players and officials indulged in a mild celebration. The players were chatting over a few bottles of beer. At one table, Tommy and T G were sitting with Gordon Watson and Billy Cook. The chairman Will Cuff walked past. "He looked across at me" said Tommy '"and said 'Have you ever been to Ireland, Lawton?' I said 'No sir, I haven't.' He just smiled and nodded and walked on. I thought 'What on earth was that about?'"

CHAPTER TEN

1938 – EVERTON **THE INTERNATIONAL STAGE**

Three days after the Arsenal game, Lawton understood exactly what the chairman had been referring to on the train home. A letter arrived from the Football League advising him that he had been selected to play at centre-forward in the Inter-League game against the Irish League at Windsor Park in Belfast on September 21st 1938. "I was just on the way out of the door going down to the ground for training when the postman arrived with a letter. Well, we didn't get many letters in those days, not at the house anyway and hardly any for me. When I opened it, I just couldn't believe it. It was a very formal invitation. 'Dear Lawton.... you are invited to play. You should report to...' All that type of thing. Oh! And it reminded me to bring my own boots! I was just so elated. I dashed down to Goodison to find out who else from Everton would be playing. But nobody else had got a letter. I suddenly realised I'd be on my own." In the meantime there was the little matter of Portsmouth at Goodison Park to deal with in order to set the new record of six successive wins from the start of a Division One season. "They were a good side. Jack Tinn, their manager, had done a good job at Fratton Park and they proved that after only about seven minutes or so because they surprised us by taking the lead. Maybe we thought that we had done the hard work by beating Arsenal, but we knew then that we couldn't take it easy. In the end, we put five past them. I scored another, so that was eight in six games, I'd scored in all six and we had set a new record."

Lawton reported, as instructed, to the Adelphi Hotel in Liverpool the following Tuesday to link up with the rest of the Football League team prior to catching the ferry across to Belfast. The rest of his teammates were familiar names to him but he did not know any of them well. Eddie Hapgood, the captain, and Stanley Matthews both made the teenager welcome, but could do little about his nerves, not so much about the game, more because of the impending sea crossing. Tommy was relieved when the ferry reached Belfast without incident, but only just in time. En route to Windsor Park, heavy rain was whipped up by a gale into a massive downpour. Hardly the best of days for football. Ten minutes into the second half, with the score level at 2-2, the rain became torrential. "I suppose there were about 2,000 spectators on the uncovered terrace on one side of the ground and they'd obviously decided they'd had enough of getting soaked through, so they just swarmed across the pitch and dashed for the cover of the stand on the other side." The game was held up for several minutes as this invasion took place, the players, engulfed by the crowd, could not believe what was happening. In the middle of the confusion, all Lawton could hear was referee Peter Craigmyle repeatedly blowing his whistle as he tried to restore order. Eventually the game resumed and the Football League swept to an 8-2 victory. Lawton scored four.

"The hold-up affected the Irish more than us, I think. After that, Stan and Len Goulden just hit top form. Stan was just dazzling down the right. Len made my third with a pass that just split the defence, all I had to do was run onto it and hit it." The headlines on the back pages the following day hailed Lawton's goalscoring brilliance and called for his inclusion in the full England team. Lawton, however, always insisted that no-one should "run away with the idea that I was the star of that game. Stan Matthews and Len Goulden were at their best that day and nobody could outshine them. Len's pass for that third goal of mine was just the sort that centre-forwards pray for."

Meanwhile, the mounting threat of serious conflict in Europe meant that the FA gave serious thought to suspending all football from the First Division to local leagues but, eventually, they gave the next round of fixtures the go-ahead.

On September 24th, Everton's unbeaten run came to an end at Leeds Road when Huddersfield beat them 3-0. Two goals in three minutes from Tom Hinchcliffe ensured there was no way back for Everton. That was Hinchcliffe's finest achievement. The two goals were all he scored that season for Town. In November, he was sold to Derby County.

"Quite frankly we all felt relieved. A run like that puts a tremendous strain on the players. Everyone is waiting for you to lose and every team is determined to be the one that beats you. I look at the clubs that have had long unbeaten runs, like Forest and Liverpool and Manchester United and there's a common factor. The managers have all been great motivators. We didn't have that. Our motivation came from within the team. We motivated each other."

Prime Minister Neville Chamberlain returned from Munich waving his piece of paper which gave people hope that another world war could be avoided. "Some people believed in that so much. We really didn't think much about it, we had other things on our minds." The following day, Liverpool came 'across the park' for the next league match. With the rest of Britain still breathing a collective sigh of relief at the avoidance of the seemingly impending global catastrophe, at Goodison there were weightier matters to dispute. Before kick-off there was a brief ceremony, prayers of thanks for the keeping of the peace in Europe, a hearty rendition of 'God Save The King' and it was down to the real business of the day. In front of 64,977, Everton won the first of two local derbies 2-1. For once Lawton failed to score, but on the blue side of the city they barely noticed as they celebrated goals by Stan Bentham and Wally Boyes, while Liverpool's came from Willie Fagan.

Liverpool had been in third place. Everton's next challenge came from fifth-placed Wolverhampton Wanderers at Goodison. "We thought Wolves were the toughest side around that season and we had to play them without three of our best players. Billy Cook and Alex Stevenson were playing for Ireland against Scotland, who'd picked Torry Gillick. They didn't postpone league games for international calls back then, so we had to bring in a lad called Arthur Barber to play on the wing. He was my age, but only about six weeks before he'd been playing in junior football down in Somerset with Weston-super-Mare. Some difference that." Wolves were a strong side under Major Buckley pre-war. In defence they had three England internationals in Stan Cullis, Tom Galley and Bill Morris. In attack they had two most prodigious goalscorers in Dickie Dorsett and Dennis Westcott. "There was always a great deal of rivalry between me and Dennis. He was from Wallasey on the other side of the Mersey and he'd been on the Everton books as a youngster. He was a year or two older than me and Everton let him go to New Brighton. Well, about the time that I got in Burnley's first team he was number 9 for New Brighton and he was scoring goals (six in his first seven games) and he never stopped when he went to Wolves. He was a strong lad, fast and with him and Dickie always changing positions, he was difficult to mark. He was always out to prove that Everton had made a mistake by letting him go and we always had great battles against him." On this occasion, Westcott was eclipsed by Lawton as he scored the only goal of the match, nine in nine league games for him from the start of the season. Everton were top of the table, and Tommy, in prime form was headline news . On the Sunday, his day off, he went to Worsthorne near Burnley to visit his girlfriend. Unfortunately, he was not able to give her his full attention. "I was on tenterhooks. It had been about three weeks since the match in Belfast and in between times, most sports writers had been putting my name forward as England's number nine." None more emphatically than Charles Buchan. In the *News Chronicle* he wrote "Lawton is undoubtedly England's centre-forward. His great headwork, moulded on the pattern of Dixie Dean, and his clever footwork, stamps him as England's leader for many years to come."

England's next international game was away to Wales at the end of October. "Some of the Everton lads like Billy Cook and Alex Stevenson were telling me not to get my hopes up. Ted Sagar said that I would definitely get an England cap but perhaps not then. I was only just 19 and England didn't exactly have a record of picking teenagers in the full side. All week though I was so pent-up. I knew they were announcing the side on the Sunday but I had no way of finding out if I was in. I just couldn't wait till the six o'clock news on the wireless.

"So I just dawdled around for a while then, when I went past a phone box, hit on the idea of calling the local paper's sports desk and asking them

1937. Looking the part – Burnley's rising young star. (Tom Lawton collection)

1937/38. Learning fast. Tommy (back row, fifth from left) at the Dixie Dean football Academy. (Gordon Watson collection)

1937/38. Like choirboys. Tommy (back row, second from right) as usual in the close company of T G Jones (back row, third from right) on their first trip abroad with Everton in Copenhagen. (Gordon Watson collection)

*1937/38. Post Dixie. Tommy Lawton – Everton's first choice centre-forward.
(Hulton Getty)*

August 1938. "We didn't even look at what we were signing." The Everton School of Science ready for another season – and what a season! (Gordon Watson collection)

October 24th 1938. Doing the Lambeth Walk. New England cap Tommy Lawton and the rest of the team at the Drury Lane theatre with Lupino Lane and the cast of Me and My Girl. (Tom Lawton collection)

March 1939. Everton, in their best training togs, prior to meeting Wolves in the FA Cup fifth round. (Gordon Watson collection)

1938/39. Everton's title, Tommy Lawton First Division leading scorer, 34 in 38 games. (Tom Lawton collection)

1939. The Football League champions. Back row 1-r Harry Cooke (trainer), Jock Thomson, Gordon Watson, Billy Cook, Ted Sagar, Joe Mercer, Norman Greenhalgh, T G Jones. Front row Torry Gillick, Stan Bentham, Tommy Lawton, Alex Stevenson, Wally Boyes, Jimmy Caskie. (Gordon Watson collection)

October 1939. Everton chairman Wilf Cuff distributes cheques to cover the players' accrued share of benefit. They were the only club to pay up every member of their staff on the outbreak of war. (Gordon Watson collection)

September 3rd 1939. Champions for the next six years. Joe Mercer, Tommy Lawton, Jimmy Caskie, Gordon Watson and T G Jones face the uncertain future.
(Gordon Watson collection)

1939/40. Who scored in every one of Everton's Division One games that season?
(Hulton Getty)

1941. Ready for battle. Tommy's first marriage was never the happiest.
(Liverpool Daily Post and Echo)

1941. In the Army now. 1548031 Company Sergeant Major Instructor Lawton and his team in between matches at Aldershot. (Tom Lawton collection)

January 7th 1942. England v Scotland at Wembley. Tommy Lawton and Scotland goalkeeper Jerry Dawson challenge for a Stan Matthews' centre. Matt Busby with a close up view, Bill Shankly nearest penalty spot. (Hulton Getty)

December 29th 1945. The Dell. They played in tough in those days. Tommy Lawton, with black eyes courtesy of Charlie Bumstead of Millwall the day before, helps Southampton's Bill Dodgin off the pitch after an accidental collision. (Duncan Holley collection)

April 1946. Mr Tommy Lawton (Chelsea and England) demobbed at Kingston upon Thames. (Tom Lawton collection)

September 16th 1946. Tommy Lawton's "Football is My Business" became a bestseller was was reprinted the following year. (Tom Lawton collection)

1947. Striding out at Stamford Bridge. So cold that winter that the players' hair froze.

January 1947. Success in the FA Cup for Tommy Lawton. One of his three goals in the third round tie with Arsenal which went to two replays.

October 1st 1949. Out of his class. Notts County v Leyton Orient at Meadow Lane and a 7-1 win for Notts. Tommy Lawton scored twice and gave Dave Davidson the run around. (Tom Lawton collection)

1948. Hero worship. Tommy Lawton and Billy Baxter meet three young Notts fans, including, perhaps, the young Trevor Mitchell? (Hulton Getty)

April 22nd 1950. Where are they now. An all-ticket crowd at Meadow Lane for the Division Three South derby between Notts County and Nottingham Forest. Tommy shakes hands with his great friend Horace Gager, captain of Forest. Lawton and Jackie Sewell scored as Notts won 2-0 to finish as champions. (Tom Lawton collection)

if the team had been announced. A voice at the other end of the line began to read 'Woodley, Sproston, Hapgood.' He was reading really slowly and I was getting more and more anxious.' Willingham, Young, Copping.' Yes, yes. 'Matthews, Robinson, Morton...' I said 'Morton. Who's he?' And the chap said, 'Bloody hell. Never heard of Lawton, Our Tom?' And I was outside that phone box dancing with delight. I didn't find out the other two names 'til the next day, but that didn't matter, I was in! The best tuppence I ever spent." The sub-editor at the Burnley *Express and News* had no idea who was calling so he can be forgiven for missing out on a first quote from England's new cap.

Sixteen days after his 19th birthday Lawton sat in the England dressing room at Ninian Park, Cardiff, as the singing of the 40,000 crowd, mainly Welshmen, built to a crescendo. He had been nervous before the Inter-League match, but he had experienced nothing like this.

Wales; John (Swansea); Whatley (Tottenham), Hughes (Birmingham); Green (Charlton), T G Jones (Everton), Richards (Birmingham); Hopkins (Brentford), Leslie Jones (Arsenal), Astley (Derby County), B Jones (Arsenal), Cumner (Arsenal).

England: Woodley (Chelsea); Sproston (Tottenham), Hapgood (Arsenal); Willingham (Huddersfield), Young (Huddersfield), Copping (Arsenal); Matthews (Stoke), Robinson (Sheffield Wednesday), Lawton (Everton), Goulden (West Ham), Boyes (Everton).

"In the week before the game, my big mate, Yanto Jones had been picked for Wales and he kept telling me that I was not going to get a kick! Now Yanto was a great player, 'The Prince of Wales.' I knew how good he was and I kept thinking 'what if he's right?' Our captain, Eddie Hapgood, came over to me and said 'Good luck, Tom. By the way, you're taking the penalties.' I think I said, 'Oh God!' but I was quietly very pleased."

In front of a partisan Welsh crowd, England were no match for Wales and lost 4-2. Derby's Dai Astley with his "mustard left peg" was outstanding at inside-forward for Wales and with T G Jones shackling Lawton, chances were limited. Midway through the second half, England were awarded a penalty and Lawton slammed it past goalkeeper Roy John. "It was about the only kick that I was allowed that day. Yanto played an absolute blinder." Sixty years on, T G recalled the game and his performance. "You just couldn't afford to allow Tommy a kick. Think what he would have done with it. He was the type of player who only needed half a chance and it was in." While Lawton himself felt he had underperformed at Ninian Park, press reports suggested that his debut had been a promising one. Charles Buchan, after the build-up he had given Lawton following the Arsenal game, could hardly do anything else but suggest that: "Lawton led the line with great skill, holding his own with Jones, his dogged club-mate." He added "Lawton has come to stay as England's centre-forward. He played with the assurance and thoughtfulness of an old campaigner." Unstinting praise.

While acknowledging that Scotland were the 'Auld Enemy,' Tommy always thought that Wales put up stiffer opposition against England during his time as an international. "They were a very talented side. They had forwards who'd cost fortunes like Bryn Jones. They had Les Jones, Dai Astley and Dai's big pal, Idris Hopkins. Today, they'd be worth millions! I mean, Bryn Jones, he hit these long, sweeping passes and Dai would be scurrying around, just hitting these short balls and darting onto the return." Wales appeared to have a surfeit of talented inside-forwards and half-backs in the pre-war years. Bryn Jones is possibly the best known, since Arsenal signed him for a world record fee. In 1937, Les Jones had been controversially signed by Arsenal from Coventry in a player-exchange deal after Tottenham had offered £6,000 for him. Astley and Hopkins were both miners from Merthyr, where they lived in the same street and shared the same birthday. Having endured the grinding poverty in Wales during the '20s, Astley had every intention of making as much as he could out of the game. In November 1936, Jimmy Seed, the Charlton manager, refused to go through with a deal that had been agreed with Aston Villa because of Astley's "under the counter" demands. The following day he was amazed to see Astley at the Valley. He had signed for Charlton's opponents, Derby County. With players earning only £8 a week in the late '30s, the temptation to ask for an extra payment as a signing on fee when being transferred was great. Tommy always insisted that he never took anything other than his accrued share of benefit and the standard £10 signing on fee from his transfers. "It was often alleged that I took more than my share but nothing could be further from the truth. Whenever I heard the rumours and stories about me, my attitude was, 'Let them say what they like.' I felt I was too big to bother about petty rumours."

He once detailed his earnings in the 1938/39 season:-

Winter Pay	per week £8	£266.00
Summer Pay	per week £6	£100.00
Internationals	per match £8	£ 64.00
Overseas expenses per day	10/- (50p)	£ 10.50
League championship bonus		£ 25.00
Points bonuses (league and cup)		£ 7.00
Total		£531.50

Tommy was quick to point out that it amounted to little more than a top comedian of the day earned in a week. "Nobody suggested that Trinder should be paid the same as a girl in the chorus line. Yet in football a star like Stan Matthews might earn the same in a week as a lad at Accrington Stanley. The system was all wrong and, no doubt, led to under-the-counter payments. We were drawing gates worth £25,000 for internationals and only getting about £10 with expenses. In any other walk of life, a man who was a success would have got a rise. But we didn't. We could have a benefit, if the club wanted to pay! And then only £650 maximum. We were lucky to play the game for a living, but that was the only reward, to be playing a game we loved." It was indeed widely suggested that Lawton earned more from his various transfers than most. The first secretary of the Professional Footballers' Association, Jimmy Guthrie,wrote "It's a fairly safe bet that there was 'a little something' for Tommy each time he moved, but should that have been necessary? It was the Lawton brain and trained body, plus his accrued skills and experience, that was sold and the selling clubs got the money."

Four days after the international in Cardiff, England were due to play against the Rest of the World at Highbury, a game to mark the 75th anniversary of the Football Association. The selectors met immediately after the Wales game to pick the side. "It was an anxious time for all of us. I was convinced that they'd leave me out and bring back someone like Ted Drake on his home ground. In the end they kept me, but dropped Alf Young and Jackie Robinson and brought in Stan Cullis and Willie Hall." The match was given a tremendous build up in the press. England had never lost at home to foreign opposition, but they had never faced a side of this calibre. The Rest of the World side was selected from all the countries affiliated to FIFA. The Home Nations did not join up until after the war, but that still left over two-million players to choose from world wide. In the event the team came entirely from Europe and Scandinavia, though Michele Andreolo was a Uruguayan who played for Italy. It was still reckoned to be the strongest eleven ever assembled for a match in Britain.

FIFA XI – Olivieri; Foni, Rava (all Italy); Kupfer (Germany), Andreolo (Italy), Kitzinger (Germany); Aston (France), Braine (Belgium), Piola (Italy), Zsellenger (Hungary), Brustad (Norway).

Tommy did not remember the game with any great relish, although England won 3-0 and he scored one of the goals, Willie Hall and Len Goulden the others. "It leaves a bad taste in my mouth whenever I think about it. The referee was Jimmy Jewell. When he gave a free-kick against Andreolo for a foul and it was a real lunge on Ken Willingham, the Italian spat at him. Deliberately. It was just disgusting and Mr Jewell just ignored it! Kept his temper and did nothing at all in view of the occasion and the dignitaries and all in the stand. Fortunately we had Wilf Copping and Willingham in our side and they never let an insult like that pass unnoticed! The continentals kicked, hacked, punched, pulled jerseys, obstructed and tried to play without the ball." Seventeen years on, Charles Buchan wrote that the match demonstrated that the most important aspect of football is teamwork. The European team comprised brilliant players but apart from the four Italian defenders they were strangers to each other. "Whenever a movement broke down, they stood in the middle of the field, waving their arms or shrugging their shoulders. England's combined team took matters easily. The forward line – Matthews (Stoke City), Hall (Spurs), Lawton (Everton), Goulden (West Ham) and Boyes (Everton) – gave them a lesson in combined play." What Buchan apparently forgot when making his observation some years after the war, was that Lawton was making only his second appearance for England. The first having hardly been successful at Ninian Park. Yet still the side turned in a decent performance. Tommy would always point out that, pre-war, the England team had very little preparation time together. "We didn't have a week to practice before a match like they do these days. We met up the night before if we were lucky. Often, in war-time, only just before kick-off! Brains made the difference. You only have to look at the great players we had – Willie Hall, Len Goulden, Sir Stan Matthews, Stan Cullis. Oh! It makes me shudder when I think of those days. The likes of Wilf Mannion, Raich Carter, Joe Mercer, Tom Finney. I mean, you couldn't buy them today. With players like them, my job was easy. Yet I'd look at the other centre-forwards who were around – Ted Drake, Bobby Gurney, Albert Stubbins, Dennis Westcott – there were seven or eight of them, and I'd think 'Well, if one of them gets in to the England team, then I'll have to wait another two years before I get another chance. I had to make sure that nobody took that number nine shirt away from me."

November 1938 was a memorable month for Tommy Lawton. He was in the Football League side that beat the Scottish League 3-1 at Molineux. A week later, he scored for England in the 4-0 defeat of Norway at St James' Park, his third goal in three full internationals. Alongside him in the England forward line, Stan Matthews had been a permanent fixture and a source of great encouragement as well as an endless supply of decent centres. The inside forwards had been ever changing and for the match against Ireland at Old Trafford on the 16th November, they recalled Jackie Robinson at inside-left and Willie Hall at inside-right.

Hall, five foot six, stocky and fair haired had made his England debut as far back as 1933, but the Ireland game was only his seventh cap. He had played well against the FIFA XI but disappointed against the Scottish League. His recall was hardly greeted with enthusiasm by the newspaper pundits.

Yet with Matthews on top form it went brilliantly well for England and especially for Hall. Matthews tormented Lawton's Everton team-mate, Billy Cook, the Ireland captain, setting up the first for Lawton after leaving four Ireland defenders trailing in his wake. Then, between the 34th and 38th minutes, Matthews and Lawton laid on the fastest hat-trick in international football for the 26-year-old Hall. He added two more, one an unlikely overhead bicycle kick, to equal the number of goals scored in a single game for England. Charles Buchan reported that it was "His shooting that day had to be seen to be believed. Personally, I have never seen anything better." He added, "Funnily enough, Hall had no really great reputation as a goalscorer." Tommy was stunned by the performance on his right. "Hall and Matthews working together like two super craftsmen, as perfectly as two busy knitting needles, a wing that for 90 minutes matched anything that England had ever before fielded; a wing that, perhaps, gave the greatest cohesion of single thought and, at the same time, of unselfish play that I've ever seen." Hall kept his place for the next three games, missing out only in Bucharest, the last match of England's 1939 tour, through injury. He appeared in three war-time internationals, partnering Lawton for the last time against Wales at Cardiff in May 1942. By then, he was plagued by injury, a result of the harsh treatment he received from defenders determined that he should not repeat his five goal exercise against them. He retired in May 1944, but thrombosis set in and he was forced to have both legs amputated. A tragic end to a fine career, though he retains the England scoring record for a single match, shared with Malcolm Macdonald among others.

Shortly before his death in 1967, Willie Hall was still insisting that his feat in November 1938, "owed much to the unselfishness of Matthews and Lawton." – 7-0 the final score. *The Daily Telegraph* reported that "We have known Matthews as a fine player, sure in his control of the ball, and beautifully balanced on his feet. This afternoon, he reached a pinnacle and at the close the crowd rose to him as one to salute the player whose wizardry had them fascinated." Opinion on Matthews was divided. Even his friend Raich Carter thought that he was "so much of the star individualist that, though one of the best players of all times, he is not really a good footballer. When Stan gets the ball on the wing, you don't know when it's coming back. He's an extraordinarily difficult winger to play alongside." Tommy sympathised with Billy Cook "who'd spent the whole afternoon chasing shadows, but he was always a sportsman. He even congratulated Stan when he scored. Sometimes Stan could make everything look so ridiculously easy." That was not to say that sometimes Lawton, like Carter, became irritated with the great man. "Yes, I fumed at times when he headed off on one of those mazy dribbles of his, but you'd forget all about that when he produced a cross that was just perfection." In the next international, he was to do just that.

In the meantime, Lawton had a little unfinished business to attend to with Everton – completing the title chase successfully.

CHAPTER ELEVEN
1939 – EVERTON CHAMPIONSHIP RUN IN

Over the Christmas period, Everton had stumbled badly as Derby County came up on the rails to take over at the top of the First Division with a 2-2 draw at Goodison and a 2-1 win at the Baseball Ground. Lawton did not play in the first game, injured and replaced by Bunny Bell. Derby won the return with an astonishing goal from Douglas Dally Duncan. 'Derby were a good side, Sammy Crooks on the right wing could catch pigeons, but that match was won by Dally on his own. He went past Billy Cook like greased lightening and fired in a shot from an impossible angle that swerved and dipped past Ted Sagar. Jock Thomson was so angry. "What a bloody fluke!" Dai Astley was near him and he said "Oh no! He's always doing that." It was neither Everton's nor Tommy's best spell of the season as he went five games without scoring, during which Everton won just once.

Their form returned however and by Easter Everton were leading the chase again. A 'full house' of six points over the holiday period might possibly have given them the title for the first time since 1932. The fixture compiler, though, had not been kind to them as Everton had to play Sunderland at Roker, then travel to London to meet Chelsea, before heading home for the return with Sunderland at Goodison.

The first leg of the Easter treble at Roker was accomplished, 2-1 on Good Friday. The team then left Newcastle by sleeper train for London. "We were all in a great mood. Sunderland had some big names, Raich Carter and all. We all got on the train really keyed up. It was impossible to sleep so Yanto brought out a pack of cards and we played well into the night, with the train roaring through the darkness. We must have got some sleep though, because by the time the steward came round with a tray of teas, the train was in Euston and we were all snoring away happily." Everton continued to snooze on the pitch at Stamford Bridge with a below-par performance. Chelsea defended well. Everton missed chances. Untypically, Lawton skied one from a Stevenson centre high into the Shed End. Joe Mercer saw his powerful drive turned round the post by goalkeeper Vic Woodley and with 15 minutes left it was still goalless. "Then the miracle happened! Alex Stevenson headed a goal! When you think that Stan Matthews headed the ball more often than Stevie you can see why I call it a miracle." "Alex Stevenson was so small," says Gordon Watson, "that we used to call him Mickey after Mickey Mouse. For that header though he was up above Bobby Salmond (Chelsea's centre-half). It was a great moment because Stevie had played so well all season, he was probably our most consistent player and that's saying something because we were a great side." A couple of minutes later, Torry Gillick put Everton two up and made certain of their second win of the weekend. The team returned to Merseyside for the Easter Monday game with Sunderland, aware that Wolves, chasing an unlikely League and Cup double, were not yet out of the hunt despite a 4-2 defeat at Preston.

Everton did all that they had to do against Sunderland, beating them 6-2. The result confirming that Sunderland's position as one of the powerhouse clubs in the land was beginning to slip. Carter was marshalling affairs from inside-right, but that "bundle of energy" Bobby Gurney, hampered by injury, appeared in only eight games that season and his inside-left, the Scottish international Paddy Gallacher, in just nine before he was sold to Stoke City. The team that had won the championship in 1936 and the FA Cup a year later, to be rated the best in the country, was breaking up and there were new pretenders to the title.

The crowd came over the wall at the end of the game, convinced that their heroes had done it, but they still needed one more win to make sure.

Tommy was away with England in Scotland when the next league game, a home fixture with Preston North End, took place. It finished goalless and with Wolves beating Charlton 3-1 at the Molineux, there was still no confirmation of the championship.

The following week at the Valley, a distinctly nervous Everton went down 2-1 to third-placed Charlton Athletic, but Wolves lost at Bolton Wanderers and Everton could not be overhauled. The team planned a major celebration back at the Langham Hotel, but even though they had won the title, the elements of professionalism came through.

Gordon Watson recalled how: "in the first minute I made a mistake that led to the Charlton goal and we were one down in no time. Well, nobody said anything then, except 'Come on lads' and that type of thing, but back at the hotel, where we'd gone for a few drinks, Billy Cook really laid into me, he gave me hell about that mistake and there was no chance of a drink until he'd got the message across. It was a hard school." Everton rounded off their season with a relaxed 3-0 win at Goodison over Aston Villa. Lawton had scored 34 goals in 36 league games – a major contribution to the campaign – but he left the scoring against Villa to Bentham, Gillick and Cook, though he did have two fierce drives beaten out by the Villa goalkeeper Rutherford.

"And do you know what they gave us as a reward for winning the title?" asked T G Jones some 60 years later. "A day trip to Morecambe. Oh! We could bring the wife if we wanted!" For Tommy, the 1938/39 Everton side was "the best. I never played in a better club side than Everton that season." While acknowledging the part played by Stevenson's consistent promptings from midfield, he thought T G Jones was the biggest factor in the title win. "Yanto was a real taskmaster. He was never satisfied with even the finest performance." For journalist J L Manning in the *Daily Sketch*, Everton won the championship because "every man was enjoying a game of football and not making a job of work of it." Though that did not mean, as Gordon Watson's brush with Billy Cook demonstrated, that they were unprofessional. Towards the end of his life, Lawton regarded football as a "commercial business, not a sport any more. But every player loves the game and whether he makes his living at it or not makes no difference to his love for the game." He may have questioned the motives and objectives of certain individuals involved in the game in later years, which made him reluctant to be in the mainstream, but he always loved football and the 1938/39 season provided one of the highspots of his eventful life.

CHAPTER TWELVE
1939 – EVERTON
THE WEMBLEY FACTOR

In retrospect, Tommy acknowledged that his best chance of winning the FA Cup came in 1939. "That Everton side had everything, Experienced men like Ted Sagar and Billy Cook, Joe Mercer and Jock Thomson at wing-half, Torry Gillick and Jimmy Caskie, two Scottish wingers and young lads like me and Tommy Jones, still learners but dead keen." Everton's progress in the Cup that 1938/39 season hinted at the possibility of success. They had beaten the favourites Derby County in round three with a Wally Boyes' goal; smashed eight past Doncaster Rovers in round four; then, after a 2-2 draw at St Andrews before a crowd of 67,144, they won the replay against Birmingham City 2-1 and were drawn away in the quarter final, to the new favourites – Wolverhampton Wanderers.

"Wolves were a big, strong side in those days, they always have been really. Major Frank Buckley was the manager and he wanted big, strapping lads who could plough through anything, like Stan Cullis. When he was a manager, Stan was the same – he wanted wing halves like Ron Flowers and Bill Slater. It's no surprise that Major Buckley sent Billy Wright home before he'd even played a game. He wasn't the Wolves' type at all, 'Not big enough' they told him, but he proved them wrong. What a loss he would have been, not just to Wolves but to England. A hundred caps, a great captain and a lovely man but, in those days, not the Wolves type."

Wolves had demolished Everton 7-0 at Molineux in the league a fortnight earlier when Lawton played inside-right to Bunny Bell, a centre-forward who had been signed in March 1936 from Tranmere to replace Dixie Dean. He never had much of chance at Goodison. On Boxing Day 1935, Bell had scored nine for Tranmere against Oldham Athletic – and missed a penalty – but although he scored nine goals in 14 appearances for Everton, he was soon eclipsed by Lawton and later returned across the Mersey to Tranmere. In the league game at Molineux both Bell and Lawton found the mud a real handicap. "The weather had been perfect all week, but when we got to the ground, the pitch was almost water-logged. I said to Joe Mercer 'What's all this about?' and he just laughed and said 'Oh, it's the Wolves' water-cart, been busy again.'" Stan Cullis remembered that Theo Kelly, Everton's secretary-manager, sent Harry Cooke, the trainer, down to Molineux on the morning of the game. Cooke saw the state of the pitch and ran straight back to the Grand Hotel to tell Kelly that the boots they had brought with them would not suit the heavy going because the studs were too short. An extra long stud was required but this could only be fitted in the boot-room at the ground. "The trainer asked the secretary of the Wolves who had the key to the boot-room, but the secretary said he didn't know. The trainer went to the groundsman... he didn't know either. I don't know how many people he asked, until he finally ended up in Major Buckley's office and, eventually, was given the key."

As a result of this episode, Everton, whose chairman was Will Cuff, also a big-wig at the Football League, proposed a rule that no club should be allowed to excessively water the pitch. While Everton regarded the Wolves watering as gamesmanship, Raich Carter among others, thought it should be positively encouraged. "It should be made compulsory. It reduces the risk of serious injury if a player takes an awkward toss on a soft ground he'll probably get away with it. On an iron hard ground that same fall can probably mean a broken limb. In any case, good football needs a yielding pitch, a light ball on a hard ground is extremely difficult to control. Sunderland always found that their Molineux pitch suited us as much as it did them." The Molineux mud however was not the main story. The papers had splashed the extraordinary tale that the Wolves players were being injected with monkey glands to enhance their stamina and performance. The public was fascinated and appalled. The newspapers fuelled their interest.

The so-called 'monkey gland treatment' had been initiated by Major Buckley. Stan Cullis has always insisted that this was pure fabrication but milked by the manager for all it was worth. "The papers were full of this 'monkey-gland treatment' and it was a big talking point, none of the other clubs had it, but I think it was just an anti-flu injection. Major Buckley was not one to miss out on a chance of publicity for the Wolves and he told the press that it was something to do with 'monkey glands' and they built it up into the most sensational thing ever." Most of the Wolves' players were nervous about the injection, some convincing themselves that it was just a stunt of the manager's, others that it was simply water in the syringe, while some, like Cullis, believed it was a 'flu jab. None of them ever knew for sure and on this occasion it worked spectacularly.

Certainly, Tommy believed that Wolves had been taking something. "Before the game, I saw Stan Cullis walking down to the dressing rooms. I knew him from the England team, so I called out 'Hello, Stan, aren't you speaking to me then?' And he just walked past me, eyes glazed and ignored me. Well, there was no doubt in my mind they were on those monkey pills or something like. They absolutely thrashed us, even though Joe Mercer and Gordon Watson had great games. At half-time, they were 5-0 up and weren't even sweating. Jock Thomson, our captain, came in the dressing room and said 'Don't worry lads, they were playing with the wind that half.' And Alex Stevenson next to me on the bench just muttered 'Some bloody wind!'"

According to Charles Buchan the 'gland business' did not amount to much. "I did not believe glands or any stimulant had anything to do with their grand play. It was due, in my opinion, to the co-operation of eleven young athletes who were great footballers." Buchan interviewed Buckley about the treatment. "I was convinced that the effect was psychological, not physical." Having lost in the league 7-0, Everton knew just what to expect come the Cup quarter final. T G Jones recalled that Everton trained at Harrogate from the Tuesday to the Thursday and travelled down by coach to Wolverhampton on the Friday before the game. Their worst fears were realised though this time the culprit was not the water cart. "It'd been fine weather all week and on Friday afternoon, the pitch was perfect, " recalled T G, then, overnight, a downpour continued well into Saturday morning and the ground, "was just a mud heap. We were up against it again." The Molineux groundsman forked the pitch as the sun came out and the pitch dried into something resembling a ploughed field. Even so, Everton dominated the first half.

"It was an important match for me," said Tommy. "I wasn't playing very well and there was some talk in the papers that 'this Lawton, well, he's OK for a young lad, but he's not the man we need at centre-forward for England. After Wolves had beaten us 7-0, the press down there (in the Midlands) were saying that Westcott deserves a chance." Westcott was having a great season, on his way to scoring 32 goals in 37 league games and everyone in Wolverhampton and for miles around believed he was better than Lawton.

According to Tommy, Everton "played well in the first half and we should have been in front when Gordon Watson sent me through down the middle, a perfect ball, but then a hand clutched my shirt and the ball ran through to their goalkeeper." Lawton was too much of a gentleman to identify the culprit, but the correspondent of the local paper, the *Express and Star* was proud to write: "Lawton was never in this game. Well, yes, he was, once in the first half. Then he looked all over a scorer until he was brushed off the ball by Cullis."

Stan Cullis was one of Tommy's most respected opponents. "Certainly the greatest centre-half I ever played with or against. Neil Franklin, Billy Wright, Bobby Moore, Franz Beckenbauer, in my opinion, Stan had them all beat. He was a fierce tackler but a ball-player too, he could hold it up until someone was in a good position, or start an attack himself. He also had tremendous confidence and that enabled him to keep his head no matter what the danger. He was always very serious about everything that he did. He was always studying and ready to discuss any new theory, surrealist art, education, whatever. And he's an expert at Esperanto. He did these adverts for hats in the paper – 'Ward's hats, the best I've ever had.' I said 'You'll have to get me one of those hats, Stan.' He said 'We don't make 'em big enough for you.' You could never have the last word with him."

There were just three minutes to go to half-time when Bob Scott, a giant figure of a 'keeper at 6 ft 4ins, gathered the ball from Lawton and cleared downfield, Ted Maguire prodded a pass out to Westcott on the left and he began to cut inside. Four men including T G Jones and Gordon Watson failed to stop him. "Westcott veered inwards," said the *Express and Star's* correspondent, "to beat opponent after opponent. All the time the crowd yelled to Westcott 'Pass it, man, pass it!' but Westcott was deaf to all entreaties and released a magnificent shot which scarcely rose an inch from the ground and found the right-hand corner of the net."

A quarter-of-an-hour after half-time, Westcott and 'Dickie' Dorsett exchanged passes, Westcott went past three Everton defenders and finished with another superb shot. "Westcott's Wonder Goals Won It" shouted the headlines – "Two of the most dramatic and picturesque goals imaginable" began the story and Westcott was applauded as "a modern day Albert Shepherd." (Shepherd, another England international centre-forward born in Lancashire, played for Bolton, Newcastle and Bradford City before the First World War). Even that was not enough for the *Express and Star* since their correspondent confidently asserted "There is no comparison between Lawton, the Everton and England centre-forward, and Westcott."

Said Tommy, "We knew what to expect when we played Wolves, everybody did. The question was, 'Could we stop them?' They used the long ball out to their wingers. Ted Maguire on the left was quick. Norman McIntosh was the deep lying inside-forward with Joe Gardner at wing half and they booted everything out to Maguire and Burton who fed Dennis Westcott, he was good in the air, and Dickie Dorsett snaffled anything that ran loose around the box." Incidentally, Wolves beat Grimsby 5-0 in the semi-final at Old Trafford, but, 'stale, nervy or both' according to one report, lost comfortably 4-1 to Portsmouth in the Final at Wembley. That same 1938/39 season Dickie Dorsett scored 26 goals in 35 league games to add to Westcott's 32. Yet Tommy eclipsed them both with 34 in 38 league matches.

Despite a fine league career Westcott never was capped for England, though he did appear in four war-time internationals, replacing Lawton for a three match spell in 1943 when he scored four goals At the end of that 1938/39 season, 'Pilot' in the *Liverpool Evening Express* described Lawton as "the most feared centre-forward in football." This after a goal he scored in the Lancashire Senior Cup Final against Bury at Gigg Lane – a ferocious 25 yard drive that barely left the ground as it flew into the net.

Even so, having enjoyed such a fine season, being an England regular with a championship medal before the age of 20, it still rankled Tommy that he was not about to appear in a Wembley final. Not for the last time, the Wolves had denied him. He noted that "On reflection, it was the best chance of winning the Cup I had, but I wasn't to know that at the time. I thought I'd got years left but Mr Hitler and his pals ruined most of them."

MATCH OF THE DAY

Scotland v England
Hampden Park, Glasgow
April 15th 1939
Scotland: Dawson (Rangers); Carabine (Third Lanark), Cummings (Aston Villa);
Shankly (Preston), Baxter (Middlesbrough capt), McNab (West Brom);
McSpadyean (Partick Thistle), Walker (Hearts), Dougal (Preston), Venters
(Rangers), Milne (Middlesbrough).
England: Woodley (Chelsea); Morris (Wolves), Hapgood (Arsenal capt);
Willingham (Huddersfield), Cullis (Wolves), Mercer (Everton); Matthews
(Stoke), Hall (Spurs), Lawton (Everton), Goulden (West Ham), Beasley
(Huddersfield).
Attendance 145,000
This was the match the 19-year-old Lawton had always dreamed of. His first
England cap against Scotland and only his fifth in all. England had failed to beat
Scotland in the previous four internationals and had not won in Glasgow for 12
years. Stan Matthews was to provide the crosses from one wing, but the selectors
turned to Eric Brook of Manchester City, who had claimed the last of his 18 caps
almost two years earlier, to provide improved service from the left. Wally Boyes of
Everton and J R Smith of Millwall had been discarded and were ignored even when
Brook reported injured – Pat Beasley being brought in for his only full
international appearance. Tommy regarded a cap against Scotland as "the greatest
prize of all" and sympathised with Brook for missing out. "A fate worse than
death, I should have thought." As a measure of the importance of the Home
Internationals in those days, it mattered little to Lawton that he might also have
missed out at club level, even though Everton were in sight of the title. In Tommy's
priorities, it was country first. Eight of the England team had never played at
Hampden before, the English press showing some concern that the famed
Hampden 'roar' would disturb the inexperienced internationals.

Certainly, Lawton admitted that he had never heard anything like it, but it did
not frighten him. Having experienced it several times on the old ground, he
described it graphically – "It seems to start behind one goal and then echoes and
eddies around and smashes your eardrums. You can almost see it. It makes your
heart thump but once the game starts it doesn't worry me at all. Some players
though do go weak at the knees." On this occasion, England's defence started
nervously, Stan Cullis being the unlikely culprit almost letting in Jimmy Dougal.
After 20 minutes in which the England defence was tested incessantly, Scotland
went ahead after what Peter Wilson in the Sunday Pictorial *called "the most*
appalling error I have ever seen on a football field." Bill Morris intercepted a
Tommy Walker pass intended for Dougal, hesitated, thought about booting it clear
but instead played it back for his goalkeeper Vic Woodley. The goalkeeper was on
his way out off his line, the pass was well wide of him and left Dougal with a
simple tap in. Dougal was the slight, quick-moving centre-forward who had done
so much for Preston during their successful FA Cup run the previous season. For

the Scots packed into Hampden, this simple goal meant so much more than victory in an English competition.

Meanwhile, Lawton was having difficulty making any impression on the Scotland centre-half Bobby Baxter. In the early part of Everton's 1938/39 season the precocious Lawton had experienced no problems scoring the goals that put his club in pole position for the First Division title, but when Everton's form slumped in mid-season, so did Lawton's. And he was still out of touch in early April. His lack of goals had not gone unnoticed and it was not just Dennis Westcott who was staking a claim. At Arsenal, Ted Drake was tipped for a recall after scoring five goals in four matches during March 1939.

Lawton decided to go back to basics. He had never experienced such a goal drought and with the help of his Everton teammates, particularly Alec Stevenson, Joe Mercer and goalkeeper Ted Sagar, he went through the drill established five years earlier at Turf Moor under Ray Bennion. "Joe and Stevie just kept pushing balls through the centre or crossing from the wings. Stevie would be shouting 'Just hit 'em, hit 'em!' and eventually after I'd peppered the stands and the terraces with miskicks and skiers, Ted was having a real afternoon of it!" By chance, the day before the selectors met to pick the England side for Hampden, Everton were at Ayresome Park to play Middlesbrough, whose centre-half just happened to be Bobby Baxter. Four-all was the final score – Everton's four all from Lawton. Now his England place was secure.

At Hampden, though, in windy conditions with heavy rain throughout the game, Lawton began shakily, like the rest of the England team. "Lawton and Beasley were right off form," said Peter Wilson. "Baxter had Lawton's address," wrote "Rex" in the Sunday Mail. Baxter was not repeating the mistakes of the previous weekend when he had allowed Lawton far too much room and the Scots should have been well ahead by half-time.

During the break both teams changed their shirts sodden by the driving rain. England had not brought a spare set so reappeared in kit borrowed from the Scottish amateur club Queens Park who played at Hampden. The famous roar built to a new crescendo but it failed to intimidate England, only inspire them. After 65 minutes Stan Cullis broke out of defence, found Len Goulden who centred for Lawton, Jimmy Carabine should have cut it out but missed it, Lawton set up the unmarked Beasley who gleefully smashed it past Dawson from 12 yards. A goal in his only international for Beasley.

With the wind at their backs, England penned Scotland in their own half. Mercer became the dominant figure in midfield and Matthews shifted more into the centre and found extra yards of space. A rare Matthews' shot was kept out by Dawson, then he won another "grand duel" with McNab to set up Goulden. The inside forward laid off for Lawton who, astonishingly, blasted an excellent chance wide of the open goal. England's last chance had gone it seemed, but with 70 seconds left, Matthews again began to weave a mazy pattern down the right, then swept past McNab. Shadowed by George Cummings, virtually to the corner flag, Matthews checked, then jinked inside, leaving the Villa full-back floundering, and centred.

Lawton had pounded through the morass in the middle, Goulden and Mercer "like two destroyers" in support. The cross was perfect, Lawton saw it all the way and "Glory be! There it was up in the corner of the net with the outstretched fingers of the diving Dawson inches from it." Matthews remembered that: "It was then that Tommy proved just what a great centre-forward and header of the ball he was. Seated in the mud on my backside I watched him rise majestically, the sinews in his neck bulging like strands of cooked spaghetti as he strained to make the height of the ball... It flew into the net and I watched a thousand tiny raindrops fall in unison onto the Hampden turf at the back of Jerry Dawson's goal." Soaked to the skin, the rest of the team dashed over to Matthews. "We were drenched, but didn't notice. Eddie Hapgood was skipping around like a mudlark. I picked up Stan and said 'For God's sake man, I'm six foot tall, not six foot three!' Now, he had a peculiar habit of blowing on his fingers and he just blew and in his high pitched voice said 'Oh, alright! I'll put that right next time!'"

"It is a long time since I saw an England side play with such united enthusiasm," wrote George Allison in the Sunday Express, "they clustered around each other as they ran wet, dirty and bedraggled from the scene of a great triumph."

"I've played all these years and this is the win I've longed for," said the captain, Hapgood, afterwards. "I could have jumped over the moon in delight." He almost did, too. One reporter thought he was like "a Maori doing a war-dance." Scotland had been denied the Home International Championship but it was the defeat by England that mattered so much to Bill Shankly. Sensing the danger as Matthews took on Cummings by the corner flag, Shankly began to position himself to challenge Matthews if necessary, only to find the ball lifted beyond him, arrowed straight for Lawton's forehead. "I heard him shout, 'Get in there!' recalled Shankly. "The ball went home like a bullet and the swish and ripple of the soaking net made a sound that frightened me... that moment was like Doomsday. I turned and saw Lawton with such a look on his face. I could have shot him!" Shankly did acknowledge: "Lawton, a great centre-forward. And Matthews. We weren't beaten by nobodies, we were beaten by great players." Shankly and Lawton became great friends over the years. "Whenever Hampden '39 was mentioned," said Tommy, "Bill would just growl and shake his fist at me and he'd mutter, 'I could have killed you for that.'" Shankly told the story often, embellished it as much as only he could. John Richards, the Wolves and England centre-forward, remembers Shankly recounting the incident "in his own inimitable way" some 30 years on "still remembering the swishing noise of the ball hitting the back of the net." Few thought it had been an outstanding game, though the conditions played a major part in that, yet Jack Harkness in the Sunday Post suggested that England had produced their best team since the Great War and mused "had we been opposed to this bunch in 1928, would there have been such a thing as the Wembley Wizards?" (In 1928, Scotland had beaten England 5-1 at Wembley with a team that included the great Hughie Gallacher and Alex James, while Harkness of Queens Park played in goal). Charles Buchan, in the News Chronicle, thought Mercer was "undoubtedly the man of the match" as did Henry Rose in the Daily Express but

Harkness went for Matthews – "Now I know why Mr Chamberlain told Hitler he could have Austria, Rhineland, Czechoslovakia and perhaps his colonies, almost anything except Stan Matthews."

Virtually all the Scottish press agreed that if Scotland had picked Torry Gillick of Everton instead of playing Jacky Milne of Middlesbrough out of position on the left wing then Scotland would have won. Tommy would not allow that even the inclusion of his Everton team-mate would have made any difference: "We were so difficult to beat, that was a great England side with a wealth of talent – Len Goulden, Stan Matthews, Stan Cullis, Joe Mercer and Eddie Hapgood would have played for England in any era." So might Lawton. George Allison thought that he "led the line with credit to himself, apart from an inclination to do a little too much off his own bat." But then he was still only a teenager.

While the international occupied most of the column inches, other football did receive coverage. Newport County clinched promotion to Division Two and the *Sunday Express* commented that "when they straighten out their present financial tangle it is highly probable that the town will rise to the team and see that they take their proper position in Division Two. It would be a pity, after working so hard to get a promotion team, to have to remodel the club and start again." Meanwhile George Casey in the *Sunday Pictorial* had the story of France cancelling their international with Germany on April the 30th at the request of their Ministry of the Interior. Casey expected the Italy v England match in Milan in May to be the next to be called off. "Politics do interfere with sport."

Young Lawton read the reports of events over the channel but never thought he would be affected and few of his colleagues were alarmed either. For him, shortly to win the championship with Everton and the scorer of the goal which saw England beat Scotland at Hampden for the first time in 12 years, life could not have been sweeter. "I shall remember that goal when I am 70, when the name Lawton is just another entry in the record books of this great game of ours." He did too. Lawton, supposedly "right off form" in the first half of the 1939 Hampden Park game against Scotland, thought that football journalists often failed to understand the way he contributed to the game. "If the centre-forward just waits upfield for the ball to be presented to him, then most of the time he won't get results. I found that I had to keep on the move, even if, to all intents and purposes I was producing nothing for myself. Yet, I often made room for others. I'll tell you. There were many times that I deliberately made a move in the wrong direction to put the opposition defence off the scent. In fact there were games when I did it so much I was accused of not trying!

"I annoyed the spectators, the critics had a real go at me but many a time my only kick, or header, at goal won the game. That's football psychology. And if that kick in the last minute produces the winner, the satisfaction is all the greater. Especially if you know that it's all part of a plan. I was personally elated by that goal at Hampden. But personal elation is the more satisfying because of the effect it has on others and disappointment is the less intense because there's always someone to share it. The team is always more important than the individual. I shall never forget that goal, one, because I scored it and, two, because of the pleasure it gave the team and the whole country. England's team spirit that day at Hampden was there for everyone to see as we came off the field, wet through, splattered with mud, everyone hugging and congratulating everyone else. One of the best moments of my whole career."

CHAPTER THIRTEEN
1939 – ENGLAND
FOREIGN FIELDS

With a championship medal and his name embellished in the folk lore of England v Scotland matches, Tommy was rapidly becoming a major star in the game. At the end of the 1939 season, he was one of 16 players selected for the FA tour of Italy, Yugoslavia and Romania. Fortunately for the very ambitious teenager, the war held off long enough for the tour to be completed, though even the "football daft" Lawton could not fail to notice the storm clouds building.

"There was a lot of discussion about whether the team should go abroad at the time. The Foreign Office and just about every politician in the land had something to say about it. I suppose they were right as things turned out. If there'd been a problem at one of the games then it would have been turned into an international incident." Tommy was elated to be included, even though it meant enduring more of those hated sea crossings. The party was widely held to be the strongest ever to represent England abroad. Tom Whittaker, the Arsenal trainer, was in charge of the players, the first opportunity Lawton had of working with the man who was later to become his manager at Highbury.

The other players were: Vic Woodley (Chelsea); Bill Morris (Wolves), Eddie Hapgood and George Male (Arsenal); Ken Willingham (Huddersfield), Stan Cullis (Wolves), Wilf Copping (Leeds), Joe Mercer (Everton), Don Welsh (Charlton); Stan Matthews (Stoke), Willie Hall (Spurs), Len Goulden (West Ham), Eric Stephenson (Leeds), Frank Broome (Aston Villa) and Les Smith (Brentford).

On May 9th 1939, four days before the first international of the tour was scheduled against Italy in Milan, the FA party left London's Victoria station on the 'Balkans Express.' Tommy was relieved that the only water crossing involved in the early part of the journey was on the ferry from Dover to Calais. On this trip he was able to observe the FA secretary, Stanley Rous, renowned as a football ambassador and diplomat, at close quarters. Tommy was impressed. "It can't have been easy for him. There were a lot of people who didn't want us to go. He had to smooth the way, make sure that we didn't get into trouble. Some of us were unused to being abroad and might have said or done the wrong thing. But it was a triumph for him. Everywhere we went, we were welcomed with flowers and cheers. War didn't seem possible. We couldn't understand why we were likely to be fighting the Italians. The people were delighted to see us." The Italian welcome began at the border station of Stresa, By Lake Maggiore, where the train stopped for the usual customs check. Within minutes, the team's carriage was filled with flowers from the dozens of people who had come out for a glimpse of the England team. En route to Milan, more crowds and more flowers arrived. Then what should have been a short walk from the station to the hotel in the Piazza Duca D'Aosta became a half hour ordeal.

"In Milan, we had to fight our way through the crowds. It was like we were film stars or something. Joe Mercer said to me 'A few of your pals come out to see us then?' I'd never seen anything like it. It was all so new and exciting. Strange to think that less than a year later, these people were marching against us." In fact, that very week, Mussolini had proclaimed his intention that Italy would march with Hitler's forces in the quest for "European peace and justice."

It began raining the night before the match. The England players were pleased about that. Like Raich Carter and Sunderland at the Molineux, the archetypal English pro likes the 'bone' taken out of the ground, heavy conditions rather than a dry, hard surface where the ball bounces or where it zips over slightly damp close cut grass. "It appeared that conditions were right in our favour but when we got to the stadium we found that in parts the new turf had sunk. That was not what we were looking for at all." The San Siro in Milan had only recently been opened. Despite a heavy downpour, the crowd was an enthusiastic, capacity 70,000. Lawton was astonished to see that the spectators were separated from the pitch by high wire fences, designed to keep the crowd on the terraces and prevent them from hurling bottles and other various missiles at players and officials they took a dislike to. As an added disincentive, the Carabinieri patrolled the wire, armed with machine-guns. "They looked as though they were only too anxious to impress us and use them. They were only probably there to protect Mussolini's son, Bruno, who was in the royal box, but it was disconcerting. But Joe Mercer was grinning away as usual. He said 'Hey, Tom, don't score too many or they'll be after you!'"

Almost exactly a year earlier in the Olympic Stadium in Berlin, the England team had given the Fascist salute before an international with Germany. Photographs of that controversial action subsequently attracted a great deal of attention, and the decision to placate the hosts in Berlin, effectively Hitler's Nazi party, was condemned. Yet the England team repeated the action for the Fascists in Milan. "Yes, we all did the Mussolini salute that day in Milan. We were ordered to. Some of the boys had done the same in Berlin – Eddie Hapgood, Vic Woodley and Stan Matthews (and Frank Broome, Len Goulden and Ken Willingham too). This time we all stood there in the rain and gave the salute to the four corners of the ground. I didn't feel any reaction and I don't think the others did either. It was only later that everybody started criticising us. At the time, the FA officials asked us to give the salute and we did. We were told that the situation in Europe was such that the slightest incident could set the whole thing off. Well, I tell you, I was more bothered about making sure that I kept in step with the other players in turning and lifting our hands than anything else."

Under coach Vittorio Pozzo, Italy, who had won the World Cup for a second consecutive time with a 4-2 victory over Hungary in Paris the previous year, were considered the best in the world on their own ground. England, not being a part of FIFA at the time, had not competed in the World Cup and disdainfully believed they were among the elite. At worst they were "The Fathers' of Football."

"It was going to be a tough match. We were told that whatever happened, we had to be gentlemen at all times and we weren't to lose our heads and none of us did, though we were severely provoked. The continentals pulled shirts, kicked and punched but we knew they'd do that. The main incident was over their second goal."

Italy; Olivieri; Foni, Rava; Depetrini, Andreolo, Locatelli; Biavati, Serantoni, Piola, Meazza, Colaussi.

England; Woodley (Chelsea); Male (Arsenal), Hapgood (Arsenal); Willingham (Huddersfield), Cullis (Wolves), Mercer (Everton): Matthews (Stoke), Hall (Tottenham), Lawton (Everton), Welsh (Charlton), Broome (Aston Villa).

Italy included ten of the side that had won the World Cup in the Stade Colombes in Paris. England had eight of the team that had achieved the famous victory at Hampden. Just as against Scotland, a Matthews cross was met by Lawton for a vital goal, a goal that was greeted by absolute silence from the crowd.

"Stan's beautiful ball across was just asking to be nodded in and I promptly did so. I'd played against the centre-half Andreolo in the FIFA game at Highbury, he was just the same in Milan. He never left me alone and was pushing and bumping me every time I was anywhere near the ball. But Stan's ball in caught him cold and his face dropped as the ball went across him and into the far corner of the net."

Biaviti equalised for Italy before half-time with a superb shot that was always heading out of Woodley's reach. England, though, were confident that they were capable of handling the best Italy had to offer. Joe Mercer was in especially good form, this was his best game ever in England's colours. After the break, Italy went ahead to the utter disbelief of everyone watching. Colaussi's cross arrowed in from the left and centre-forward Silvio Piola darted in, outpacing the defence but, seeing the ball still out of range, reached out and punched it into the net, but then promptly followed through and thumped George Male in the eye. Piola had scored twice in the 1938 World Cup final but he knew this goal was as important as any other that he had scored. The referee Dr Bauwens, from Germany, signalled a goal.

"The ball came over from the left, Piola could not reach it with his head, but he tried and ended up punching it into the net. Everyone on the ground saw what happened. We couldn't believe it. We were just standing there waiting for the referee to rule it out and give a free-kick, but he didn't. Then our skipper, Eddie Hapgood went over to him, they went over to the linesman and the Italian players, even the crowd thought it would be a free-kick to us. But the linesman said it was legal. Well, all hell broke loose in the crowd. They were overjoyed. They were shouting 'Viva Goering...Viva Ribbentrop.' We had no choice, just to get on with it." With Male off for attention, the ten men salvaged a draw when Willie Hall equalised, again from a Matthews centre after Goulden's shot had been saved.

"A draw was the least we deserved from that match. Afterwards, we were told that up in the royal box, Stanley Rous had to restrain Crown Prince Umberto from going out on the pitch to order that the goal be annulled. The FA officials applauded the players for their attitude. "I think we all knew that if we'd reacted any other way to Piola's goal, there'd have been a riot." Conversations between the players of both sides after the game left the England internationals in a state of consternation. Most of the Italians conceded that they earned about £30 a match, almost four times the wage of an English professional. The following day, the team travelled to Venice, Lawton's first glimpse of the city. The scenery was beautiful, but the food was not to the liking of the England team. "The stench of garlic was everywhere and everything was cooked in oil. Joe Mercer would walk past a cafe and hold his handkerchief over his nose. We just wanted some home cooking and a cup of tea." The English abroad.

The entertainment in the evening was a gondola trip to a casino on an island. Opulent in the extreme, the setting was too lavish for many of the England players who felt completely out of place. Tommy was fascinated by the setting and the people.

"There was a rather attractive, beautifully dressed girl playing roulette. She was the centre of attention, nonchalantly flipping blue and white chips from a stack at her right elbow. After watching for a while, I thought that as the chips were in Everton's colours, we should try our luck, expecting that we'd break the bank. So we got a kitty together and I went over to the cashier and I asked him for enough chips to cover the cash. It was so embarrassing, there wasn't enough to cover one chip! In the end, we managed to find enough money to buy five, which we lost quite quickly, while this woman was still betting away. No emotion, not a trace. It was only when she left the table that we discovered who she was and why she could afford to lose all that money. She was Barbara Hutton, the Woolworth's heiress."

Then it was across the border to Yugoslavia, where three days later England were due to play in Belgrade. "Yugoslavia was a different kettle of fish to Italy. A much poorer place. There were a lot of troops about, but they had old fashioned firearms and scruffy uniforms. A pathetic sight really, if it wasn't so ominous. We wanted to go to a Turkish bath and were taken to an old tin bath in the open air where these fat old men were having what looked like their annual wash and brush up!" In Belgrade,

England, unchanged from the side that drew with Italy five days earlier, were beaten 2-1 by Yugoslavia. "Their team was the complete opposite to their army! They were quick, well organised. They won fair and square, playing like a Scottish team with the ball on the deck and while they had the speed, they also had the ball control. It was too hot for us, we had buckets of iced water around the ground so we could cool off a little, but the main thing was probably the hard ground coming after the soft pitch in Milan and we had Stan Matthews and Eddie Hapgood injured." After the tour, Tommy wrote: "The Yugoslavs were good, but they had the fault of all continentals, they took too long to shoot. If only they shot as readily as Tito's men against the Germans, they will play a big part in post-war football." At that stage, the side's reputation as the strongest ever to leave England was in serious jeopardy. Hapgood, the captain, who had played in Belgrade for the most part with an ankle injury, brought the team together for pre-match "brainstorming" session.

"It was a real pep talk. Two matches and we hadn't won, something had to be done about it. And we did it." Six days later in Bucharest, having made four changes, England beat Romania 2-0 with goals from Goulden and Welsh. "It was probably our first real warning of the rise of continental football. We didn't know it then, but for many of that team it was their last international, officially at any rate. Only two of us who went on that tour, Stan Matthews and me, played for England after the war. And only one other man, Raich Carter played before and after. Just the three. That's what a difference the war made to people's lives and careers. Six years wasted, though I've always said, that some of the internationals we played in during war-time were the hardest games of all. And the England team then was probably better than before the war and as good as anything afterwards."

At the end of the tour there was still no respite for Lawton and Mercer. Everton had arranged a close season visit to Holland to play a game as League Champions. The club had agreed to bring as many of their medal winning first team as possible. Leaving Bucharest at eleven o'clock Thursday morning with the rest of the England team, they travelled through Budapest and onto Basle in Switzerland, reaching there at three o'clock on the Saturday morning. Their England teammates continued on their way home, while Mercer and Lawton waited for the through train to Amsterdam. Fifteen hours later they were there, a journey that had taken 54 hours overall. Lawton was in no state to play. "I was exhausted and just sat in the stand. But Joe turned out, looking as fresh as ever. he played for all 90 minutes." Not yet 20, Tommy Lawton's football progress had been rapid. It was all about to come to a sudden halt.

CHAPTER FOURTEEN
1939 – EVERTON
CUT OFF IN THEIR PRIME

Tommy's favourite football quiz question in later years was: "Which player scored in all his club's league games in one season?" With a chuckle he would give the answer – "Me!" Only three league matches were possible in the 1939/40 season before the onset of the Second World War brought an abrupt halt to proceedings. Everton drew 1-1 at home with Brentford, then beat Aston Villa 2-1 away. On Saturday September 2nd 1939, Everton went to Ewood Park and drew with Blackburn Rovers 2-2. Lawton had scored four of Everton's goals (Stan Bentham claimed the first at Villa Park) and so assumed an unlikely world record. Even to a young man as focused on football as Lawton, it appeared inevitable that war was now looming. Players were enlisting in the Territorial Army. In fact, Liverpool joined the TA en bloc. Football became a minor topic of conversation.

The Friday before the game at Ewood Park, evacuation orders to move children from the big cities in Britain had come into effect. A day later, the German invasion of Poland began but the Home Office decided that the situation was not critical enough to cancel fixtures, thinking that an afternoon's entertainment would allay fears on the home front. Everton made the relatively short journey to Blackburn and back again but the evidence of preparation for war was all around, with the roads jammed by traffic, military and civilian. Trenches were being dug, tank traps were being cemented into position to delay any invading army. "I don't think anybody expected that war would come so soon. We just wanted to play. We were the champions, I think that we thought that nobody, not even Hitler could touch us!" With a home game scheduled midweek, Everton reported for training at Goodison on the morning of Sunday, September 3rd. Except that there was no training that morning. The players did not even bother to change out of their smart Sunday suits but, armed with their now regulation gas masks, gathered around the wireless to listen to the grave tones of Prime Minister Neville Chamberlain. "No sooner had he finished speaking than the air raid sirens went off. We all went out onto the pitch to see if we could spy any Jerry aeroplanes. Andy Tucker, one of the trainers, came dashing out shouting 'Get back in! The boss says you've got to get back in!' They thought then that there was less danger from bombs if you were inside. Why they thought that I'll never know."

When war was declared, the assembly of crowds was banned and the FA and the Football League decided to cancel the rest of the season; all players' contracts were suspended. The Everton directors, being scrupulously fair minded, arranged to pay every member of the playing staff their accrued share of benefit, one of the few clubs in the country to do so. Tommy had been with Everton for less than two years and picked up £300. Charlie Gee received the full amount, £650, but never kicked a ball for Everton again. It was an utterly bewildering time for Tommy. At the peak of his powers, an established international, he loved Everton and Goodison Park. Yet, here he was, almost 20, with no future. Just three years after his league debut, it had all ended so quickly. "All my prospects of fame and fortune were shattered at one fell swoop. I'd signed advertising contracts for shaving soap and porridge oats, they were cancelled. But there were thousands of people worse off than me, so I just decided to get on with it." Meanwhile, his £300 seemed a fortune, certainly enough to live on until he received his call up papers. Tommy's Everton teammates Joe Mercer and T G Jones had gone to work in civilian industry, Mercer at the Cammell-Laird shipyard, Jones in an aircraft factory. Tommy's friend, Frank Swift of Manchester City, had joined the police force. On his first day on point duty he managed to confuse the traffic to such an extent that he walked away from the scene, leaving the jumble of buses, lorries, cars and vans to sort themselves out. Peter Doherty, also of Manchester City, was at an ordnance factory in Warrington, Raich Carter of Sunderland joined the Fire Service. For that, Carter was severely criticised, to such an extent that he felt obliged to apologise "I am not proud of my war service. I made a mistake and I admit it."

His crime? To opt for being a fire fighter rather than enlist in one of the armed services. Carter later joined the RAF, but initially football crowds "made my ears burn with slurs and smears and jibes about the fire brigade." Carter explained that after being laid off by Sunderland, he needed a wage to support his family. He could start work as a fireman straight away, whereas he would have had to wait, without unemployment benefit, to be called up. The explanation fell on deaf ears. The taunts continued.

By September 14th, the FA relaxed their ban on organised games and allowed regional matches within a 50 mile radius and friendlies in "neutral and reception areas" to be played. Crowds were restricted to a maximum of 15,000, all ticket, in the larger grounds. 8,000, or half the capacity of the stadium whichever was the smaller, elsewhere. Two days later, Everton made the trip up the coast to Blackpool and lost 2-1 in a friendly where Lawton kept up his record of scoring in every match he had played in so far that season. Admission to the war-time friendlies was set at a maximum of 30/- (£1.50). Everton played three more games in Lancashire, against Preston, Liverpool and Burnley while the 50 mile radius restriction remained in force. Lawton scored in each match, and also in the first of the League West games against Stoke City, when the regional competitions began on October 21st.

Stanley Rous, secretary of the FA, urged the players who had yet to join up, to apply for the Army Physical Training Corps with the promise that they would automatically become Sergeant Instructors. Joe Mercer and Don Welsh of Charlton were among the first to take Rous' advice and were sent to Reading for training.

It was there that they discovered Rous had no authority to promise three stripes automatically. The specialist instructors who had spent years qualifying were understandably resentful that footballers, internationals or not, could just walk in and attain the equivalent rank. Mercer and his colleagues, among them Cliff Britton and Billy Cook also from Everton, were told there was no "fast track" for them. Not quite understanding the consequences of their action, they simply refused to take orders. Mutiny in war-time carries the stiffest of penalties. Fortunately, Rous intervened to settle the dispute and the players were made "Temporary Sergeant Instructors" though the resentment from the regulars still lingered.

In November 1939, Tommy played in his first war-time international, against Wales at Wrexham, England winning 3-2, Lawton naturally on target. The following month it was Scotland at Newcastle. Another win, 2-1, another goal. In the meantime, he played three times for Leicester City, returning to Everton for the Christmas fixture with Tranmere Rovers. Lawton scored four in the 9-2 victory, but by then he knew that he was about to be called up "I'd played for England, so I thought, I'll fight for England. I wound up my personal affairs, cursed Hitler and all his works and, occasionally, sat down to think of what had been, and what might have been."

Tommy was one of the last footballers to be recruited for the Army PT staff, in January 1940. The train journey south from Liverpool to Aldershot was long and difficult, through snow storms, with various changes and delays due to fears of enemy action. The only compensation for the 13 hour journey was that from Crewe onwards, he had the company of Frank Swift, who had decided life as a policeman on point duty in Manchester was not for him! "Neither of us was very happy about our new life, but once we'd met up with the 'Footballer's Battalion' we cheered up a bit." The first familiar face Lawton recognised was Bob Pryde, who, as Blackburn's centre-half, had marked him at Ewood Park the day before the war had started three months earlier. 1548031, Private Lawton T, was soon to find out that this was not going to be an easy life. Prior to being issued with his uniform, Tommy was approached by an officer who chatted cheerfully about a match he had seen during Everton's championship season. "I thought if all officers were as matey as him, then the Army and I would get along fine." Lawton changed into his new gear and strode out onto the parade ground where he spotted the officer again and enquired how he looked in his uniform. The reply was forthright, "When you meet an officer, the first thing you do is salute!" Initially, he scrubbed gym floors, polished anything that stayed still long enough and was put through a tough course of square-bashing and gymnastics. "I despised the discipline and the bull, but enjoyed the comradeship – and the football." More than 50 years on,

Cyril Griffin from Salford in Lancashire, recalled Tommy's arrival at Aldershot. Griffin had been called up a couple of weeks before Lawton and was in the same barracks. "We knew he was coming. One of the sergeants had said when we reported that we weren't to expect any special treatment, even though "that Tommy Lawton" was about to be with us. Sure enough, he arrived, looking like a choir boy. He was only about 20 at the time I suppose. A big lad though, hair very neatly parted down the middle and a wristwatch! He had a Smith's watch on! There weren't many of those about." Early in Tommy's spell at Aldershot with the Army, Griffin remembered, "A corporal came into the barracks. Tommy was polishing his boots because we were on parade later. I'd never known anybody polish his boots and shoes like he did. You'd look up from your bed and reading the paper or whatever and there he'd be, brushing away. Anyway this corporal came in and said some unit or other were playing on the field that afternoon and they were short. They wanted a winger. "Who plays on the right wing?' he asked and Tommy stood up. This corporal took one look at Tommy and said 'Don't be stupid, Lawton. Everyone knows you're not a winger!' And next to Tommy was a lad from Bradford called Jack Greenwood. He was a thin, wiry type and though he could play football, he was like me, he hadn't played professionally or anything. This corporal said 'Greenwood! Can you play on the wing?' And Jack just nodded. 'Get your boots then and come with me.' And off they went. I mean it was just ridiculous, the army all over. I used to laugh when I thought about this corporal turning up at the ground with Jack and saying 'That Tommy Lawton tried to fool me into thinking he was a right winger, but I know better! I've got you this chap instead. And the team saying – 'Bloody hell, we could have had Tommy Lawton!'"

In fact, within a week of arriving at Aldershot, Lawton was told to report to London to link up with the rest of the British Army side that was to go to France for three games against the French Army to entertain the British Expeditionary Force. Eighteen players were in the party – among them, Matt Busby from Liverpool, Wolves' Stan Cullis, Denis Compton of Arsenal and Billy Cook and Joe Mercer from Everton. On the train from Victoria to the ferry port at Dover, Cullis approached Tommy and Busby, all three notoriously bad sailors, with the idea of buying three anti-seasickness pills for a guinea. It was, he said, a cure that "positively could not fail." Busby and Lawton agreed and took the pills as soon as they were on the ferry. Cullis brought out a pack of cards and they settled down to a game of brag that became more and more boisterous as the trio realised they were not being affected by sea travel whatsoever. After an hour-and-a-half, Cullis announced that the ship should be docking any minute and they ought to go up "and take a look at France." The three arrived on deck and were just able to see shaded lights of a blacked out harbour. "Calais,"

Lawton cheerfully pointed out. "Calais!' said a voice from the stern, "this is still bleedin' Dover, we haven't bloody well left yet." Tommy claimed that he spent so much time on deck being ill that trip that he almost contracted pneumonia!

The matches were keenly contested, though Tommy did not have a good game in either Paris, Lille or Rheims. The draw in Paris was due to a great performance from goalkeeper Reg Allen of Queens Park Rangers, a man who later became a paratrooper before he was captured and spent four years in prison camps in Italy and Germany. A Joe Mercer goalline clearance two minutes from time saved the British team from defeat. Of the French Army side, Tommy was impressed by their goalkeeper, an Austrian, Rudolph Hiden. The war came home to him fast. He was amazed to learn that nine of the side had been serving in the Maginot Line only three days before. The game was watched by a crowd of 35,000 French and British troops. It was the last big game before the Dunkirk evacuation.

There were some lighter moments. The team was entertained at a British Officers' club in Paris in the evening with a famous French actress due to give a cabaret performance. Naturally, all the players were keen to catch a close up glimpse of this renowned beauty. Bert Sproston, the Manchester City full-back, dashed over to the table where Lawton, Busby, Cullis and Mercer were sitting. "Guess what?" he said. "I've seen her and she spoke to me!" "Well, what did she say?' they asked. Sproston proudly told them "She said, 'Get out of the way.'" Tommy found the whole experience "unusual and strange. The real war hadn't begun then, but Paris was blacked out. Even so there were thousands of troops milling about enjoying leave before going back to their fighting stations, trenches, gunposts, aerodromes or whatever. The atmosphere was unlike anything I'd known before. They knew what was coming and were just saying 'Oh well, let's get on with it.'"

CHAPTER FIFTEEN
1940 – WAR
DOING HIS BIT

Tommy was upset that so many people went out of their way to point out that he, as a fit, able-bodied man spent his time playing football in England rather than joining characters of a similar age who were fighting in the front line. "I was ordered to stay in England and do my war job. I didn't have a choice. But wherever I went there'd be someone who'd say 'Why are you here and not in the desert, in the front line, in the navy.?' We got it all ways." Although the abuse never reached the proportion of that hurled at Raich Carter, Lawton still felt obliged to point out that: "I never asked to stay in England. But the lads who watched us play in all the exhibition games must have been so annoyed that we weren't going out with them to face the bullets and the bombs. They made that clear at times. But I didn't have a choice. I was ordered to do my war job. Play in the charity games for England, The Army, Command and other Unit sides with dozens of other well known players and raise money for the Red Cross and all the other service charities."

The Aldershot manager, Billy McCracken, the former Northern Ireland international, made sure that he had first choice of the best players that arrived in the town for their training. "I'd got a pass to the barracks, so I got in to meet Billy Cook and Wilf Copping. One of the officers in charge was Michael Green, the cricketer. I'd walk in the gate, give him a salute and he'd say 'Morning Mac! Who do you want for Saturday?'"

Michael Green was an amateur who played county cricket for Gloucestershire, was later secretary of Worcestershire and managed MCC sides to South Africa and Australia after the war. He was a fine all-round sportsman, playing for the Army at both rugby and football.

Because he had been required by the Army, it was not until March 6th that Tommy Lawton made his debut for Aldershot in League South 'B' against Chelsea. Frank Swift was in goal and Jimmy Hagan at inside right. Within three minutes, Hagan had been brought down in the area and Lawton had fired home the penalty, the first of two goals he scored that day as Aldershot won 5-1.

The following week, Aldershot were at Southampton, without Swift, but with the Hagan-Lawton partnership up front. Lawton again took a penalty, but while the shot was powerful enough, the goalkeeper, one Eugene Henri Bernard, an amateur, made a fine save as the ball cannoned off his legs and looped over the bar. This Hampshire derby was won by 'The Shots' 3-2.

Lawton's first posting after the Aldershot training was to the 8th Cheshires at Birkenhead. At the time he was quoted as saying that he felt he was lucky to be so near home because then he would be able to play on a regular basis for Everton in the regional league competition which had been set up for the war years. There was another reason he was pleased to be back in Liverpool. He wanted to be able to spend as much time as possible with his new girlfriend, Rosaleen. Things were getting serious between them. Between March and June 1940, Lawton appeared in all Everton's 13 league and cup games, about one a week. The League was divided into eight divisions, Everton being in the Western Division along with some of their most familiar rivals like Manchester United and Manchester City, Liverpool and Stoke City. "There were some queer results in that section. We were beaten by Crewe, Chester and Wrexham! And Fulham knocked us out of the Cup when they beat us hollow, 5-2." Tommy played in a few representative games in the 1939/40 season but was disappointed to discover that the FA had no intention of awarding caps for England international matches.

The "phoney" war did not last long. Before long the name 'Dunkirk' was on everyone's lips, then in late summer came the Battle of Britain. In June 1940, one of Tommy's friends from Liverpool, Tom Cooper, an England international full-back who had joined the military police, had been killed when his motorcycle was in collision with a bus in Aldeburgh. The horrors of war were coming closer.

When the 1940/41 season began, the effects of rationing and conscription were beginning to make themselves apparent. The grounds were looking scruffy, with paint peeling from the walls in the stands and the dressing rooms. Railings and stanchions had been requisitioned to aid the armaments industry. Paint was in short supply and there was little likelihood of any being allocated for use on something as inessential as a football stadium.

The playing staffs were depleted. Players appeared for their own clubs when they could, but that depended on where they were stationed and their opportunities for leave. Even then they were only able to play at grounds within easy reach of their units.

Each club employed one man during games specifically to sit at the top or on the roof of the stand to look out for enemy aircraft. Heinkels, Dorniers and Stukas soon became common sights and sounds over the skies of British cities as the air raid sirens wailed. A weird, almost unreal, atmosphere prevailed as the season began.

The league was divided into two, north and south, with clubs playing as many opponents as they felt they were able or could afford to. League positions were calculated on goal average, not points, because of the discrepancy in the number of games played. The suggestion that professionals should not be paid by their clubs for the duration of the war was not adopted. So the pros still received their 30 shillings (£1.50) a match.

Lawton played for Everton for most of the first half of the 1940/41 season. During a three week course at Aldershot in October he played alongside Swift and Hagan once again in three League South games, the first at The Dell against Southampton. Ted Bates remembered Lawton collecting a pass from right-winger George Raynor on the half volley "That ball, no exaggeration, hit our cross-bar and landed practically back in the centre-circle. Our goalkeeper, Charlie White, is still stood there and the bar was 'Throb! Throb!' God, didn't he hit it?"

Before long, he was back in Everton's colours once more, scoring four against Manchester United at Goodison in a 5-2 win. Then, at the end of November he was in Scotland for the first time since the famous victory at Hampden. Lawton failed to score as the Army beat the Army in Scotland at Ibrox 4-1. "It was the last time I played against Joe McCulloch of Celtic. He was killed just before the end of the war, driving a tank back to his unit after a game in Holland." On Christmas Day 1940, Lawton played for Everton against Liverpool in the morning (and lost 3-1 at Anfield), then dashed down to Crewe with Tranmere to score both their goals in a 2-2 draw.

By January, he knew he was about to be transferred back to Aldershot within a couple of months. He took what leave he had and joined the ranks, marrying his fiancee Rosaleen, a Merseyside girl who worked in the jewellery department of a local store. In the photographs, Lawton was in his uniform, all ready to go to war. Unfortunately, his marriage turned into a battle ground too. The couple enjoyed a brief honeymoon in Tommy's favourite part of the world, on the Clyde, but it was impossible for Lawton to stay away from football for long and whilst there he played for Morton – and scored in the 3-3 draw with Hamilton Academical.

The Army released Tommy to play in just one match that season for England – on February 8th 1941, Scotland the opponents at St James' Park, Newcastle. The England team contained some familiar names, like Cullis, Mercer and Goulden. And some less familiar including an inside-forward from Middlesbrough – Wilf Mannion. It was the first time Lawton and Mannion had played together. Mannion had been one of the British Expiditionary Force evacuated from Dunkirk. After a period of rehabilitation, he was playing football for Middlesbrough and having been an England reserve back in 1937, was delighted to link up with the national team again. Lawton and Swift arrived together from Aldershot, as usual. The jokes and comic routines began as soon as they were inside the dressing room door. They were also quick to welcome Mannion into the fold. "We had a lot of time for him. Bryn Jones had called him a 'boy wonder' and he could really play, but also he'd seen action, you know, in France. We did our jobs, keeping up morale and all that. But lads like Wilf and Eric Stephenson were where it hurt." In a fiercely contested match. Lawton scored for England but two goals for Jock Wallace ensured Scotland won 3-2.

He played eight games for Aldershot before the end of the season alongside some other big names, notably Cliff Britton, Stan Cullis and

Jimmy Hagan. Hagan and Lawton built up a friendship and understanding which prospered further when they played for England in wartime internationals.

A week's leave in April 1941, found him back on Merseyside. Liverpool was suffering from the frequent bombing raids, but the League North match against Blackpool at Goodison went ahead and Lawton was still in Liverpool the following Saturday, when he was due to turn out for the Football League against An All British Eleven at Anfield.

"That was a strange match. We won it 9-7 and they had Stan Cullis! Inside-right for us was Dickie Dorsett, Stan's team-mate at Wolves. Before the game, we said, 'you've got some chasing about to do today Stan, you're not going to see it!' And he was calling us, like, 'No, you're up against good players for a change today, you don't stand a chance.' Well I scored three and Dickie got a couple and Stan chased his tail all day." Providing the crosses from the left wing at Anfield for Lawton and Dorsett that afternoon was Huddersfield's Harry McShane, later to play for Manchester United, the father of actor, Ian McShane. Lawton was not at all keen on life in the Army at Aldershot. There was far too much square bashing for him, as opposed to the football training he had been used to. "We were footsore at times and blistered, but there were some good times. We had many a laugh and above all there was so much companionship." The companionship was most welcome. His marriage was not working out and his beloved grandfather, James Hugh Riley had died at the age of 64. Tommy was pleased that his grandfather had lived long enough to see him reach the pinnacle of his profession, though not long enough to see him play at Wembley. Quite what he made of Lawton playing for Aldershot for £1.50 a match has not been recorded.

"Whenever we played for Aldershot, we'd corner Billy McCracken and try to wheedle expenses out of him. There'd be seven or eight thousand at these games and all we got was the bus fare from camp. So we'd try it on, but 'Mac' wasn't having any. He'd make out we'd agreed to play for nowt! Then he'd get out his cash box and pay us in coppers, cursing and swearing. He said 'Dick Turpin was gentleman compared with you lot!' It was all good natured, but think about it. There were thousands of people paying their thirty bobs to see us. And all we got paid was thirty bob each, eleven thirty bobs! It wasn't going to make a big hole in the kitty to give us enough to get back to camp and have a meal and a beer." A welcome relief from the system of orders and discipline came when he was selected for the British Army team to play The Army in Ulster over in Northern Ireland in September 1941. The team was near international strength, with Swift in goal, the half back line of Britton, Cullis and Mercer with Mannion and Denis Compton alongside Lawton in attack. Such an attractive line up brought in a crowd of 12,000 to watch them win 6-1.

McCracken tried to make sure Lawton turned out for 'The Shots' whenever he was available. "He had the pick of many good players stationed at Aldershot, but that season we failed to finish higher than fourth in the London League and didn't even qualify for the London Cup finals. Perhaps it was all the chopping and changing, but any side that had the pick of the likes of Jimmy Hagan, Cliff Britton and myself on a regular basis should have done better." On January 17th 1942, Lawton was called up for the international against Scotland at Wembley, his first appearance for England for almost a year and, almost 20 years since he had sat around the table in the family home in Bolton when he had first heard the word "Wembley." His ambition of playing in the stadium for the first time looked likely to be thwarted as it snowed heavily for the four days before the game. A postponement looked a distinct possibility and there was no guarantee that Lawton would be able to have leave to play in a rearranged game. Eventually, it went ahead, the lines cleared of snow and marked out in blue instead of white. "It was a freezing cold day," remembered Lawton. "By then we were used to normal dressing rooms being cold, because of the rationing on fuel, but at Wembley! Those big rooms got really cold and even afterwards, when there was warm water in the bath, it was still unbearable."

The proceeds from the match were intended for the Clementine Churchill Red Cross Aid To Russia Fund. Before the game, the teams were presented to the wife of the Prime Minister. "As we broke away for the kick-in, she went to the microphone. I couldn't hear what she said but from the roar of the crowd, it was obviously something important." Sure enough, Mrs Churchill had announced that her husband was flying back to Britain having signed the Atlantic Charter after a secret meeting with the US President Franklin Roosevelt at The White House. In great secrecy, Churchill had left Britain the previous month on board the battleship HMS Duke of York for his first meeting with the President since the entry of the USA into the war after Pearl Harbor. It was a visit which captured the imagination of the British population at a crucial time. The war was becoming a desperate struggle, there were frequent rumours of invasion pending. For obvious reasons, few had known of Churchill's journey across the dangerous Atlantic until he actually arrived. It was a major boost to morale in war-time, with the signing of the Charter, effectively the basis for the United Nations Declaration, especially stimulating.

Scotland had picked an unusual looking side with Everton's left winger Torry Gillick at centre-forward while Jimmy Caskie, who was just about to leave Goodison for Rangers because he had been unable to displace Gillick at Everton, was on the right wing.

"Torry and Jimmy were little midgets, about five foot four the pair of them, a couple of little imps. We were standing in the tunnel waiting to go onto the field when Jimmy said to Torry 'Good job, they're not sending us two out first.' And Jimmy was puzzled. 'Why not?' And Torry said 'Because the crowd will think the Japs have invaded!'" Fifty seconds gone and England were ahead. Wilf Mannion put Jimmy Hagan through and he outpaced the Scotland defence over the tricky surface and slammed in an unstoppable shot.

In the slippery conditions, the player with the ability to stay on his feet was at an advantage. England with the skilful Mannion and Hagan at inside forward to feed the wingers Stanley Matthews and Denis Compton always looked likely winners. And they were, 3-0.

In the middle, Lawton revelled in the service he received. First, he headed in a Compton centre. Then he met a Matthews corner. Simple? Well, it looked it. "When you had a chap like Tommy Lawton in the middle," said Denis Compton years later, "out on the wing you didn't have to bother too much about finding him with your cross. He was always in the right place. As long as I put it in the air and into the box, it was guaranteed, Tommy would find it." If his playing colleagues were appreciative of Lawton's efforts, FA officials demonstrated the opposite. Mr Ewbank, the FA treasurer, was a stickler for formality and protocol. Expenses claims were ruthlessly examined by this bird-like official in a winged collar. At the end of the game against Scotland, Tommy was summoned into his presence.

Lawton had claimed 12/6d (63p) for the train fare from Aldershot when it was actually only 7/4 (36p). "Ewbank called me into the office where he had a Bradshaw's Rail Guide on his desk. He was snooty to say the least. He was not my kind of person and he knew it. 'Now look here Lawton' he said. They always called you by your surname, even when they wrote to you asking to play for England! 'I think this fare is only 7/4d.' That really got my goat. The match raised £26,500. They'd paid me thirty bob (£1.50) and they were quibbling about a few pennies. I said 'Well, there's five bob (25p) for refreshments or aren't I supposed to eat?' He said 'That's still only 12/4d accounted for, what about the other twopence?' I told him I'd been caught short on the way, twice, and it'd cost me a penny both times. But then I got angry with him and I told him 'Here's what you can do, you can take my match fee and my expenses and put it all in the kitty for the fund.' And I just stormed off."

It did not do Tommy's chances of playing for England on a regular basis much good. Stanley Matthews remembered the incident and suggested that it "hammered a couple of nails into his international coffin." Matthews also remembered Ewbank: "The sort of person who, if he went riding with the Four Horsemen of the Apocalypse wouldn't liven up the mood of the party!" He also recalled being lectured by Ewbank on "the emoluments that accrue" when having the honour of playing for England. "I felt as if I was playing out a scene from David Copperfield."

Life was a bore for Tommy back at base but there were signs that he was about to spend less and less time there. "Barely a week went by when there wasn't some kind of representative match arranged. After Wembley, I played for the British Army against the Belgian Army side at Aldershot along with Stan Cullis, Jimmy Hagan and Denis Compton, so we had quite a team. The next week we played the RAF, then the FA and so on. There was always a match that somebody wanted us to play in." But the game that Lawton most wanted to play in was for England against Scotland at Hampden Park towards the end of the season. "I hadn't been back there since we won in the rain in 1939. What a change since then! War really had made a difference. There was no question of a luxury trip to Scotland, first class compartment, a carriage separated from the rest of the passengers on the train. No, instead, we were told to make our own arrangements to get to the Central Hotel in Glasgow by ten o'clock on the Friday night. We were told to eat before we set off because there wouldn't be any food on the train. Bring your own refreshments – and boots, of course!"

There was a less than capacity crowd at Hampden, only 91,000 but even so, that was some 20,000 more than the local police had officially stipulated to be in the ground. They were treated to one of the most memorable matches and probably the most competitive of the war years between the old adversaries, settled in the closing stages when Scotland won it 5-4 with a late winner from Bill Shankly that made up somewhat for 1939.

Tommy was satisfied with his performance "I had a grand game and scored a hat-trick. A pity that Jock Dodds did the same for them or we might have won!" Unusually, Lawton was on the losing side for a second successive international when Wales beat England 1-0 in Cardiff. Tom praised the Wales manager: "Ted Robbins was a great man. He was the type of chap who would go out of his way to say hello to you. The Welsh lads would do anything for him. This time he'd had trouble getting a team up so he'd put together an odd side. He had brought in three lads that I'd not heard of before – Squires of Swansea, Lowrie of Coventry and Lucas who played for Swindon."

Frank Squires was serving with the 8th Army in North Africa and played in the same services team as Tom Finney and Bryn Jones. It was predicted that George Lowrie would be as good as Bryn Jones, the war probably prevented that, but in March 1948 his goalscoring prowess persuaded Newcastle to buy him from Coventry for £18,000, then the third highest fee of all-time. Billy Lucas was a small, powerful wing-half with brilliant ball control. "It was Lucas who scored the goal that mattered but we should have won. I hit the bar twice and then George Poland pulled off a brilliant save in the last minute from my header. George was one of the players whose career was ruined by the war. The summer before it all started, he'd signed for Liverpool for a big fee for a keeper (£3,000). Then during the war he broke his arm and that was it. He never played again." For Tommy it was important that "football was being played at all at that level. I suppose it just illustrated the mood of the nation, they can drop bombs or do what they like, we're going to the game."

CHAPTER SIXTEEN
1942 – WAR DROPPED BY ENGLAND

The football hierarchy met in Nottingham, a city that was reasonably safe from German bombs, in June 1942. On the agenda, the arrangements for the new season. They decided to revert to the system of localised leagues to save costs and the valuable war resources, especially fuel. It meant that spectators would not see the variety of teams and players they had become accustomed to in the previous war-time season. A larger list of representative fixtures was arranged, Tommy thinking that if he stayed fit and in decent form and was able to obtain leave at the right time, he would play in most of the big games.

He was certainly fit enough. Persuaded to take part in the Aldershot District Military Athletic Championships, he surprised on-lookers, and himself, by winning the 100 yards by a considerable margin and then took the long jump title. Not quite Jesse Owens, but good enough. He had not attempted athletics in competition since his school days almost ten years before and then not in such an organised manner. He was delighted, but then, throughout his life, he was always determined to be a winner at whatever he approached.

Walley Barnes, later captain of Wales, played for Southampton in the 1942/43 season. His first ever league game was against Aldershot, normally it would have been a "no contest' but on this occasion Barnes, lining up with his new Southampton teammates, mainly young unknowns, had more than an inkling that a thrashing was likely as Aldershot included England's half back line – Cliff Britton and Joe Mercer of Everton, with Stan Cullis of Wolves at centre-half. Up front, Jimmy Hagan was inside-right with Tommy at centre-forward. Seven-nil the final score and Barnes thought Southampton lucky that they did not lose by ten.

Two months later, in November 1942, Aldershot played the return at the Dell, this time without Cullis and Mercer, while Southampton were strengthened by the appearance of Charlie Mitten of Manchester United, Ted Bates (later Southampton manager) and Bert Tann, then of Charlton. On this occasion, Southampton won 2-1, but the highlight for Barnes was not the victory but the display by Lawton. "Reputations alone have never interested me," he insisted. "But when Tommy took the ball in his stride, crashed through the defence and hammered the ball past George Tweedy, from that moment I began to understand why his reputation was so high." Tweedy, of Grimsby Town, was no ordinary stand-in goalkeeper. As big as

Frank Swift, he had played for England in 1936 against Hungary.

After captaining the FA, then playing for the British Army in Ireland and Scotland, Lawton was selected by England for the first of the season's internationals against Scotland at Wembley in October 1942. It turned out to be a very poor spectacle for the 75,000 there with defences on top throughout and finished in a goalless draw. Tommy blamed himself and the other England forward for not winning the game. "Our close control was not good enough. I had only one chance, laid on by Stan Matthews, but I hit the cross-bar. It was the sort of day when the most spectacular sight was the flight of Spitfires circling the ground." Two weeks later, another international, this time against Wales at Molineux. After the sub-standard performance at Wembley, the FA selectors had been encouraged to make changes and Lawton was pleased to be retained though "I couldn't begin to imagine what they were thinking about by choosing three centre-forwards!" Jimmy Hagan had been dropped along with Maurice Edelston and Denis Compton and in came Ronnie Rooke of Fulham and the 'Spurs amateur Jackie Gibbons. "That meant we had three up front to score goals, no inside forwards, no providers. I didn't think it would work. We were ahead early on after I'd scored but after that we just faded out of the picture." The goal was well worked, brilliantly executed at speed with Jimmy Mullen, of Wolves, making his international debut on his home ground, playing a major role. Wales though had the better team spirit and the better organisation and won with two goals from Horace Cumner of Arsenal.

Cumner had glimpsed the horrors of war first hand. A Royal Marine, he had been badly burned when a hydrogen container exploded on his ship five weeks earlier. "Horace wasn't expected to be out of hospital, let alone be able to play. But there he was and he got the goals. It was a great effort, he was a quick, direct player. After the war, he played with me and Jackie Sewell at Notts County." It was the last that Lawton saw of the international scene for a while. The selectors' triple centre-forward plan had backfired, so all three were dropped for the next match against Wales at Wembley in February 1943 and Denis Westcott of Wolves at last received his chance to play for England and took it brilliantly well by scoring a hat-trick in England's 5-3 win. "It was a really depressing period for me. Everybody's goal is to play centre-forward for England. I thought I'd never get another chance." Lawton had to be content with scoring goals in the war-time league competition which he did with relish. "The most exciting game that I played in during the war years was for Aldershot against the Arsenal in a league south match in November 1942. Arsenal turned up without Bernard Joy, Eddie Hapgood and Alf Kirchen. We had four internationals in our forward line, me, Dave McCulloch, Jimmy Hagan and Jimmy Cunliffe. We were 3-0 up after half-an-hour and they hadn't had a sniff of a chance. Then they scored six in a row and we ended up going down, 7-4! Don't ask me how, I can't explain how it happened. I just know that it did." Tommy played with some of the best inside-forwards of all time, among them Raich Carter, Wilf Mannion, Len Goulden and Len Shackleton, but one always had the feeling that he rated Jimmy Hagan as highly as any of them.

In December 1942, Aldershot met Luton in the war-time league and the Lawton-Hagan combination proved lethal. "We rammed home nine goals on that day. I got six of them and they were all made by Jimmy. He was brilliant, unselfish, I don't think he ever played a better club game." One of Tommy's last games at Aldershot was for the British Army against the Belgian Army. Again he was in excellent goalscoring form bagging another four. Soon he was posted north again, pleased to be back home, with an opportunity to make work the marriage with his young wife and with the chance of playing regularly for Everton once more.

It was not until October 1943 that England recalled Lawton for the game against Scotland at Maine Road. "It was a surprise when I heard I was back in as only a few days earlier England had beaten Wales 8-3 at Wembley and Don Welsh, playing at centre-forward had scored two. So I was fortunate to be in the side against Scotland although I didn't realise how fortunate until after the game. I think it was the finest England side that I ever played in, not just on paper, but as a team on the field. That display against Scotland was one of the best ever in international football."

MATCH OF THE DAY

England v Scotland
Maine Road
October 4th 1943
England: Swift (Manchester City); Scott (Arsenal), Hardwick (Middlesbrough); Britton (Everton), Cullis (Wolves), Mercer (Everton); Matthews (Stoke), Carter (Sunderland), Lawton (Everton), Hagan (Sheffield United), Denis Compton (Arsenal)
Scotland: Crozier (Brentford); Carabine (Third Lanark), Miller (Hearts); Little, Young (both Rangers), Campbell (Morton); Waddell (Rangers), Gillick (Everton), Linwood (St Mirren), Walker (Hearts), Deakin (St Mirren).
Lawton walked into the dressing room at Maine Road in his uniform, hung his cap on the peg and looked around at his colleagues. "I was telling myself that this was where I wanted to be. In this sort of company, among the best players. I had got another chance to establish myself in the England team and I had to take it." After the previous victory against Wales, one national newspaper had suggested that the England team had deliberately starved Stanley Matthews of the ball. Lawton regarded this comment with suspicion. "I thought it was comic. I had a word with Joe Mercer before the game in Manchester and he just laughed at the idea that there was some sort of conspiracy to keep the ball away from Stan. It was all to do with some comments made by the Wales left-back Billy Hughes. He was boasting before the game about what he was going to do to Stan and how he wouldn't get a kick. So the lads decided to see what Hughes would do if Stan never got the ball at all! Anyway it worked.

"We all had moments when we've been exasperated with Stan because he'd taken the ball off down the wing as if he was playing on his own, but then he'd produce a moment of sheer genius that nobody else could hope to match. That day at Maine Road he played as well as he'd ever done. People talk about the Cup Final in 1953, but I think he was even better in that game against Scotland. It was 90 minutes of sheer wizardry."

If Matthews had seen little of the ball against Wales, he was scarcely without it in the five-star show against Scotland. England were one up after a quarter-of-an-hour when Lawton back-heeled for Hagan to slot into the net. Ten minutes later England were four up and Lawton had completed a hat-trick, including one from a near prone position on the ground in the six yard box with his back to goal. Usually, Lawton was not given to the acrobatic, athletic certainly, spectacular and powerful often, but this was an exception.

The goal which completed the hat-trick was not intended for him. Matthews had been the star of the first half as he ran the Scotland defence ragged. Lawton supplied Carter on the edge of the area. He made ground, then stood with his foot on the ball and called for Matthews, who sidled into space on Carter's right as the ball rolled into his path. It was intended to be a demonstration effort to prove that Matthews was indeed part of the team. Matthews did not score many at the best of times (only 11 in his total of 54 full international appearances for England) but his shot cannoned into the post and ricocheted straight to Lawton standing in front of an empty net. Carter scored the fifth, then missed a penalty. Hagan, then Lawton made it 7-0 and eventually Matthews claimed the goal that capped a wonderful individual display and rounded off a magnificent team performance. "Stan weaved his way through, feinted to pass about four times, but carried the ball right up to Crozier and casually slipped it past the goalkeeper. It was bedlam. The whole stadium rocked with the applause as Stan loped back to the middle to be mobbed by the rest of us. Even the Scotland defenders applauded him. It was a great moment but he just ducked his head in that shy manner of his and got on with it."

The game remained vivid in Tommy's memory as one of the greatest he ever played in. One particularly important figure in the Football Association agreed. Charles Wreford-Brown was an England selector, a few days short of his 77th birthday. Very much of the old school, he had played for Oxford University, Old Carthusians and Corinthians and won four caps for England as a centre-half in the 1890s. Wreford-Brown had been playing and watching football for more than half-a-century and was quick to congratulate the team on its fine display. "This England team showed perhaps the greatest combination and team work in the whole history of international football. I myself have never seen anything like it before." Tommy often disregarded comments from "big wigs in blazers." But he made a note of that one. The general verdict was that England had played exceptionally well at Maine Road. Stan Cullis thought it was "the finest football I'd ever seen." Frank Swift regarded that England eleven as the best he ever played in and journalist Ivan Sharpe, who had reported football almost since the days of Wreford-Brown, thought that the 1943 team was "perhaps England's best since 1907. For this there was a reason, services football brought them into action more *frequently than is possible in normal times. They developed understanding." Ivan Sharpe's comparison with the England team of 1907 is an interesting one which unfortunately must be consigned to the history books. England in 1907 included such luminaries as Bob Crompton, Ben Warren and Bill Wedlock in defence with Jock Rutherford from the great Newcastle United team of the time on the right-wing with his inside partner Vivian J Woodward, the gifted, elegant Tottenham forward who won gold medals with the British team at the 1908 and 1912 Olympics. It was obviously a team of some calibre, going unbeaten for 18 matches over a three-year period up to 1910.*

CHAPTER SEVENTEEN
1944 – WAR BANNOCKBURN, CULLODEN AND HAMPDEN

For the 1943/44 league season, the FA had lifted the maximum wage to £2 a game, but that was restricted to only 14 of the players in the season. (Aldershot used no fewer than 84 in 1943/44). Lawton played only his second game for Aldershot that season on November 27th at home to Southampton. Six internationals turned out for Aldershot that day – Britton, Cullis, Hagan, Lawton, McCulloch and Cunliffe. With Lawton scoring six goals, Southampton were swamped 10-1. Hagan and Cunliffe, with two apiece, notched the others, leaving McCulloch, strangely, without a goal in such a rout. Aldershot played Ernie Bell on the right wing. He had appeared for them pre-war but in the meantime had spent most of the war in a prisoner of war camp in Germany, from which he had been repatriated. Lawton was in a rich vein of form at the time, having scored 25 goals in his last eight matches. No wonder 'Arbiter' (F W Carruthers) in the *Daily Mail*, claimed "Lawton is the best England centre-forward for 20 years." Lawton knew he was good, but never encouraged such comparisons. "Was I better than Geordie Camsell and Pongo Waring? Or better than Dixie – I don't think so."

A student at Swansea University, George Edwards had played a couple of games as an amateur for Swansea City before the war and had earned an amateur cap for Wales against England at Cheltenham in the 1938/39 season. When he joined the RAF he was stationed at Wellesbourne Mountford near Stratford upon Avon and soon found himself playing football four times a week. "Early in 1944, I was picked to play in a Services XI against Leamington Town and the news soon filtered through that our centre-forward that day was to be Tommy Lawton." Lawton, having 'passed out' from Aldershot, was being sent all over the country to organise the Army's gyms and training quarters. George Edwards had never met anybody of Tommy's stature before "apart from Denis Compton, perhaps, when he played at Swansea for Arsenal Reserves in 1938 soon after having a great summer against Don Bradman and the Australians. So when I met Tommy, I almost called him 'Sir!' I was just starry-eyed, in complete awe of him. I didn't know what to say to him. In situations like that, well, you do say some silly things and as we were about to go out on the field I asked him about how I should cross the ball, where would he like it? Before I'd finished the question he said "Well, Stan Matthews always manages to do it with the lace away, son, lace away!' Well, that old joke just lightened everybody, they all laughed and we won the game quite easily. There was a serious side to his comment though. With the lace in the leather ball sometimes twisting the knot out front, it was quite easy to head the ball and receive a nasty cut. Anyway I never forgot it and neither did Tommy."

It was back to Hampden Park in April 1944 for the second international of the year against Scotland. Two months earlier at Wembley, England had beaten the Scots in comprehensive fashion 6-2, the latest in a line of defeats for Scotland, who had not beaten England since the famous 5-4 win at Hampden in 1942. This match assumed crucial importance to the Scots. No fewer than 14 members of the Scottish FA met to pick the side for the England game. After all day deliberations they announced the team.

Scotland: Crozier (Brentford); McDonald (Celtic), Stephen (Bradford PA); Macaulay (West Ham), Baxter (Middlesbrough), Busby (Liverpool); Delaney (Celtic), Walker (Hearts), Dodds (Blackpool), Duncanson (Rangers), Caskie (Everton). England showed changes too with a new full-back pairing. England: Swift (Manchester City); Taylor (Wolves), Leslie Compton (Arsenal); Soo (Stoke), Cullis (Wolves), Mercer (Everton); Matthews (Stoke), Carter (Sunderland), Lawton (Everton), Hagan (Sheffield United), Les Smith (Brentford).

North of the border there was great expectation for the match, the attendance an incredible, considering the circumstances, 133,000 at Hampden. It was the largest paying attendance for any event during the war. Tommy recalled that "the Hampden Roar was just terrific. It was the first time that I was conscious of the crowd noise there. Perhaps it was because the Scots outplayed us for the first 20 minutes and the crowd really got behind them." England's new full-backs, Frank Taylor and Leslie Compton, struggled to contain the Scottish wingers Jimmy Delaney and Jimmy Caskie. It was Caskie who scored the first goal with a dipping, swerving shot that bounced and screwed past Swift into the net. "We were just submerged by the deluge of sound that greeted the goal. It was deafening. The Scots may have been inspired by it, but then so were we. Tommy Walker shot wide and Swifty took the goal kick quickly and found Raich Carter in the centre-circle. He slipped it through to me, about 20 yards out and I just had a bang! Suddenly, there the ball was, climbing up the back of the net behind Joe Crozier. That shut 'em up." Lawton it seemed was destined to be the curse of the Scots at Hampden yet again. Especially when Stanley Matthews meandered into the middle and rolled a pin point pass wide of Bob Baxter in the direction of Lawton inside the area. Lawton was quick enough to beat both Jim Stephen and Crozier to the ball to tuck it into the net. Two-one to England who went further ahead only a minute later when Jimmy Hagan set up Carter for a left foot shot that flashed in from 25 yards. England had scored three times in only ten minutes.

The Scots, determined not to lose to England again, had employed the strong-arm tactics to try to hustle England out of the game. "The first half was tough, but it was a Sunday school picnic compared to the all-out struggle the second half turned into." Scotland had the wind behind them after the break, but the England defence, under severe pressure for half-an-hour resisted superbly. The crowd was in a frenzy, feeding on a diet of incessant Scottish attacks but Swift was dynamic in goal, Cullis, relishing the battle, cleared everything within reach and Compton and Taylor came through their first tests at international level with aplomb, despite the abuse that was hurled at them from the terraces. "Whenever our defenders went in, there was a storm of booing. When a Scot went over the ball, it was obviously a fair do! All part of the game!' Scotland reduced the deficit when Jock Dodds beat Cullis to a Caskie cross and headed past Swift. "Somehow we held on. It was the toughest international game I ever played in and that includes the internationals against the continentals. half-an-hour after the game though, we were all together in the bar, everything forgotten, in those days, there were no vendettas." It was an impression that Tommy liked to convey about his time in the game, but it was not always strictly true. Stan Matthews recalled a win for England at Hampden after which he chatted in the bar with Billy Steel and Billy Liddell. George Young was annoyed with his colleagues and came over to say so. Liddell protested that: "Scotland had lost at Bannockburn and Culloden, but this was only a football match." Young was in no mood to listen. "Aye, but after Bannockburn and Culloden we weren't told to put suits on and make small talk over sandwiches!"

The guest of honour at the match was Field Marshall Montgomery, just months away from D-Day. Lawton was pleased to hear Monty speak of the worthwhile contribution sportsmen were making to the war effort. "He said that those who were fighting overseas and those who were at work on the home front were members of the same team. One couldn't do without the other. He said there were two things that had to be done. To fight the Germans and to keep the people at home from worrying." There was increased optimism in the country that the worst was over and that the pendulum of war was swinging in the Allies' favour.

Lawton played just four more games that season. One of them an international against Wales at Ninian Park, which England won 2-0. "I scored one, Les Smith the other. There was no T G Jones for Wales, so I was up against Bob Davies from Forest. Bob was from North Wales, and a tough nut. He was in the parachute regiment. I don't think I'd played against him before, but later he was the physio at Forest when I was in Nottingham and we got to know each other well. If it hadn't been for the likes of T G and Tommy Griffiths, he'd have played a lot more for Wales."

CHAPTER EIGHTEEN
1945 – WAR
THE END IN SIGHT

At 25, Tommy was now an elder statesman to the youngsters coming through, destined to be the new breed of player after the war. Lawton had grown up fast, "But then you just had to get on with things. Some of the lads I played with were not coming back, I was one of the lucky ones, I came out alive, a lot of my mates didn't." Among his footballing friends who died in the war were Tom Cooper, the Liverpool full-back; the Bolton captain, Harry Goslin, killed in action in Italy; Eric Stephenson, a major in the Gurkha Rifles, Tommy's inside-forward when he won his fourth cap, drowned in the Burma campaign in 1944; and Albert Clark of Blackburn who lost his life on D-Day.

The 1944/45 season began with a flurry of games for Everton, Western Command, Combined Services and for England. On September 9th 1944, a strong Combined Services team was chosen to play Ireland in Belfast. "We needed some good lads out there because Ireland had quite a team. Tommy Breen from Manchester United was in goal, Davie Cochrane of Leeds on the wing and their inside-forwards were Alex Stevenson and Peter Doherty. So they had a chance."

The Combined Services line-up: Swift (Man City & England); Scott (Arsenal & England), Barnes (Arsenal & Wales); Macaulay (West Ham & Scotland), Joy (Arsenal & England), Busby (Liverpool & Scotland); Matthews (Stoke & England), Carter (Sunderland & England), Lawton (Everton & England), Mortensen (Blackpool), Mullen (Wolves & England).

There were nearly 50,000 in the ground at Windsor Park to see Doherty dominate the first half, scoring both goals for Ireland, although with two from Raich Carter, the Services were level at half-time.

After the break, the football was simply dazzling. Jimmy Mullen put the visitors back in front, only for Doherty to complete his hat-trick. With half-an-hour to go, Mortensen made it 4-3. Cochrane equalised a minute later. "It was one of those games that never stopped. Doherty was brilliant for them. Raich was in top form for us, then Stan got going." Matthews made four goals in the last ten minutes, two more for Carter, another for Mullen and the eighth, the best of the game for Lawton. "He was inside our half when he set off on one of runs. He beat four men just outside the area, left them on the ground, drew Tommy Breen out, shaped to shoot and said, 'Yours Tom.' All I had to do was sidefoot it home. Two days later we played the Irish League at Cliftonville. I was up against Jimmy Dykes who played for Scotland pre-war. In the paper the next day they said "Dykes held Lawton in a grip of iron." I had to laugh. Further down it said 'Apart from his goals, Lawton wasn't really in it." I'd scored twice and we'd won 4-0!" Dykes was working for the local brewery. After the match he invited the Services' team to taste his product. "It wasn't the normal stuff we'd got used to in the war. It knocked you out. Laurie Scott, Matt Busby and I were in a dreadful state, worse than normal, on the ferry back across."

In the absence of Stan Cullis, Joe Mercer captained England for the first time and Stan Mortensen made his debut against Wales at Anfield on September 16th. In drizzling rain, more than 38,000 spectators saw Wales rip into a two goal lead after only a quarter-of-an-hour. "It was a sensational performance, they just flew at us and rattled two past Frank Swift in no time." The goals were scored by Don Dearson, of Birmingham, direct from a corner after five minutes then Billy Lucas, of Swindon, set up by Leslie Jones, produced a deadly accurate shot. England scrapped for a draw gained when Raich Carter and then Lawton scored,

"Reg Flewin of Portsmouth had replaced Stan Cullis and the papers blamed him for our shaky start. I don't think he played that badly, but he never got another chance. This was the game where Stan Matthews nearly headed a goal, though he didn't know much about it. The ball came flashing across from Jimmy Mullen and Stan had his back to goal and it just hit the side of his head and flew wide of the post. I was flattened towards the end by Walley Barnes. I was coming through and we both collided and down I went. He came up to me as I was coming round and said "I'm sorry Tom, if I could have got out your way, I would have!'"

MATCH OF THE DAY

England v Scotland
Wembley
October 14th 1944
England: Swift (Manchester City); Scott (Arsenal), Hardwick (Middlesbrough); Soo (Stoke), Joy (Arsenal), Mercer (Everton); Matthews (Stoke), Carter (Sunderland), Lawton (Everton), Goulden (West Ham), Les Smith (Brentford).
Scotland: Cumming (Middlesbrough); Stephen (Bradford PA), Cummings (Aston Villa); Thyne (Darlington), Baxter (Middlesbrough), Macaulay (West Ham); George Smith (Hibs), Walker (Hearts), Milne (Hibs), Black (Hearts), Caskie (Everton).
The problems started for Scotland on the day before the game when Bill Shankly, picked to play at right half, reported with a knee injury. A lengthy fitness test at Stamford Bridge, overseen by the Scotland team doctor and trainer, determined that he was not fit enough to play. Just 24 hours before, the team had stood down Matt Busby who was available to play. Now they were forced to turn to their only other option, Bob Thyne, or face the indignity of playing at Wembley with only ten men, or, worse still, having to 'borrow' an Englishman.

Sergeant Thyne of Darlington was included in the party simply for a taste of the big match atmosphere. He had been a promising centre-half but having been called up for the infantry found himself heading for the beaches of Normandy on D-Day. Six days into the battle for France, he was in a trench which was heavily shelled and received a direct hit. He was invalided home with a badly injured leg and not surprisingly suffering from shell-shock. By all accounts he was still convalescing four months later when he turned up at Wembley and borrowed Shankly's kit. It was certainly an astonishing feat to play in an international so soon after having suffered such severe wounds. Unfortunately, there was no fairy tale ending to this element of his story. He looked out of his depth in the game and finished on the losing side in common with most of his Scottish colleagues during the war years. The game had started well for the Scots as they were ahead after only four minutes, the first time in six matches they had taken the lead at Wembley. They held onto the lead until well into the second half as Cummings shackled Matthews down the right and prevented Lawton in the middle receiving any service at all.

Eleven minutes after the break though, Lawton scored the equaliser. "I was just loafing around in the middle waiting for the ball. The wind was blowing the rain into our faces in the second half and I thought back to Hampden and decided that if the chance came I'd give it a belt. It was a greasy ball and it might pay dividends. Next thing, Frank Soo found me and called out 'Your's Tom!' It just went my way after that." Another Lawton understatement. In the Sunday Graphic *the next day, Roy Peskett wrote that "Tommy Lawton, England's dynamic centre-forward, giving the greatest display of his life, pulled back a match which looked well won by Scotland 34 minutes from time. In the 11th minute of the second half, he fastened onto a long pass from Frank Soo, eeled his way past Stephen, beat Baxter in his stride, and with 93,000 throats roaring him home, smashed the ball past the Scottish keeper. The England team stood still and clapped Lawton back to the middle. Even some of the Scots patted him on the back as he made his triumphant way to the centre spot.*

It was more than a goal... it was victory. Four minutes later Lawton scored again, and from then on it was a rout. England scored four more goals, one by Lawton and the other three made by him."

Two weeks later, Bob Thyne played for the Army in Scotland against The Army at Hampden, renewing acquaintance with Lawton, Swift and Mercer, and he also appeared in the next international against England at Villa Park in February 1945 and according to Tommy "showed what a talented player he was." It was not until November 1944 that Tommy was on Merseyside often enough for a consistent spell in the Everton side. As one of the most experienced players in the team, he was frequently appointed captain. He was also writing his first newspaper column in the *Liverpool Evening Express*. After the game against Bolton Wanderers at Burnden Park in January 1945, he singled out the "pluck of Stan Bentham" to emphasise the spirit in the Everton team. "Had Stan not returned to the field at Bolton after having three stitches put in the cut on his forehead, no one would have blamed him – but he came back out with blood running down his face and said 'I'll play anywhere, skipper, outside-left if you like.'" Boy's Own stuff, different times, different manners.

Tommy also complimented Lol Hamlett, the Bolton centre-half. "After the game, he ran to me and said that although he had hoped to stop me scoring, he was delighted that we had such good tussles in a sporting way." These days that all seems rather Baden-Powellish, highly unlikely that Duncan Ferguson and Paul Ince might behave in a similar way after a game. Perhaps, despite the carnage of the war, they were more innocent times. For the record, Everton won the League North match 3-1 and Lawton scored his third goal in a week against Hamlett. In his next match for Everton, two weeks later at the Gwladys Street End of Goodison Park against Stockport County, Tommy scored his 400th goal in senior football. It was one of a quartet for him and of the nine that Everton rattled in on an afternoon when they beat Stockport 9-2 in another League North game. For a man who always insisted that records meant little to him, Tommy made a point of noting that it was at the opposite end of the ground that Dixie Dean scored his 60th in the 1928 season.

Perhaps he noted it because it was a year of such momentous happenings. The end of the war in Europe and the Far East, the atom bomb, in such a year it would be pleasant to be recognised for an important achievement. Lawton was to appear just three more times for Everton that season – and just another eight games in all. England and The Services teams claimed him for matches from Belfast to Florence and it seemed, he was weary of playing and travelling. Gordon Watson recalls heading across the river to the HQ of the Cheshires with Harry Cooke, specifically to have a word with Lawton. The intention being to ensure that he played the following day in a Liverpool Cup match at Anfield. "We were at the guard gate and they sent for Tommy. I remember Harry saying, 'He's not bothered about playing for us.' And I didn't believe him. Tommy Lawton didn't want to play! About a minute later he came walking across the yard towards us and I saw what Harry meant. He didn't want to play. He said 'Well I've got a few jobs to do here' and he made a few excuses. He did not want to play for us and that was it. In the end we just left it."

Lawton had much on his mind. His marriage was going through a very rocky period. In early February he had played in his 15th war-time international, again against Scotland at Villa Park. It was the first time in almost six years that the ground had been full to its 66,000 capacity, the grandstand seats having been replaced after being used in Birmingham air raid shelters since the days of the blitz. To Tommy though, the ground, not surprisingly, appeared "bomb scarred and shabby." Petty Officer Bobby Brown, an amateur goalkeeper with the Queen's Park club of Hampden Park, was the hero of the day, but, he could not prevent England winning 3-2. For once Lawton was not among the scorers, Stan Mortensen with two and Sailor Brown did the trick. But Lawton was among those denied in a frantic second half as Stan Matthews and Les Smith produced frequent chances. The night before the game at Villa Park, Frank Swift had made a point of seeking out the young Scottish debutant keeper, proffering a few words of advice and encouragement. It certainly worked wonders, especially in the last 20 minutes when he made a series of brilliant saves. "He looked like a schoolboy in a sweater that was far too big for him and long shorts. He was given a lucky horseshoe before the game and carried it with him, even at half-time! I hadn't seen such an inspired display by a young keeper since John Mapson before the war for Sunderland." Sailor Brown had been brought in as replacement for Carter, although the Sunderland man was available and in good form. Carter was never told why he was omitted for the match and it took a determined press campaign to restore him to the side. In the *Daily Sketch*, L V Manning wrote that Carter had been the "key man in every international since 1943. A month or two ago Carter (not Matthews and not Lawton) was by common consent the man whom Scotland and Wales must beat first to make a game of it, and the learned and not so wise were raving about the Matthews-Carter wing." For Tommy, the dropping of Carter was inexplicable. "Raich was the perfect team man. He would send through pin-point passes, or be there for the nod down. He was a scheming inside-forward, but he had the extra dimension with one of the hardest shots in the game with either foot."

In March 1945, Tommy made his first trip in an aeroplane. Along with Matt Busby, Joe Mercer and Stanley Matthews he was in an FA Services team chosen to play two games in Belgium to entertain the Allied troops making their way through the Low Countries en route to Germany.

A bad enough traveller by sea, Lawton was quaking with nerves by the time he arrived at Northolt Airport in the afternoon of March 23rd. "We were flying out by RAF Dakota, which, in those days, looked like a big aeroplane to us! The lads like Stan and Matt who'd done this before, were very matter of fact. 'Nothing to it, Tom. You don't even know you're up there.' So I thought, it must be OK then. Except that the steward says to me 'Make sure that Mae West is pulled tight, otherwise it'll strangle you when we come down in the drink!'"

The flight was uneventful, Lawton even daring to look out of the window to see the damage war had wreaked on the Belgian coastal towns. In Brussels they were welcomed warmly, but it was still obvious to the players that there was as much relief from the troops and the local population as delight that star footballers were on view again. "You could see in the faces of the people that they'd gone through a terrible time. Then we only knew the half of it. Six years of terror and hunger, the strain was bound to show." The all-star team played two games in two days, the first against the 'Diables Rouge' (Red Devils), was won 8-1 in Bruges, Lawton scoring four. The next day in Brussels he scored all three in a closely contested 3-2 win over a semi-representative Belgium side.

Lawton was back with Everton for the 1-0 defeat by Liverpool in the Merseyside derby at the end of March. More than 51,000 packed Anfield for that one, another sure indication that one of the most gruesome periods in history was coming to an end. Everton finished second and Liverpool third, with Derby County the leaders in the League North (Second Championship) that season. The rest of Lawton's season was spent playing for the England, the FA and the Army, with two more overseas trips lined up before the end of May. First though came yet another fixture against Scotland at Hampden Park.

MATCH OF THE DAY

Scotland v England
Hampden Park
April 14th 1945
Scotland: Brown (Queen's Park); Harley (Liverpool), Stephen (Bradford PA); Busby (Liverpool), John Harris (Wolves), Macaulay (West Ham); Waddell (Rangers), Bogan (Hibs), [(sub Johnstone (Clyde)], Tony Harris (Queens Park), Black (Hearts), Kelly (Morton).
England: Swift (Manchester City); Scott (Arsenal), Hardwick (Middlesbrough); Soo (Stoke), Franklin (Stoke) Mercer (Everton); Matthews (Stoke), Carter (Sunderland), Lawton (Everton), Brown (Charlton), Les Smith (Brentford).
Europe had awoken that morning to the news of US President Roosevelt's death in Washington. There was an air of disbelief around the packed stadium, though the roar as the teams emerged in the torrential rain was as raucous as ever at Hampden. For Tommy, there then followed one of the most impressive scenes he had ever been a part of. "With the players lined up in their positions, and with the vast crowd standing hatless in the pouring rain, a minute's silence was observed in memory of the late President. After the strains of the Last Post had died away, the crowd reverently sang 'Abide With Me.'" A Lancaster bomber flew over the stadium, dipping its wings in salute as the flags of Britain, Russia and America rippled at half mast.

The poignancy of the pre-match ceremony heightened the tension on the pitch and the start had to be nothing short of dramatic. Within 40 seconds of the kick-off Scotland were a man short. The 22-year-old Hibernian forward, Tommy Bogan, making his debut for Scotland, saw his chance of making an early impression and chased a long ball into the England penalty area. Frank Swift came out to cover and Bogan collided with the big keeper, tumbling over and lying motionless on the ground. Swift picked him up and, to a storm of booing, carried him to the touchline. Bogan, unconscious, was then taken to the dressing room on a stretcher and did not return. Fifteen minutes later, Scotland's reserve for the game, Les Johnstone, was allowed onto the field. By then England were ahead, Raich Carter, restored to the side, scoring from about 20 yards. Substitute Johnstone levelled for Scotland before half-time, but after the break, England overwhelmed the Scots, going back in front with another Carter produced Lawton special, he always seemed to produce his best at Hampden.

112

Lawton beat centre-half John Harris and broke into the area. Suddenly, he was on his own, bearing down on goal. "Perhaps this is the hardest position a centre-forward finds himself, carrying the ball through on a lone dash. He has to make and stand by a decision himself. Whether to shoot from long range when the keeper is off balance while moving out, or to take the ball right up to him and slip it into the net." In this instance, Lawton, moving at pace over a treacherous surface was into the area, clear of the defence and had only Brown to beat. "I suddenly stopped my run and quick as a flash the boy dived at the ball. I was prepared for this and whipping it back, ran it round the keeper before tapping into an empty net. Young Brown, a great sport, grinned at me as I made my way back, 'I might have known you'd do something like that!' I answered, 'Sorry!'"

The final score, 6-1 to England after another goal from Lawton, plus one each for Matthews and Brown, with a penalty from Smith, reflected their superiority and also the disorganisation of the Scots. With the score 3-1, Mercer collided with Willie Waddell in the area and the Scots won a penalty, "rather fortunately" according to Lawton. Their captain, Matt Busby, asked Waddell to take the kick. He refused. Busby called up Tony Harris, but he turned and walked away without answering. Then he asked Archie Macaulay, who told him "No, you're the one to take it, Matt." So Busby took on the responsibility himself. In Swift's early days at Manchester City, it was Busby who had practised with him and taught him how to stop penalties. He tried to vary his approach with a couple of feints, thought of a double bluff but it was no surprise that Swift kept this one out too.

A week later, Lawton, along with five of his England teammates from the Hampden game, was in Belgium again for another couple of games against the Diables Rouge. They were joined in Liege by a number of players who were stationed in North West Europe, including England's pre-war captain, Eddie Hapgood who Tommy had not seen for almost two years. In the event, Hapgood did not play in either game on the short tour, Tommy was captain as both matches were drawn 1-1 and 0-0. The most memorable moment, for Tommy, being when the antiquated bus in which they were travelling to one of the games broke down. "We were told that it was an old coach that had been left behind by the Germans. Well, they were obviously pretty good judges. We all piled into some RAF cars, squeezing in with our kitbags and sure enough, we got lost! By the time we arrived at the ground, the old bus had made it before us!" Prior to the next England match against Wales, Tommy, along with Frank Swift, Joe Mercer and Raich Carter, reported to the Great Western Hotel in Paddington on Friday May 4th 1945, there was a definite feeling that "something was up." As they, plus Stanley Matthews, Frank Broome, Bert Williams and Stanley Rous were sitting in the lounge, the 'wireless' announced the surrender of the German forces in North-West Europe. "Bill Baron, the manager of the hotel, immediately ordered the floodlights outside the hotel to be switched on, the first sign of celebrations." The team joined in the party, Swift and Lawton's double act being the centre-piece. The following morning, in pouring rain, they left Paddington for Cardiff on the eight o'clock express.

113

It rained all the way into Wales and was still raining as the teams ran out onto a Ninian Park mudheap. The crowd was in festive mood, nothing could dampen their enthusiasm. The goal nets were festooned with leeks, some of the spectators had swung on one of the cross bars and it was bent in the middle. George Edwards making his debut for Wales on the left-wing recalled that the atmosphere was such that "I lost all feeling in my legs from my knees downwards. I couldn't feel a thing. I don't know how I ran out on that pitch. Once the game started, I was fine. The rain stopped and we were on top in the opening stages." But after seven minutes, Neil Franklin's free-kick found Carter and he beat Cyril Sidlow from close range. Wales were level before half-time when Mercer was adjudged to have handled in the area. Play was held up while the referee tried to locate the spot and in the end paced out the 12 yards ("looked more like 10 to me," commented Tommy) and Horace Cumnor scored.

Twenty seconds after half-time, Lawton intercepted, fed Sailor Brown, who made 35 yards before Carter took over, lobbing the ball out of reach of the advancing goalkeeper. Carter added a third but then George Edwards set up a grandstand finale. "In the first half, I was on the 'Bob' Bank side, and turned infield to go past Laurie Scott. He caught me with his arm and I went down, bleeding from my mouth. At half-time, Ted Robbins, (FA of Wales secretary) walked to the board room past the press box and they wanted to know about the injury. Ted just said 'Oh, he'll be alright, just lost a couple of teeth, he'll be back.' The truth is, I hadn't lost any teeth but it made a good story when I scored with ten minutes to go." Every paper carried something along the lines of "lost two teeth, but not his bite in front of goal" after Edwards drove powerfully past Williams, deputising for the injured Swift. According to Tommy, the ball hit the only remaining leek hanging in the net "and shot it straight into the hands of an excited Welshman. I bet he still has it framed – or pressed into the family Bible." Edwards recalls it differently: "I saw my father and mother leap into the air, because they were right in line with the shot, that's all I saw. I suppose there might have been a leek but I didn't see it." England survived the late Welsh pressure to win 3-2. "That was a very good England side,' said Edwards. "Though not the best I played against. That was the following year at Maine Road."

For Edwards it was back to the RAF camp at Abingdon to review the match with his colleagues and opponents Neil Franklin, George Hardwick and Bert Williams. While, straight after the game, Tommy, along with Joe Mercer, George Smith and the Wales goalkeeper Cyril Sidlow had dashed to the station to catch the 5.30 back to Paddington to link up with the rest of the British Army team due to fly out the following day from RAF Lyneham en route for Italy where they were due to play a series of games against sides drawn from the Army units over there. Oh, what a lovely war!

The letter from the War Office informing Lawton of his selection for the tour, arrived with the following instructions. "Uniform will be worn by all ranks. If necessary arrangements will be made for a temporary issue in Italy of khaki drill. Baggage is limited to 55lbs per man and provision should be made for an adequate supply of towels, soap, razor blades toothpaste etc. Players will also supply their own football boots,which should be properly studded; gym shoes or plimsolls, shin guards,and athletic slips (jock straps)."

It was a standard letter, Lawton had long since been used to supplying everything he needed for a trip apart from his team shirt, shorts and socks. By comparison, today's stars have it easy, with their kit neatly packed into skips by a baggage man and laid out for them neatly before their arrival at the stadium. Lawton, Swift, Busby and the rest knew of no other way of life. In any case they felt immensely privileged to be selected for such a trip. The RAF Warwick took about six hours to reach the Bay of Naples, landing at Pomigliano where they were greeted by Stan Cullis, stationed out there. While the trip was a morale boosting one for the Army stationed in Italy, it was also an educational experience for the players. Sight seeing around Pompeii provided a lasting memory, as did the Church of the Madonna. VE day itself was celebrated on what had only recently been enemy soil, though the chances of a major party that night were scuppered when all troops were confined to barracks for three days and nights. The first game of the tour in Naples, against No 3 Army District (selected from units stationed between Bari and Gibraltar) was won comfortably 6-0, despite Frank Swift taking over in their goal for half-an-hour when No 3's keeper was injured. It may have been a closer game had three of Tommy's old acquaintances, Bryn Jones, Ray Westwood and Albert Geldard been able to play for No 3. They instead were otherwise engaged in the Mediterranean Championship semi-final. It really was the end of the war in Europe! Which only served to improve the team spirit and camaraderie within the party as they drove to Rome. By now, Joe Mercer, who owned his own grocery business in Hoylake, was in charge of rations, Cliff Britton of transport, which meant a five-ton covered lorry to take the party of 18, and Swift and Lawton were the baggage men. Swift, of course, contrived to lose his own boots on the trip.

The 150 mile trip went through Cassino, the scene of some of the most vicious fighting in the Battle for Italy. For Tommy the most tragic sight was of the cemetery containing the bodies of the dead. White crosses on the graves of British and American soldiers. Black on the Germans.'

On the road to Rome, the truck laboured through the town of Caserta. "Vic Wright, our Army 'pilot' mentioned that it was the place where one of my cricketing pals, Hedley Verity, had died the year before. Soon after he had been killed, I was in Leeds with Arthur Wood, the Yorkshire wicket-keeper who played with Hedley and was in the Green Howards with him too. We had commiserated with each other and I wrote Arthur a letter from Italy saying that we'd been to Hedley's grave and laid some flowers there. It was a sad moment on a very happy tour." A visit to the Vatican in Rome was probably not top of the list of priorities when he was first told he was going to Italy, but it is a memory that never left him. "I was overwhelmed by the magnificence of the place. The sweeping marble steps and the intricacy of the architecture. It was breathtaking, a real contrast to the poverty and squalor we'd seen all around us in the rest of Italy. We were all gathered in one room when the Pope, in his embroidered robes, was carried in by his Swiss guards and proceeded to bless us all. It was quite an experience for me, a Church of England working class lad from Lancashire, to be blessed by the Pope." In Rome, they beat the Army in Italy 10-2, Lawton scoring five of them, then it was back in the truck for the run over the Appenines to Ancona. The comradeship that was to bind this collection of players together for ever was established during this trip. They stopped off for a nude swim in a mountain stream to remove some of the chalk and dust picked up on the journey. "Starting to look your age, Matt," they joked with Matt Busby. "After the war, I saw little of Matt but I always knew that we were friends. Whenever Manchester United were in Nottingham, he would leave tickets for me and my son, Tommy, to go along as his guests. When we met it was as if time had stood still." One hotel on the tour had a huge communal bath, around which various athletic carved figures were positioned, each about 16 feet high and in various poses. Frank Swift climbed out and compared himself with one of the statues. "This bloke's got nothing on me," he declared. The rest laughed at Swift's proud boast. Even he was dwarfed by the giant figure in more areas than one.

The patience of the squad was tested when Joe Mercer lost the only tin opener they had. "It was a disaster. All the food was in tins. We were giving Joe all sorts of flak. We didn't have a nail, a knife, anything that could get us into these tins. In the end it was getting quite desperate and Joe was even in danger of losing his permanent grin. The boys were hungry and there's nothing worse than a gang of hungry footballers. Somebody came up with the bright idea that we should use the lorry to open a few tins, but Cliff Britton wouldn't let us. He said it could puncture the tyres. In the end we convinced him and laid out the tins of bully beef so that he could drive slowly over them and just pop them open. Of course, he goes smack over the middle of them and the beef that wasn't flattened into the sand was splattered all over the place. He did it right the next time and we were able to eat, but Joe was relegated from Mess Sergeant to Orderly."

After playing one game in Ancona, the squad set off for Florence for a fixture with the Fifth Army. The result was a 10-0 victory for the tourists, but it was not a game that gave Lawton and his colleagues any pleasure at all. "We got nettled by the remarks from the crowd of servicemen. They were shouting 'Come on the real soldiers,' and calling us 'The D-Day dodgers.' Rather than play exhibition football and make a game of it, we went all-out for goals. Looking back you can hardly blame the lads in the crowd. They had not had an easy time in Italy, seen many of their mates killed and we'd spent the war safely at home. Though none of us had asked to do that." Lawton and Joe Mercer left the tour early, flying back from Rome to London in time for the England international against France at Wembley. The rest went on into Greece, playing their series of matches ever closer to front line, often, according to Matt Busby, with the noise of gunfire drowning out the sound of the referee's whistle. The BBC commentator, Raymond Glendenning praised Lawton, Matthews, Busby, Hagan and their colleagues for being "our first ambassadors to liberated Europe. On and off the field, they've done more for this country's prestige than is generally realised." All the more surprising then, that Lawton never received any official recognition from HM Government for his services to the nation and the nation's game.

Mercer and Lawton arrived back in London on May 25th, the day before the France game at Wembley. "We were told to go straight to the FA in Lancaster Gate to see Stanley Rous. He had a quiet word with Joe. I didn't know at the time, but he told Joe that the selectors wanted me to skipper the side." It was put to Mercer that, in view of the great season Lawton had enjoyed, it should be recognised with the England captaincy and that Mercer himself was the man to tell him. It appears an extraordinary method of handling affairs, judged 55 years on, but different times, different manners, underlined when the manager of France, Gaston Barreau, informed Lawton that he would feel "privileged to be beaten by such distinguished opponents."

England: Williams (Walsall); Scott (Arsenal), Hardwick (Middlesbrough); Soo (Stoke), Franklin (Stoke), Mercer (Everton); Matthews (Stoke), Carter (Sunderland), Lawton (Everton), Brown (Charlton), Les Smith (Brentford). France: Da Rui; Dupuis, Swiatek; Samuel, Jordan, Jasseron; Aston, Heisserer, Bihel, Siklo, Vaast.

All of the French team had stories to tell from the war. Da Rui had been captured at Dunkirk, but escaped from the Germans after three weeks in jail. Dupuis was in the French Resistance, a roof-top sniper during the battle for Paris. Siklo, born in Poland, had been in a labour camp for six months until he managed to escape.

Lawton was the first man to captain England from centre-forward since the legendary Vivian Woodward before the first World War. "We did not play well that day. They hustled and bustled and we just never settled into our normal pattern." England went ahead through Carter after ten minutes, missed a succession of chances, including a penalty, saved by Da Rui in inspired form, and conceded an equaliser before half-time when Vaast rifled past Williams. Lawton was fortunate to beat Da Rui with a long range header but other chances were squandered and eventually Heisserer, in attack in the closing stages, grabbed the equaliser.

England were slated in the press for their below-par performance. France were not expected to put up much of a show and a 2-2 draw was extremely unsatisfactory.

The 1945/46 season started early for the England team with a two match tour to Switzerland in July. For the first time since the war began, the team was in 'civvies.' Switzerland being a neutral country, uniforms of a 'belligerent' nature were banned. So the FA had to provide clothing coupons for every man in the squad.

Although the war was over in Europe, matters in the Far East were taking a little longer to settle and the trip was all but cancelled when the Air Ministry discovered they had no plane available to fly the team to Zurich. A day later, the Swiss government despatched one of their own aircraft to pick up the team from Croydon (now Gatwick), the first Swiss plane to land in England for six years. "When we arrived in Zurich we were taken to the Hotel Gotthard for a meal. It was the best meal any of us had enjoyed for many years. Everything that was rationed or just not available in England was on the table. Melon, salmon, sides of beef, everything we could have wished for. What a way to start a tour. We may not have played very well, but we ate like kings and it was, I think, the best overseas tour that I ever made."

The England players who made the trip were: Swift (Manchester City); Scott (Arsenal), Hardwick (Middlesbrough), Kinsell (West Brom), Soo (Stoke), Franklin (Stoke), Mercer (Everton), Ted Fenton (West Ham), Finney (Preston), Brown (Charlton), Smith (Brentford), Mickey Fenton (Middlesbrough), Hunt (Sheffield Wednesday), Watson (Huddersfield), Lawton (Everton). Tom Finney who had been flown back from Austria only two days earlier to make the trip, was about to appear in the same team as Lawton for the first time. "In Berne, Tom Finney was up against Willie Steffen, the best left back in the world. He still came out with credit and it was obvious that he was going to be around for years to come. He and Frank Swift were about the only plusses though. We were tired after the experiences of a long war. The Swiss had spent three weeks training in the Alps and were too quick and too fit for us. And they used a formation, with a deep lying centre-forward that had us foxed. It's a system that lots of sides have used since. The way to combat it, I thought, was to use our inside-forwards' speed to wrong-foot the defence." The result, a 3-1 win for Switzerland. The verdict? That England were beaten by a cleverer team.

On the tour, Tommy met the two Swedish milers, Gundar Hägg and Arne Andersson in the Perroquit night club in Berne. Andersson assured him that the mile in under four minutes could be achieved "but only if he and Hägg helped each other. We hadn't heard of Bannister, Brasher and Chataway then." Two days later on the Grasshoppers Zurich ground, England met the Swiss 'B' team. This was the side that had taken on their supposed superiors in a trial match the previous week and won 3-1. Playing with the smaller sized continental ball, England emerged with a 3-0 victory. Tom Finney scoring his first goal for England, while the others came from Willie Watson and Micky Fenton. During the war, the maximum wage had 'peaked' at £4 a week. For the 1945/46 season, it increased to £9 a week, while the minimum admission charge was 1/3d

(6p). Given the vast attendances that were common at the time, it was scant reward for the players who had kept the game alive in war-time, doing their bit for public morale.

In September, Tommy was on England duty again in Belfast, partnering Stan Mortensen up front in a Victory International against Northern Ireland. It was Mortensen who scored the only goal of the game five minutes from time, but the lasting impression from the match, was the display of Peter Doherty. "Peter was brilliant that day, he always seemed to reserve his best for us. But he had an added incentive, because he was anxious to move from Manchester City and he wanted to put himself in the shop window if you like. Doherty eventually had his transfer request granted and he moved to Derby County. One of a number of players who were transferred that season including Raich Carter, also to Derby, and Tommy himself.

The Combined Services side to play the League of Ireland at Cliftonville two days after the international at Windsor Park, contained most of the familiar faces – Swift, Franklin, Mercer and Matthews, but a new name replaced the unavailable Raich Carter at inside-left, Billy Wright of Wolves.

In the first minute, Lawton was up for a ball through from Mercer and deftly flicked it down into the path of Wright. "I was so nervous, I panicked completely and hit it well behind our left winger, Willie Watson." The crowd jeered mercilessly and Lawton went over to Wright to say "Don't take any notice of them; you can't call yourself a footballer until you've had a bit of that." Wright appreciated Tommy's concern, "He was the greatest centre-forward of them all. An appearance by Tommy, home or abroad, was the signal for the 'House Full' notices to go up. He took some tremendous hammerings during the course of his career, but never once can I recall Tommy losing his temper or his poise or ever deliberately fouling an opponent. He taught me that no one can ever afford to lose his sense of humour, as well as a hundred and one different things about the game without ever realising it."

Tommy was philosophical about the attitudes of football crowds. "They pay the money so they think they have the right to say whatever they like. In Italy, the 'Tommies' had called us all sorts of things but at any match someone in the crowd will say "Oh, he's not as good as so and so.' You know when I played at Wolves they would say 'Dennis Westcott's better than you mate' or in Newcastle they'd go 'You're not a patch on our Jackie.' At least they turned up to watch a certain player in those days, even me! You know, some of my pals would turn up and they'd think I was just grand. Others would be there running me down, especially if I had a stinker. They'd be shouting 'You're hopeless, big-head!' and worse. Then I might hit one in and I'm the greatest they've ever seen. They're great the public, but they're fickle. They pay at the turnstiles though and without them the game would be nothing."

In summer of 1945, Tommy had reluctantly come to the decision that he would have to leave Merseyside. "The marriage just wasn't working out, in fact it was purgatory. During the war I wasn't around much and we'd been married four years without seeing anything of each other. So, to improve the situation, I thought it would be better if we left the north of England altogether. Home was hell, something had to be done." Lawton submitted one transfer request in July 1945 but was persuaded to withdraw it. He was called into Theo Kelly's office. "He was sitting behind his desk at the end of this long room. He looked at me over his glasses and said 'You want a transfer do you, Lawton? Well, let me tell you, we've been trying to give you away for four months and nobody wants you. There's the door, go out and get your training done and stop wasting my time." I felt that small. Here I was, the best centre-forward in England, so I was being told, and nobody wanted me!'"

Small and naive apparently. As soon as the rumour mill started, numerous clubs were phoning Goodison Park. When nothing improved on the home front, Tommy decided to ask again for a move. This time it was granted. "The papers were full of it. Why does Lawton want to go? Everybody had a say, except me of course. I couldn't tell the truth, that I really wanted to stay. On reflection I should have stayed and transferred the wife. Everton wanted to keep me. They'd only had two full seasons out of me, the rest were war years. We still had a good side, we could have won the title again. But in the end I told the press that the reason I had to move was that my wife was ill and the doctors had said we should move to the south." Years later, Lawton said that he had been "loath to wash dirty linen in public." Some people knew the reasons behind the move, but generally in the manner of the day, the press accepted Lawton's version of the cause.

He was still to be demobbed from Seighton Camp in Chester when Chelsea came in with an offer, £11,500. England full-back George Hardwick had helped broker the deal. When Tommy had told him how unhappy he was in Liverpool, he had spoken to the Chelsea manager, Billy Birrell. "I was really pleased that I managed to get him to Chelsea. I knew how keen he was to move so I had a word with Billy, an ex-Middlesbrough player. I was hopeful of a move to Chelsea myself, but Middlesbrough wouldn't let me go. At least I got Tommy to the club." The deal was agreed, and the forms signed under the watchful eye of Dixie Dean at his pub. Tommy played his first match for Chelsea at Stamford Bridge on Saturday November 10th 1945. Birmingham City were the visitors in a War-time Football League South game and won 3-2. But to the delight of the 53,813 crowd, over 22,000 more than for the previous home game, Lawton scored twice.

Four days later, Moscow Dynamo were due at Stamford Bridge. It was a surprise when the team had arrived. They had been expected for three days and it appeared that they had decided not to come. Eventually they landed at Croydon on November 4th. Stanley Rous of the FA had the job of finding them accommodation in London at short notice. They started off in Wellington Barracks in Hyde Park, objected to the spartan conditions and were eventually 'billeted' in the ballroom of the Park Lane Hotel, then owned by the Arsenal chairman, Sir Guy Bracewell-Smith.

"Dynamo were a mystery team. Everybody was fascinated by them. When I arrived at Stamford Bridge that Tuesday afternoon it seemed that everyone in London had taken the day off to see these Russians." The crowd was conservatively estimated at 85,000. Many more than that broke in and found vantage points. Some precariously perched on the roof of the stand. Others vaulted the pitch walls and watched from the greyhound track. "The Russians did something that was unheard of then. They went out on the pitch for a warm-up session in track suits and with several balls. Afterwards that became standard practice here in England, but then it was unknown. The crush was so great around the pitch that the police had to clear a path for us even to get on the field. Then, after the national anthems, each one of their players stepped smartly forwards and presented each one of us with a posy of flowers. Well, we all stood there looking very embarrassed. The crowd was roaring with laughter and in the end our trainer, Norman Smith, came out to take them from us and went off looking like a harvest festival."

Chelsea had borrowed two players, Joe Bacuzzi and Jimmy Taylor from Fulham, because their defence had been hit with injuries. "We were a bit disorganised at the start, so when they came at us in the first 20 minutes we were lucky to survive. They were quick, had brilliant control and were a great team. We should have been four down in no time." Yet Chelsea scored twice in ten minutes before half-time. Lawton winning an aerial battle with Tiger Khomich, the Dynamo keeper, to set up Goulden. Lawton admitted that he headed it out of Khomich's hands. The way the game was played in England in 1945, that was legal. Then Reg Williams forced full-back Stankevich into an error and scored the second. Dynamo missed a penalty before the end of the first half "the crowd surging around and behind the goal had much to do with that." Midway through the second half, Dynamo were inspired by Kartsev in midfield. He scored from long range, then brilliantly made the equaliser for Archangelski. With eight minutes left, Lawton was up above Khomich in the area again, to nod Chelsea into the lead, 3-2. "We thought we'd won it, but then Bobrov, about 25 yards offside, I'm not joking, beat Vic Woodley and the referee gave the goal. I went charging after the ref, Commander Campbell. I was screaming 'You can't give that.' He said, 'It's for diplomatic reasons.' I was so angry. 'And you've diplomatically robbed us of a win bonus.'"

The Russians impressed Lawton. "They flashed the ball from man to man and waited for the opening. Their tactics were very similar to those in basketball, but for football, so fast." *Isvestia* reported that "Chelsea played with a strengthened team. determined to beat Dynamo at all costs, the club had spent thousands of pounds to secure some of Britain's best footballers. For instance, Chelsea paid £14,000 for Tommy Lawton, so that he could play against Dynamo." Chelsea made about £3,500 from the game, enough to cover almost a third of Lawton's transfer fee.

Dynamo went on to play in a series of matches in Britain, before departing almost as abruptly as they arrived, though not before a round table conference at the Great Western Hotel on December 3rd. Various club managers were there to meet the Dynamo staff and players and swop ideas and theories. Tommy was there too, at a table with the Dynamo centre-half, Mikhail Semichastny. "I think we all learned a lot from their visit." And Tommy had made a firm friend.

For the month after the visit of Dynamo, Tommy was in prime goal scoring form. four in two games against Brentford; a hat-trick against Swansea; on Christmas Day two more against Millwall at Stamford Bridge; then, in the return at the Den on Boxing Day, another hat-trick in an 8-0 win. It was all too much for the Millwall goalkeeper, Charlie Bumstead. He went up with Lawton for a cross from Reg Williams. Lawton's head met the ball, Bumstead's fists met Lawton's head. The result? Lawton's second goal of his hat-trick and a pair of black eyes that he took with him to Southampton three days later. Chelsea lost 7-0 with the same team that had beaten Millwall 8-0 at the Den. Doug McGibbon scored six of the Southampton goals, most of them from centres by Peter Buchanan. The Scottish international had been loaned by Chelsea to the Saints when they turned up one short and proved devastating on the right-wing. Not one of Lawton's more memorable games. Except for a press photograph at the time. Lawton is pictured helping off Bill Dodgin having collided with the centre-half who had kept him under control throughout the match. Never booked, never sent off, always the gentleman.

CHAPTER NINETEEN
1946 – ENGLAND
MORE GOALS BUT
NO CAPS

The 1945/46 season was still officially classified as "war-time." For the victory internationals against Belgium at Wembley in January and Scotland at Hampden Park in April, no caps were awarded. Belgium had never played England before in a full international and on this occasion the Wembley crowd of 85,000 saw little of the visitors, or much of the match at all, as thick fog came down at half-time. "We kidded Jesse Pye that he couldn't claim the second goal because nobody had seen it! There was one great save by Swifty from their inside-left, Sermon. The shot came in from about 30 yards and Frank kept it out. I said 'How did you manage that?' And he just grinned 'Oh, I heard it coming!'"

The tragedy which had been waiting to happen in British football occurred on March 9th 1946. Starved of entertainment during the war, crowds were flocking to games. During an FA Cup tie between Bolton and Stoke at Burnden Park, 33 people were killed and more than 500 injured, crushed against barriers or trampled underfoot, when a mass of people surged through a suddenly opened gate.

"We had played at Arsenal that day and when the news came through that there had been these deaths at Bolton, we were all stunned. Me especially, because I knew that many of my friends and relatives would have been at the game. From then on, the clubs were told to put their grounds in order. Nothing had been done to the grounds for years during the war. The clubs just wanted to take the money and do nothing for the fans. Bolton should never have happened but we should have learned from it and made sure that Hillsborough didn't either."

At Hampden, Lawton teamed up with Len Shackleton on one of their rare appearances together for England. "Shack'was the only man I know who came close to having Stan Matthews' ball control. But, like Stan sometimes, I just couldn't weigh him up at all. I never knew what he was going to do next. He was as awkward and bewildering to his team-mates as he was to the opposition. He was a masterly inside-forward but far too much of an individual both on and off the field." It was Shackleton who gave away the free-kick that led to Jimmy Delaney's winning goal for Scotland 22 seconds from the end of the encounter at Hampden. "The Hampden Roar just exploded around us. All the misery of the war years for the Scots against England evaporated then. It probably even made up for 1939. Even the Glasgow coppers on the touchline were smiling and they didn't do that often."

Switzerland had been promised a game at Wembley after they had defeated England in 1945. The date set was May 11th 1946. "It was one of the first times, if not the first, when we went away before the game to train. The FA sent us to a place in Twyford (Bucks) with Tom Whittaker in charge. I was captain. We talked about how to beat their system and I said that we needed to get our inside-forwards up quickly on Willie Steffen. It worked." It did work, but not until deep into the second half. Switzerland went ahead through a goal by Friedlander. Then Carter and Lawton combined for Carter to crash in the equaliser The other inside-forward, Sailor Brown scored the second from a Lawton flick on. Lawton himself scored with a magnificent effort from 30 yards, before Carter made it 4-1. "I don't remember a thing about the game after the first half-an-hour. I got clobbered and spent the rest of the game wandering around with concussion. I couldn't even go to the banquet at the Dorchester after the game!"

Tommy recovered soon enough and was able to play against France in the victory international in the Stade Colombes to celebrate the end of the war. "Bert Williams was in goal as Frank Swift had gone off to Norway to do some coaching. The French had a big centre-forward, Ben Barek who just flattened Bert at every opportunity. It was 1-1 with about five minutes to go, when Barek bundled Bert, the ball and anything else in his way into the net. We couldn't believe it was a goal, but the ref signalled it was. Bert was all for landing a punch on Barek, but George Hardwick pulled him away at the last minute." Swift had gone to Norway at the request of the FA to coach some of their clubs. Lawton was surprised that the FA asked him to perform the same duties in Switzerland. "I wasn't really a coach. I'd had reasonable success coaching in the Army, but somebody like Joe Mercer would have been a better bet than me. We worked at most clubs in Geneva, Lugano and Berne and we worked really hard. I was fitter than ever, I'd even lost a stone in weight."

Tommy was 26 and ready to resume his career at the pinnacle of English football. In that summer of 1946, Walter Winterbottom was appointed England's first ever permanent team manager. It was one of the few issues that Lawton and Frank Swift disagreed over. Swift thought Winterbottom "knew all the secrets of coaching and how to pass them on to others." Lawton thought he was a "good PT instructor." The relationship between England manager and star centre-forward did not get off to a good start. Lawton returned from Switzerland with a groin strain and pulled out of Winterbottom's first England squad session prior to the Bolton Disaster Fund match on August 24th. Reg Lewis, the Arsenal inside-forward, took his place. On August 31st, Lawton kicked off the 1946/47 season for Chelsea against Bolton Wanderers, his home town club, at Stamford Bridge with two goals in the 4-3 win. It was exciting stuff for the 62,850 crowd.

Bolton should have won, they hit the bar three times. Lawton's two were matched by two from the young Nat Lofthouse.

The Players' Union was threatening a strike if their demand for compulsory arbitration in the wages dispute was not met. The clubs countered that they would fulfil the fixtures with amateur players if necessary. The situation was at an impasse.

On September 7th it was back to Merseyside for Lawton and Chelsea – to Liverpool at Anfield. On a baking hot day, there were close on 50,000 inside the ground and a considerable number outside. The Reds supporters were not disappointed as Liverpool, prompted by Bob Paisley raced into a 4-0 lead by half-time. Lawton had done little, apart from acknowledge a warm welcome from the crowd, but a "ticklish header" of his was tipped over the top by Charlie Ashcroft, making his debut for Liverpool in place of the injured Cyril Sidlow.

Early in the second half it was 6-0 to Liverpool. Paisley and Billy Liddell "were making a big difference"according to the *Liverpool Echo*. With 20 minutes left, Chelsea, with Lawton rampant, had brought the score back to 6-4. Lawton having made goals for Goulden and Argue. plus two for Machin and brought a fine save out of Ashcroft. "The crowd having looked on Chelsea's effort with benign disinterestedness' were suddenly thinking in terms of a 6-6 draw. Then, with three minutes left Willie Fagan scored Liverpool's seventh – "The end of a memorable day." 'Bee' in the *Liverpool Daily Post* thought "Lawton has gone back a little in heading which once promised to reach the Dean pinnacle" but he praised him for being "unselfish, the most generous of all centre-forwards." The *Sunday Express* announced that "Chelsea obviously need half backs." At Anfield, they had Ray Goddard, newly signed from Wolves making his debut, and, after the match, completed the transfer of Tommy Walker from Hearts for £6,000. Walker had been expected to move to Charlton but their manager Jimmy Seed pulled out of the deal when Walker demanded a £1,000 signing on fee.

Chelsea left Liverpool for the Spa Hotel in Buxton, prior to the Monday night game with Sheffield United. Midweek matches had been banned the previous season so as not to interfere with production in essential industries. Now the restriction was lifted. Apart from his two goals against Bolton, Tommy had not started the season well, an injury, a missed penalty at Manchester United, and a blank at Anfield. He kick-started his season with a goal at Bramall Lane as Chelsea scrapped for a 2-2 draw, then another in a 3-0 win over Leeds at Stamford Bridge. Timely reminders to the England selectors that he was still very much in contention for a place. The squad for the first official internationals after the war, back to back games against Northern Ireland and the Republic of Ireland, the first with Walter Winterbottom in charge was announced on September 20th.

Compared with the experimental line up that had drawn with Scotland 2-2 in the Bolton Disaster Fund match, the 14 contained mainly familiar names: Hardwick (Middlesbrough, the new captain), Swift (Man City),

Scott (Arsenal), Wright (Wolves), Franklin (Stoke), Cockburn (Man Utd), Matthews (Stoke), Carter (Derby), Lawton (Chelsea), Mannion (Middlesbrough), Langton (Blackburn Rovers). The reserves were Welsh (Charlton), Shimwell (Sheffield United) and Finney (Preston). Finney replaced Matthews in the 11 when he failed a fitness test.

The team's headquarters in County Down, the Slieve Donard Hotel, within sight of the Mountains of Mourne, provided an ideal setting. "We trained on the lush grass of the lawns, played a little golf and discovered a new game – pool." Lawton and Swift, according to George Hardwick, proved adept at the pool table. "In other words, they hustled money from their teammates." Tommy suggested that Raich Carter and Laurie Scott won most of the games. "Some of my shots would not have met with approval by Joe Davis." The first match against Northern Ireland at Windsor Park, Belfast attracted such a crowd (57,111) that it appeared unlikely the game would ever start. The crowd had swarmed over the barrier and onto the running track and the kick-off was delayed until the spectators were back behind the perimeter walls and order had been restored to the satisfaction of the referee, Willie Webb, the Glasgow engine driver.

Lawton and Carter were the exceptions as it was the first official cap for men like Swift, Scott and Franklin who had become fixtures in the war-time England side. The England forwards were in magnificent form – Lawton's performance was described as being that of a "genius," Finney had a fine match, Carter and Mannion amazed the crowd with their high-speed dribbling skills. It was Mannion who scored a hat-trick, but all five England forwards were on target in a 7-2 win. "It was a grand way to begin again after the war. For once, Peter Doherty had a quiet game. The lasting memory for me of that match though, is the sight of young lads going around the ground selling toffee apples and oranges. Things we hadn't seen in England for years." The next day it was on to Dublin. Again it was food that attracted the attention of Lawton and his England colleagues. "We were taken to the Gresham Hotel and there was an eight course menu, at least five more than we had been used to during the war. 'Big Swifty' said to the waiter, 'Have you really got all this?' There was soup and various choices of fish and beef, lamb, chicken or turkey. Cheese and fruit. It was the only meal I remember with an England team that was eaten in complete silence. It was one of the finest meals I ever had." History of a different kind was made the following morning when the FA party was presented to Eamon de Valera, the Republic of Ireland's Taoiseach, at Government House, the first time that he had agreed to meet a 'foreign' football team, some 30 years after he had been a central figure in the battle for Irish independence.

The first ever meeting between the Republic of Ireland and England was a disappointing affair, played out in persistent drizzle. Bill Gorman and Johnny Carey who had played for Northern Ireland in Belfast two days earlier reappeared at Dalymount Park. Tommy renewed acquaintance with Alex Stevenson, while two brothers Kevin and Michael O'Flanagan were in the forward line. "Kevin O'Flanagan was a great character. He was called the 'Flying Doctor,' he had a surgery at Ruislip. How he found time to be a doctor, I don't know, because he was a sprinter, long jump champion, a golfer. He played on the wing for Arsenal and in between played rugby for London Irish! He set an amazing record, playing rugby for Ireland against France one week and then football against Scotland at Hampden the next. He was always the life and soul of any party. He played the piano very well. A lovely chap."

The game was won nine minutes from time when Mannion's shot was parried by keeper Tommy Breen. Mannion squared it for Lawton who let it run onto Finney, who finished with a crisp shot.

The game was not an especially memorable affair, but Tommy always remembered an incident on the team's return to Liverpool. "They were sorting out the expenses and Mr Ewbank, the treasurer, called out 'Oh! Lawton, over here if you will." I thought 'Oh, what am I supposed to have done now?' And he says ' Here's the penny you're owed from the last game when we didn't have enough change to recompense you in full." I said, 'Thank you very much.' And thought about having it framed."

For the third official international and the first at home since the war, England kept an unchanged side which meant there was still no Stanley Matthews. In his place England had a more than adequate replacement in Tom Finney. There had been calls for changes for the Wales game at Maine Road, but, even though Matthews was fit again, the selectors kept the same 11, with Bobby Langton of Blackburn on the left-wing, Finney on the right, while Lawton's inside-forwards were Raich Carter and Wilf Mannion. This was the match that Finney described as containing the best co-ordinated inside forward display he had ever seen.

"Press reports were none too enthusiastic," said Finney. "But England didn't need wingers that day, so well did that inside trio play." Two goals from Mannion, sandwiched Lawton's first half effort. Wales were never out of it until the third went in. Lawton was extremely pleased to score again against his old Everton team-mate, T G Jones. "He was such a good player, he had a complete all-round game." George Edwards, on the left wing for Wales, recalled being at the George Hotel in Knutsford when Stan Richards arrived, having been called up from Cardiff when Trevor Ford reported injured. "I was in the foyer when he came in, looking very dishevelled. It had been a long, tiring journey up by train at the last minute. They'd got hold of him by flashing a message on cinema screens in Cardiff."

"The England forward line that day was simply superb – Finney, Carter, Lawton, Mannion, Langton. How much would they cost today? They'd all be millionaires driving around in Rolls-Royces!" In the second half, Edwards led the Welsh revival, Richards shot wide from his cross, Aubrey Powell. of Leeds, headed another Edwards centre towards the corner of the net, only for Swift to save brilliantly.

Lawton collected a Henry Cockburn pass in the centre-circle, turned past T G and laid on a second for Mannion. "Lawton," said Edwards, "was commanding in the middle. Finding space and on the end of everything. When we talk about England players today, there's just nobody to compare with the talent England had available in 1946. After those five forwards, there was Matthews waiting to come in, Len Shackleton, Stan Mortensen. Nowadays, Kevin Keegan, basically, hasn't got that sort of talent at his disposal. Walter Winterbottom didn't have to do anything with that team – he just send them out to play."

Two weeks later at Huddersfield, Winterbottom made just one change for the game against Holland, Harry Johnston of Blackpool, Lawton's friend since they had played together in the Lancashire Schoolboy trials in the early '30s, replacing Henry Cockburn at left-half. The match was played at Leeds Road to celebrate the Jubilee of the West Riding FA. "We trained at the Majestic in Harrogate. All the good work of getting us well prepared for the match was nearly undone because our coach driver was determined to get us to the ground in record time. It was pouring with rain and at times we were screeching around corners on two wheels. Swifty went down the bus to him and said 'Hey mate, where's the bloody fire?' The sight of Big Frank staring down at him calmed him down a bit and we got there in one piece." The match was won comfortably 8-2, Lawton scoring four in what was described at the time by Frank Swift as "one of the finest displays I have witnessed from a centre-forward." The President of the Netherlands Football Association, Karel Lotsy, agreed. "In 30 years of football on the Continent and in England, I saw today a forward line such as I have never seen before." In his speech after the game, he went on to thank Britain for all the help given to Holland during the war. He said some of the debt had been repaid by those of the Dutch underground who had lost their lives. "What he didn't tell us, but which most of us knew,' wrote Frank Swift, "was that he had been an active underground worker."

May 10th 1947. Aberfoyle Hotel, Loch Ard. The Great Britain team for the match of the century. Back Row l-r: Billy Hughes, Jack Vernon, George Young; middle row: Billy Liddell, Raich Carter, Billy Steel; front row: Tommy Lawton, George Hardwick, Archie Macaulay, Wilf Mannion, Stanley Matthews. Young and Carter were travelling reserves. Frank Swift and Ron Burgess, who both played, are unaccountably absent from the photograph. (Tom Lawton collection)

November 15th 1947. "The worst move I ever made." Tommy Lawton makes his Notts County debut at Northampton. (Ian Davies collection)

January 3rd 1948. Getting to know you. The superstar with a common touch, after joining Notts County. (Hulton Getty)

May 10th 1948. World champions Italy had three weeks at a mountain retreat. England trained at Highbury for a day prior to leaving for Turin. l-r: Swift, Aston, Ramsey, Howe, Wright, Franklin, Nicholson, Cockburn, Finney, Lawton, Langton, Mannion, Mortensen, Pearson, Matthews and Scott. (Hulton Getty)

March 1951. Parting of the ways. Tommy Bids farewell to Jackie Sewell, sold to Sheffield Wednesday for a record £35,000. They played together 126 times for Notts and between them scored 147 goals. (Tom Lawton collection)

1952/53. Tommy Lawton appeared 53 times for Brentford and scored 19 goals as his brilliant powers appeared to be on the wane. (Hulton Getty)

May 5th 1951. With dynamite in his boots – Tommy Lawton's free kick against Leicester City. 24,092 at Meadow Lane. The cameras in those days might not have matched today's technology but there is no mistaking the power of Lawton's shooting.
(Tom Lawton collection)

September 23rd 1952. Tommy married the love of his life, Gaye Rose, at Caxton Hall. Jackie Sewell was best man. (Associated Press)

1952. A Brentford goal shows that Tommy Lawton lost none of his power in the air.

September 19th 1953. "Just a young lad we've taken on." Still a star, Tommy trots out for his Arsenal debut, against Manchester City at Highbury. 65,869 were there to watch. (Press Association)

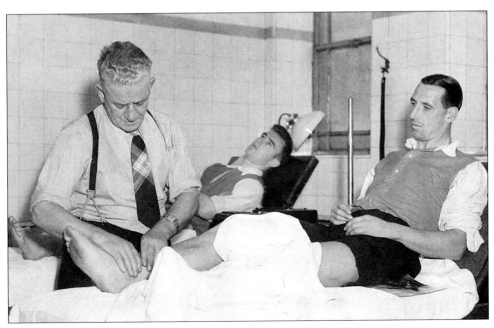

September 22nd 1953. Arsenal trainer Billy Milne attends to Tommy Lawton's ankle injured during his debut. In the background Bob Common awaits his turn. (Hulton Getty)

October 5th 1954. Midnight in Moscow. Tommy, still smoking BBC commentator Raymond Glendenning's cigarettes. (Tom Lawton collection)

October 6th 1954. Tommy's 35th birthday. A surprise celebration lunch and the present of a camera from Moscow Dynamo. (Tom Lawton collection)

*January 29th 1955. High hopes. Arsenal at Paddington en route to Wolverhampton for the
FA Cup fourth round tie. l-r: Tommy Lawton, Jack Kelsey, Cliff Holton, Jim Fotheringham,
Walley Barnes and Dennis Evans. (Press Association)*

February 5th 1955. The Lawton leap against Preston North End at Highbury.
(Tom Lawton collection)

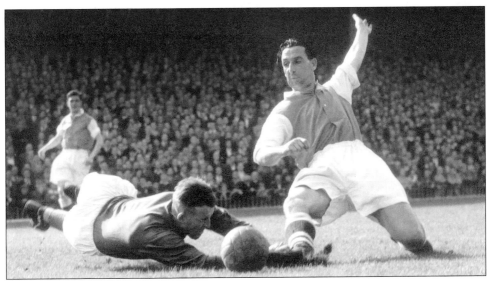

September 17th 1955. Nearing the end. Tommy Latwon's last match at Highbury, a 3-1
defeat by Portsmouth. Norman Uprichard, a former Arsenal trainee, kept Lawton out.
(Hulton Getty)

May 7th 1957. Many happy returns – but not for long. Tommy Lawton is welcomed back to Meadow Lane as manager by (l-r) F Sherwood (director), Len Machin (chairman), C H Heath (secretary), S Dickinson (chief scout) and Frank Broome (assistant manager). (Tom Lawton collection)

1956. Training at Kettering. Dixie's tricks passed on to another generation. (Tom Lawton collection)

January 26th 1963. The pools panel comes into operation. Tommy, along with other former internationals like Tom Finney, predicted the result during the big freeze under the chairmanship of Lord Brabazon of Tara. (Associated Press)

1966. Goodison greats. Three Everton leaders spanning the generations from 1924 to 1968. Between them Tommy Lawton, Alex Young and Dixie Dean made 797 appearances for the club and scored 534 goals. (Liverpool Daily Post and Echo)

June 14th 1972. Desperate days. Rock bottom after the bad cheque affair. Tommy Lawton sentenced to three years probation. (Press Association)

1980. A who's who of England's golden age, How much would they cost if they were in their prime today? l-r: Tom Finney, Raich Carter, Billy Wright, George Hardwick, Tommy Lawton, Joe Mercer, Len Shackleton and Nat Lofthouse. (Tom Lawton collection)

1981. No caps – just a certificate. Tommy Lawton and wife Gaye with the record of his war-time internationals. In 23 appearances for England he scored 25 goals.
(Tom Lawton collection)

1995. The doting Grandad. The birth of twins Anthony and Zöe to son Tom brightened Tommy Lawton's final days.
(Tom Lawton collection)

CHAPTER TWENTY
1947 – CHELSEA AGAINST THE WORLD AGAIN

With the New Year of 1947 came the most appallingly bitter winter. Conditions such that the season became the longest ever – eventually winding up in mid-June. Throughout the 'Big Freeze' in January and February of 1947, heavy snowfalls during games making visibility impossible and obliterating pitch markings were common. Sweat in the players' hair froze.

Tommy was already aware that Chelsea were not strong enough to mount a challenge for the championship, their best hope of an honour was in the FA Cup, but they appeared to use up all their luck in the third round. A massive 70,000 crowd was at Stamford Bridge for the tie with Arsenal. Ian McPherson put Arsenal ahead in the first half – a gift from the Chelsea defence. It was not until late in the game that Tommy Walker equalised to earn a replay at Highbury. Four days later, Arsenal were again in the lead – this time for 75 minutes, then Chelsea's John Harris lobbed a high ball towards the Arsenal area, Walley Barnes failed to control it and Walker was onto the loose ball instantly.

The Scottish international found Dicky Spence about 20 yards from goal. Lawton was striding over a gluepot surface, calling for the ball and Spence scooped it into his path. Lawton met it perfectly on the half-volley and it whistled past George Swindin. Barnes took responsibility for the goal, but pointed out that at the time, Tommy was at the height of his powers. "It was inevitable that, given even a half chance, Lawton would score. George Swindin played brilliantly that day, but he was given no chance." More than 59,000 turned up for the decider, at White Hart Lane on January 20th, so more than 180,000 spectators watched the three matches of the tie. The second replay followed the pattern of the first two games with Arsenal on top, but this time they failed to score. Astonishingly, in the first ten minutes, they hit the bar twice, the post three times and Reg Lewis slammed a penalty wide. Arsenal's hearts were in their boots when Lawton scored with a header. The goal being given even though a linesman was flagging for hand-ball. Diplomatically, Barnes labelled the goal "doubtful." For the first time in the tie, Chelsea were ahead. Moments later, Lawton scored again, left foot from ten yards, to put Chelsea into the next round.

Tommy was delighted that Chelsea had managed, eventually, to dispose of Arsenal. Any team captained by his former Everton team-mate Joe Mercer was liable to be formidable opposition. "Joe was a football maniac. A terrific tackler and a great passer of the ball over a short distance, or with the long ball. He was so bandy legged that I remember one goalkeeper he scored against saying 'He runs three different ways at once.'" Mercer was well aware of Lawton's ambition to win the FA Cup at Wembley. "With this lot, you must have a chance," he said to Tommy when they were in a cab to Euston after the game. Mercer was on his way back to Hoylake, where he lived, Tommy was heading home to Kenton in North London where he and Rosaleen had a trim semi-detached club house in John Betjeman's "autumn-scented Middlesex."

On January 25th, FA Cup holders Derby County were at Stamford Bridge in the fourth round on a bitterly cold day. Chelsea looked certain to go through until Raich Carter bundled in a goal in the last minute to make it 2-2. Once again, his England colleague had come between Tommy and his cup ambitions, Carter having been so influential at Goodison in 1938. "I don't remember Raich having a bad game. Great when you were playing with him, but he was always in brilliant form whenever he played against us! He was a lovely player and how many times did he play for England? Only about ten or 12 times (actually 13) it was a disgrace that a man of his talent was left out so often. Len Shack didn't get that many chances, either. If they were around today, they'd walk into the England side and just about everybody else's as well."

It was just as cold at the Baseball Ground four days later. The pitch was frozen hard. "Early on their keeper (Alick Grant) went off with a dislocated shoulder when he fell after taking a cross. Frank Broome went into goal and made one great save from me. I thought I'd scored but he was down and across just like Frank Swift!" Derby's big, burly centre-forward Jack Stamps scored the goal that spelled the end of Chelsea's hopes. Stamps was highly rated by Carter: "he wasn't just a battering ram of a centre-forward. He could play equally well at inside-forward."

The value of Stamps' powerful physique had become apparent in the final against Charlton the year before, when, in extra time, he shrugged off tired defenders and scored twice to ensure the FA Cup went to Derby for the first and only time.

On February 1st 1947, Chelsea travelled across London to play Charlton Athletic at the Valley, one of only three games played that day in the First Division because of the weather. In goal for Charlton that day, as he had been for the previous 12 years, was Sam Bartram, a red-head from Boldon in County Durham. A fine goalkeeper, agile and quick, always in command of his area, he made 800 appearances for his club and it has never been understood why he was not picked for England. Yet even he could be unsettled by Lawton. "Tommy's heading was so good he could make you look foolish," Bartram recalled shortly before his death in 1981 at the age of 67. "He had a fine understanding with Len Goulden at Chelsea. Against us in '47, Len was about to take a free-kick and Tommy pointed at the top left hand corner of my goal and said 'That's where it's going, Barty!' The ball came over, he was still climbing as his marker, Harry Phipps, was beginning to drop down, he arched his neck, forehead met ball, there was a thud and, top left, that's just where it went! He hit it so accurately that I couldn't stop it, even though I knew where he was aiming." Chelsea won the game 3-2, Lawton's goal being just one of the 26 he scored in 34 league games that season, then a club record.

Football salaries did not provide much of a reward for a star player. Terms had not improved by any great extent at Stamford Bridge where Chelsea paid Lawton £10 a week and in summer £8 a week. International matches brought in £10 a game plus 15s (75p) expenses. £1 bonuses were awarded for every point gained in the league and each win in the FA Cup. "At least I was doing what I wanted to do, and compared with a miner on three quid a week, we were pretty well off, though the rent on the club house was thirty bob (£1.50) a week! But in those days there was so much money coming into the game, though we didn't see much of it even though attendances of 50 or 60,000 were regular." Profits were enormous in those days. No club had a total wage bill of more than £350 a week and the most successful and popular teams pulled in about £5,000 a match from gate receipts.

On March 11th 1947, the National Arbitration Tribunal announced the findings of its investigation into players' wages. They agreed with the Players' Union under Jimmy Fay, when they insisted footballers were under paid and recommended a maximum of £12 a week during the season and £10 in the summer. "It was better than pre-war but still not brilliant. If you are at the top of your profession you should be paid accordingly. Even the benefit system didn't work properly. Cricketers' benefits weren't taxed because they weren't part of their contracts, but ours were. And they were awarded at the whim of the club. So you'd get players who played 600 games for their club and still got nothing over and above their wages. Ridiculous!"

Chelsea's moderate 1946/47 season drew to a close with them anchored in the bottom half of the table. Lawton was reasonably satisfied with his own contribution, 26 goals in 34 league matches, but problems were beginning to emerge at Stamford Bridge and, personally, he was becoming very unsettled again.

While Charlton and Burnley were contesting the FA Cup Final at Wembley, Chelsea were in the Midlands prior to playing Wolves at the Molineux. "We were in the Grand Hotel before the game, listening to the one o'clock news on the wireless. Somebody said that the Great Britain team for the match with FIFA was to be announced. This team had been debated in the papers for weeks. The thing was, that players from the four Home Nations had to be selected, so no one was certain of getting in." It would have been unthinkable however for a Great Britain side to take the field in 1947 without Lawton. He was, by some distance, the best centre-forward in the country and very possibly the world.

But then, Stanley Matthews was thought good enough for the British side, but not for England! Against France at Highbury on May 3rd, Tom Finney returned on the right wing and scored one of the goals in England's 3-0 win.

The British side prepared at the Forest Hills Hotel on Loch Ard. The pupils at the local school in Aberfoyle were in for a treat as the team practised on their small, bumpy pitch. The match was to celebrate the return to the FIFA fold of the home nations after an 18-year absence. Of the England team that had played against the Rest of Europe in 1938, only two were selected for this game at Hampden, Stan Matthews and Tommy Lawton.

Great Britain: Swift (Man City & England); Hardwick (Middlesbrough & England), Hughes (Birmingham & Wales); Macaulay (Brentford & Scotland), Vernon (West Brom & Ireland), Burgess (Tottenham & Wales); Matthews (Stoke & England), Mannion (Middlesbrough & England), Lawton (Chelsea & England), Steel (Morton & Scotland), Liddell (Liverpool & Scotland).

Rest of Europe: Da Rui (France); Petersen (Denmark), Steffen (Switzerland); Carey (Eire, captain), Parola (Italy), Ludl (Czechoslovakia); Lemberechts (Belgium), Gren (Sweden), Nordahl (Sweden), Wilkes (Holland), Praest (Denmark)

The British reserves, were Raich Carter and the Scotland centre-half George Young.

Britain forced four corners in the first five minutes as Matthews ably demonstrated his skills to Steffen. Willie Allison in the *Sunday Mail* suggested that: "Steffen might have stayed in Switzerland for all he accomplished in checking him." Lawton began the move that put Britain ahead, combining with Steel to set up Mannion who beat Da Rui, though Europe levelled, after a mistake by Hardwick. Mannion slotted in a penalty, Steel rifled in a 25 yard shot and Lawton scored (from about a foot out) to make it 4-1 before half-time. This was the game which made Billy Steel. Previously he had appeared just nine times for Greenock Morton and once for Scotland, against England at Wembley in April. His performance in this match, when 'Billy 'Steels' The Thunder On A Day Of Days' according to the *Sunday Mail*, induced several English First Division clubs to bid for him. If they were not convinced of his worth themselves, they only had to read 'Rex' in the *Sunday Mail* who waxed lyrical on Steel's sensational goal. "Three yards outside the area he instepped a wonder-ball that roared over everyone's head, seemed to take an interminable time to gumboil the back of the net, but fell down limply behind a goalkeeper who hadn't even started to move. Da Rui expected the pass, as all of us and the players did. Steel had dummied every blinking one of us – and sky rocketed his personal selling price to astronomical heights!" Rex estimated that Steel was now worth £20,000. In the end he moved to Derby County, who had been searching for a replacement for Peter Doherty, for a record £15,500. "Billy was a bit of a lad, but he had it all. He could be a bit fiery, well, he was Scottish, but he was as crafty as Raich (Carter) and as cheeky as Wilf (Mannion). He was only small, size five boots, but he could tackle and shoot. He learned a lot from his time at Derby with Raich, but he wasn't all that popular there in the end. Lee Leuty said 'Oh, Billy, he only plays when we're in London.' He liked to see his name in the papers did Billy!"

After the break, faced with an open goal, Lawton uncharacteristically missed badly from eight yards, then saw a header brilliantly saved by Da Rui. A Parola own goal eventually made it five, before Matthews laid on the sixth for Lawton, a header that Allison reported: "No goalkeeper could have stopped." Rex, remembering Matthews-Lawton combinations at Hampden in the past, called it a goal that "wrote on the historic scroll of this historic match. Never have so many owed so much to these two!" It was not Lawton's finest match. He scored two, missed at least two more, but was a constant threat. W G Gallagher in the *Daily Record* thought that "if Tom Lawton had been the centre-forward we have seen on previous Hampden visits, the Rest would have lost as many goals again." Lawton's marker, centre-half Carlo Parola, thought that "Faced by the greatest centre-forward of the day, the brilliant Lawton, I felt I had won my sporting battle as completely as could be." That was not a verdict shared by Lawton. "I played well enough that day and he scored an own goal if I remember right!' Parola went further, suggesting that Lawton was "annoyed that I was frequently beating him in the air." He was convinced he did his job that afternoon, "containing the dashing Lawton" while blaming the "nervous' Da Rui and his "depressed teammates, devoid of energy" for the defeat. Lawton's goal, claimed Parola, was not his fault "because at that moment I was involved in dealing with another opponent." Indeed.

A week after the Hampden game, the England players met up again at Northolt Aerodrome in north-west London to fly to Europe again. Switzerland was the first destination. The team was disturbed to find that their first evening's entertainment in Zurich was at the ballet. George Hardwick described the players in the theatre as having an attention span of about ten minutes. Walter Winterbottom could see there might be a problem and instructed the team to see it out until the interval.

Lawton and Swift were the first to make the exit, heading upstairs to a large cafe. "Stan Mortensen played 'Chopsticks' on the piano, an encore was demanded and he played it again. In fact, that was all he could play! By the end of the evening, we were dancing the 'Hokey Cokey' and enjoying ourselves immensely." The game was not so enjoyable, Switzerland again beat England, 1-0, the Swiss using the small pitch to their advantage and, again deploying the withdrawn centre-forward, confused England tactically. "We should have had a draw. I put the ball in the net and Bobby Langton, well on-side at the time I shot, followed it up.

He was going to get the ball back to the middle so the Swiss couldn't waste any time. Blow me! The ref whistled him up for offside."

The shops in Zurich's Banhoffstrasse were stacked with goods of every description, everything that had been unavailable in the UK during the war, watches, food, jewellery. Lawton was determined to buy his wife a present, in this instance a particularly flimsy item of underwear. "I didn't even know the name for it and even if I did, I was too shy to ask for it, so Frank Swift volunteered to help out. I should have known better." Swift was renowned as a mime artist and with Laurie Scott and Raich Carter an appreciative audience, began to go through his routine in the lingerie department of a Zurich store. "Frank was good at miming a man eating a bag of hot fish and chips, or a girl taking a bath. So when I asked 'Have you, er, you know, er , Miss, have you got...'" Frank started the bath mime and everyone started giggling. When the assistants brought out boxes of stuff, Frank would hold these garments up. It was at the same time, the funniest and most embarrassing afternoon."

From Zurich it was onto Lisbon for an international against Portugal. For the first time, Winterbottom decided to play both Matthews and Finney in the same team, with remarkable results. The 10-0 win was accomplished with four goals each from Lawton and Mortensen and despite the Portuguese switching to the smaller sized continental ball after the first goal went in and substituting their goalkeeper when their original choice retired with pride badly dented.

Chelsea had planned a club tour to Sweden in the summer of 1947. Lawton was reluctant to join them. "I had gone about 18 months without a break. I'd just come back from playing for England in Portugal and I wasn't well, I'd picked up a touch of food poisoning. We'd moved house to Kenton, but domestically things were still in trouble. Leaving the wife in London while I went off to play a few friendlies in Sweden would not have been a good idea." Tommy told Billy Birrell that he did not feel fit enough to go; the manager brought in the club doctor who ruled that there was nothing physically amiss. Tommy tried explaining that he felt jaded, that the rest would do him good, set him up for the following season. Birrell insisted that he travelled with the rest of the team. Tommy refused and consulted his own doctor who brought in a specialist to rule that he needed to rest for some weeks. Birrell, a stern disciplinarian, who even in team photographs appeared wearing a black bowler hat, told Lawton "We'll make you go, have no fear about that." Precisely the wrong tactics to use against Lawton who had despised "the discipline and the bull" in the Army only recently.

Chelsea's chairman Joe Mears and a director Jack Budd visited Tommy at home and tried to bully him into agreeing to go on tour. "I'd be reported to the FA, my wages would be stopped, I'd be blacklisted by other clubs, all kinds of things. What they didn't tell me was that they had signed a contract and one of the terms was that I had to play a certain number of games in

Sweden or Chelsea would be paid a lower fee. I never knew that until later. As it was, their attitude just put my back up and things were never the same again." Lawton was, by the standards of the day, outspoken about his treatment by Chelsea. He was writing his own newspaper column in the *Star* and many of his articles centred on the way players were underpaid, mere chattels of the clubs. Of his own case he thought: "A lot of the publicity was wide of the mark. There were a lot of 'know alls' around who thought they knew what was going on and just spread rumours. There was supposed to be animosity between me and the other players. There wasn't, it was between me and the board and the manager."

Tommy never retained the affection for Chelsea that he had for his other clubs, even though he admitted later in life that he realised the impasse at Stamford Bridge was not all of the board's making. "I brought trouble on myself. I felt I was too big to take unreasonable orders." Lawton was feted wherever he went in London. At the peak of his powers, an England international when the England team was rated the best in the world and, as centre-forward and goal scorer, a headline-maker and star. The turmoil surrounding his problems at Chelsea was the only public sign that his life was not in order. At home, the relationship with his wife was becoming more and more strained. Everybody wanted to know Tommy Lawton except Rosaleen Lawton who preferred the company of other men. Tommy thought he had no choice but to ask Chelsea for a transfer. It seemed the only way of solving the difficulties that had developed once the barriers had gone up at Chelsea and of easing his problematic marital state. Another club house, another move, another start.

Chelsea refused to grant his request. He was told to "buckle down, get on with the job." Joe Mears doubted that any club would want to sign him following all the publicity. Tommy tested the water himself. "Arsenal were a club that had always appealed to me, ever since those days back in the office at Turf Moor when George Allison phoned up." By chance, Lawton had met the Arsenal manager Tom Whittaker at a function and Whittaker had declared his interest in signing him. Lawton spoke to Birrell, only to be told that Arsenal had not made an enquiry for him. "I exploded. 'You're a liar,' I said. 'I know they have because Tom Whittaker told me.' I recounted the story of my, entirely legal, meeting. Birrell just said: 'Listen, there's one club you're not going to and that's Arsenal.' Even so, I was still hoping that I could move to Highbury until Joe Mercer told me that Arsenal just did not have the cash to spend on expensive transfers and even if they had, they would go for Wilf Mannion who wanted to leave Middlesbrough."

Lawton was distraught. It was the move that he most wanted. After missing the first two games of the 1947/48 season through injury, Lawton was back for the match with Derby at Stamford Bridge at the end of August. The attendance, 59,919, was some 23,000 more than for the midweek game against Blackburn. In the first half Lawton scored the only goal, a typical header, outjumping Leuty to beat goalkeeper Townsend.

By mid-September, Chelsea were still looking for their first away point of the season when they travelled to Sunderland for a midweek fixture. Lawton's goal made certain of a 3-2 win. Outside the ground, he was signing autographs before boarding the coach for the long journey back south when Bill Murray, the former Sunderland full-back who had been taken over as manager in 1939, asked him into his office. "What he said was one of the finest and most touching compliments I have ever received. He said that any player who was in dispute with his club, yet played as I had against Sunderland, was the type of player that he wanted." He put forward a good proposition. Sunderland were prepared to make sure that he was set up in business when he retired from the game. Just turned 28, Lawton was hardly considering retirement, but Sunderland's offer sowed seeds. He began to think about life after football although he turned down Murray explaining that he did not want to move so far north. The excuse being that he had lived in the south since joining up and he thought of it as home. He had always said that the reason for the move to London from Liverpool was to benefit Rosaleen's health. Two years later, he was hardly in a position to claim that it would be improved by a move back north. However, the discussion with Murray had convinced Lawton that he was wanted by other top clubs and he repeated his request for a transfer.

Lawton played his last first team game for Chelsea at Anfield on October 11th 1947. It was not a very happy return to Merseyside as Liverpool won 3-0, Priday, Stubbins and Liddell scoring the goals. When he walked into Stamford Bridge on the following Monday, Lawton learned that his renewed transfer request had been granted.

"The first manager to call me at home was Billy Murray from Sunderland. Would I change my mind, would I go to Roker Park? He telephoned me on several occasions, but I just kept saying 'No, I don't want to go that far north.'" Lawton, in charge of his own career was starting to make mistakes, his mind distorted by outside pressures. "Oh! I would have liked to have played in the north-east," he said long after his playing days "The people up there love their football without any question. All the great players they produced – Carter, Mannion, Shackleton, Milburn, Scoular, Mitchell and going back donkey's years, Camsell. I used to love playing there. If you did something good, the crowd applauded, they knew their football."

Chelsea dropped Lawton into the reserves, announcing that they did not want to use a player in the first team who had requested a move. The official line was that a player on the transfer list would not be trying his best. Lawton disputed that. "If I didn't do well and try my damndest, no club would want to buy me. That, surely, is common sense from the business point of view? There's no such thing as 'playing for a transfer.'" On October 31st 1947, the FA picked Lawton to play against Northern Ireland at Goodison Park on November 5th – it was to be the first time that the 'Lisbon Lions,' the forward line that had destroyed Portugal in May, was to appear in England. Each individual was now a major draw – Matthews, Mortensen, Lawton, Mannion, Finney.

Meanwhile at Arsenal, Tom Whittaker heard that Lawton had been dropped from Chelsea's first team and was in the reserve side to play Arsenal at Highbury the following day. "I increased the order for programmes to 20,000!' The respective first teams were engaged at Stamford Bridge and the Chelsea board were delighted with a near 'full house' – 67,277 – for a goalless draw. Over a gin and tonic or two they suggested that, of course, it was not really necessary to have a Lawton to draw the crowds. Then the news filtered back from Highbury – the attendance was 22,274 and Whittaker's opinion was ratified as almost all the programmes were sold. Suddenly, Lawton's fee was increased. The asking price became a new British record – £20,000.

At Goodison four days later, Lawton scored with a volley from 15 yards, the centre from Matthews, in the 2-2 draw against Northern Ireland. "I was desperate to play well on my old home ground. I was on show, but we went one down and couldn't score 'til about five minutes from the end. Wilf Mannion equalised, then I got what we thought was the winner. Stan Matthews made it, going one way then the other. The cross was perfect, I couldn't miss." In fact, Lawton's 11th successive international since the war saw England pegged back in the final minute when a brilliant diving header by Peter Doherty from a left wing Tommy Eglington centre made it 2-2. A week later, Bill Birrell called him into the office at Stamford Bridge and handed him a list of clubs. Lawton looked at them, somewhat bemused, until Birrell said "Cross out the ones you don't fancy."

According to Tommy, "Many of the First Division sides were on the list, but, unfortunately, Arsenal wasn't one of them. That was the one club that Chelsea wouldn't allow me to join." Among the big names on Birrell's list was one surprise – Notts County of Division Three (South). Their manager, A W Stollery was anxious to talk terms. Tommy knew him well. "Arthur Stollery had been masseur at Chelsea and was a very good friend. One morning, I was on the table having a massage, he came and said 'I've got the sack!' Well, I wasn't getting on too well with Chelsea myself and I thought it was an unjust sacking, he was good at his job, he was a fine masseur and a wonderful organiser of the medical side of things. He knew his stuff, he was skilled at his job." The pair of them went for a quiet drink at a country pub Tommy occasionally frequented, 'The Case Is Altered' in Eastcote, a few miles up the road from Kenton. There, Stollery told Lawton that he was thinking about asking the FA for a management job. Tommy had made a promise – "firmly and sincerely, I said that if ever I have the opportunity and your club has the wherewithal, then I'll sign for you. He said, 'Is that a promise?' I said 'Of course it is." Stollery had persuaded the Notts' directors to make the cash available for Lawton, the actual offer being £17,500 plus the Northern Ireland wing-half Bill Dickson valued at £2,500. Tommy had no share of the fee, only receiving £10 for signing on and his £300 accrued share of benefit. He had, however, learned from his talk with Billy Murray at Roker Park and asked Notts to fix him up in business, which they did, with a Nottingham typewriter company. There was one more matter concerning Lawton. "I was always very jealous of my England number nine shirt so I went to Lancaster Gate, number 22 then, 16 now, to see Stanley Rous of the FA. I said 'Sir, I'm a little concerned. Several First Division clubs want to sign me but the one I want to go to can't afford me, so I've opted for a Third Division club. How will this affect my international status?' And he said 'Tom, if you're playing in the Football League you can be selected, it doesn't matter what division.' I said 'Thank you, sir, that's all I wanted to know' and walked down Bayswater Road with my mind made up.

"People were always whispering that I'd gone to Notts because I got something out of it, a big signing on fee, a share of the gate or whatever. They said there was one turnstile at Meadow Lane which was 'The Tommy Lawton gate' that I got all the money from. That was all rubbish. I went to Notts County to fulfil a promise, simple as that." On November 13th 1947 at the Great Western Hotel in Paddington the England centre-forward, Tommy Lawton, signed for Notts County of Division Three (South).

The fee was confirmed as a new British record – an incredible £20,000. If Lawton had moved to another First Division club it would have been sensational, but to drop to the Third Division was quite unbelievable. Alan Shearer deciding to join Bristol Rovers is, perhaps, the nearest current equivalent. It is though, still, a highly unlikely equation. That he cost 25% more than the record fee Derby County had forked out for Billy Steel from Morton only a few months earlier demonstrates the enormity of the fee, but then consider how on earth a club from the Third Division (South) found the cash and the nerve to mount such a bid. On November 19th 1947, he became the first Third Division player to appear for England. The game was against Sweden at Highbury. Tommy sat in the dressing room under the peg labelled '9,' his feet being warmed by the underfloor heating. "I was thinking, it should be Lawton of Arsenal and England. It was a great honour to be the first Third Division player to play for England, yet I didn't think of myself as a Third Division player. I felt at home with these lads – 'Big Swifty,' George Hardwick, Billy Wright. Stan Matthews wasn't playing, he was injured but we still played well, we were 3-1 up at half-time, then they came back into it." Lawton was in top form, setting up Stan Mortensen after 20 minutes. The Blackpool inside-forward was brought down and Lawton scored the penalty. Before the break, another astute Lawton pass found Mortensen and he beat the goalkeeper with a powerful shot. In the second half, Sweden scored from a penalty, but a piece of brilliance from Mortensen in the closing minutes made it 4-2, a left foot shot finishing off a superb 40 yard run.

The transfer was the talk of the football world. Ken Shearwood, the Pegasus centre-half in two Amateur Cup Finals, was fascinated by the

Lawton technique. Unfortunately, he never played against him though a confrontation between the two, Shearwood the big raw-boned amateur who played like a professional and the athletic, supremely fair Lawton would have been quite a sight.

After playing for Oxford University against a strong FA XI on November 18th 1947, Shearwood asked his opposite number, Leon Leuty, then with Derby County, how he coped with Lawton in the air.

"Tommy," said Leuty drily. "Well, you go up with him, but you don't win it often." Leuty, who played for the Football League and for England 'B,' later crossed swords with Tommy at Notts County and took over the captaincy from him in 1951. Leuty died tragically early at the age of 35. He played two games of the 1955 season before suffering with what was described as a shoulder injury. He never played again. By Christmas he was dead from leukaemia.

CHAPTER TWENTY-ONE
1948 –TOMMY AND ENGLAND GREATS

"What did I score? 22 goals in 23 matches, something like that, not a bad average but a pity that they don't include the war-time internationals in the official figures – it'd be much better. Nevertheless, I played in some great sides. All you have to do is look at them; before the war with people like Willie Hall, Len Goulden, Stan Cullis and Sir Stan. I'll tell you, the man from Stoke was the greatest two-legged player there's ever been. Matthews may have frustrated at times with his persistent dribbling..." but Tommy was insistent. "Stan Matthews is the greatest player the world has ever seen. Forget about Pele and Di Stefano, he was better than them all. What would he have been worth these days? It makes me shudder when I see ordinary players being transferred for five and six million and I start thinking about the players I played with – Raich Carter, Len Shackleton, Joe Mercer, Jimmy Hagan – I bet they didn't have 30 caps between them but what would they be worth now? I mean Len Shack; it was my last cap and his first against Denmark in Copenhagen, my swansong. It finished 0-0 on a muddy pitch, I missed four, Shack missed four. I think the next time we played together was in 1954, for 'Old' England."

This was a match against 'Young' England at Highbury on the night before the Cup Final. The 'Old England' forward line was the one that played in Copenhagen in 1948, apart from Wilf Mannion at inside-right for Jimmy Hagan. "I don't think I'm boasting when I say we pulverised the young lads," was Tommy's considered verdict. "And we could have won much more easily than the score of 2-1 suggests. Matthews was magical, Mannion and Shack produced every trick in the book." The winning goal came from a Matthews centre which Lawton headed into the bottom corner of the net.

The following season Old England really rubbed it in, winning 5-0 at Highbury. Lawton scored twice, revelling in the gala atmosphere, as Frank Swift came out of retirement to play a half in goal and Harry Johnston, Tom's old friend, came down from Blackpool to play along with Stan Matthews and Stan Mortensen. "My job for England was easy, anyone could have done it. I was surrounded by so many great players – Matthews and Finney – you can't make them big enough compared with the players of today. I mean, you could guarantee that Matthews playing away for Stoke or Blackpool would add an extra ten thousand to the gate and this was in the days when gates were pretty good anyway! But the characters of those days – Doherty at Manchester City, Mannion, Shackleton, Carter, Finney – all used to add to the gates. Even me! I used to drag in a few of my pals!"

For a man so proud of playing for England, Lawton's decision to move to the Third Division so prematurely and jeopardise his international career was a strange one. His England career over, the memories remained. "I was lucky, the service was so good. There must have been about 20 inside forwards or wing halves just queuing up to be capped and most of them never made it. The difference between then and now is that anybody who had some brains and talent could see that being a footballer made a difference – the difference between thirty bob a week (£1.50) for a miner or eight quid (£8) to play football. We weren't rolling in it, but we were better off than most. In fact it was the life of Riley for doing the thing we most wanted to do!'"

CHAPTER TWENTY-TWO
1947 – NOTTS COUNTY THE MAGPIES' GOLDEN AGE

From the King's Road, London to the King's Meadow Road, Nottingham. The disparity in locations was as pronounced as the two clubs involved in Lawton's extraordinary transfer that was as sensational as it was surprising. The capital thoroughfare brushed by Chelsea's Stamford Bridge ground before leading to the bright lights of the fashionable West End. Tanks and military hardware rumbled across the cobble-stones of the East Midlands street, causing seismic disruptions in the adjacent terraced accommodation as they made their way to and from the Royal Ordnance Gun Factory, formerly owned by Cammell Lairds. That it was situated in The Meadows district of the city was appropriate for its population was the source of much of Notts County's support that would wend its way through the narrow lanes and past the high density housing which characterised the working class region.

Lawton had turned his back on the aristos of Chelsea for the carrot crunchers at Meadow Lane. Yet for him, the issue was never in doubt. He felt he owed a friend, although history tended to testify to the contrary where Lawton was concerned, a favour. In this case it was Arthur Stollery, part of the backroom team at Stamford Bridge. "At Chelsea he was the masseur and a close confidant," Lawton recalled. "We talked endlessly not only about football but about personal matters. One day he woke up and found he had been sacked. Imagine that, and for no particularly good reason as he could fathom out. But that was football in those days."

Before Lawton took his leave of London, he travelled to Nottingham to meet Harold Whalmsley, the County vice-chairman, and to peruse what would be his new territory. After the train journey in the opulent first class compartments on the former Great Central line to the grand Victoria Station, a legacy of the old Queen's reign built in her honour at the turn of the century, a taxi whisked Lawton across the city centre and down Arkwright Street, the main arterial route of The Meadows.

As he sat and contemplated the view, the commercial epicentre of the neighbourhood with its shops, public houses and characters, the image of his own roots in the back-to-back housing of Bolton most likely sped through his innermost thoughts. In a sense he was home, among people who ultimately welcomed him as if their own prodigal son had returned.

The people's champion he may have been, but by then he was no longer one of the people as such. Wealth, not on the scale (or more aptly totally off it), of the millennium remuneration that modern professionals can expect, but nevertheless a relative prosperity had visited Lawton during his illustrious career.

His home would be among the more genteel society in Mapperley Park, a des res in one of Nottingham's most prosperous communities whose inhabitants comprised the professional and business classes. Outside lavatories and an absence of running hot water on tap, everyday trappings for the hoi polloi, were no longer inflicted upon him. He would invite colleagues, acquaintances and good friends back there – partly to impress maybe but also, for the likes of young Jackie Sewell, his naive and as yet aimless young partner elect in the County forward line, perhaps to inspire." I tried to tell him, not directly but in a subtle way, that such as all this could be yours." £20,000 was a substantial amount to invest for the oldest league club in the world whose stadium certainly did not let the side down in terms of its antiquity. Nevertheless it was prudent business as the 28-year-old England international confirmed his celebrity status, literally overnight, in the mean, deprived streets of The Meadows and Nottingham in general.

Historically the timing couldn't have been better for the County board. The spartan demands of rationing still drained the population in post-war Britain. Despite the unassailable fact that they had won the Second World War, sacrificing loved ones, home and most of their cherished possessions in the process, there was no significant indication that the unrelenting austerity would ever end.

The severe frost and snow during the winter of 1947 was bad enough. That it was followed by the hasty thaw in February that swelled the waters of the River Trent, enticing them to burst its banks, merely rubbed salt into their wounded pride. During March of 1947, Meadows folk were marooned like drowned rats in their sodden homes, furniture, carpets and parlour pianos all but destroyed by the stench and filth of the sanitation that forced its way into the their front rooms and kitchens as it fled the all-consuming Trent. Small wonder they embraced the impeccably tailored and legendary Lawton in November with such zeal, a flamboyant lifeboat amidst a sea of mediocrity and deprivation in a country still ravaged by conflict.

Tommy's fame was probably at its height at the time of the transfer. In the late '40s, though, the trappings of fame were considerably less than those available to the top players of today, with their pop star lifestyles. Lawton was aware of his responsibilities and behaved and dressed accordingly. His shoes were always immaculately polished, his hair slicked back, with a ruler-straight centre parting. He never went out without having shaved first. When he was in public, he wore his club blazer or a suit, usually pin-striped and double-breasted. If he needed an overcoat, it would be long and belted, big over the shoulders, which, together with the loud ties he preferred, gave him the look of '30s Chicago mobster. Knowing Tommy's liking for the cinema, it was probably a look he deliberately cultivated.

"None of us in the dressing room believed he would be coming," Sewell recalled of an expectant County squad. "Clearly there was some tie with him and Stollery but when he did arrive, by crikey what a presence! The man was immaculate in his dress sense, Crombie coats and so forth. He looked like a movie star, he just had natural charisma."

Sewell had joined Notts, aged 17, just after the war under the regime of Major Buckley. He had worked down the pit in Whitehaven before that and his first trip from the village of Kells, on the Cumberland coastline, was to have trials in Nottingham, a football career that was diametrically opposed to that of Lawton's cosmopolitan soccer sojourn.

"I just looked at this bloke and thought he is strong enough to get me kicked out of the team if he wants to. He had that sort of reputation. But then I was a bit younger then, living in digs in Bulwell and fairly carefree. Looking back, though, I was no different from the rest of us – totally in awe of the man."

Like Sewell, Nottingham had never experienced the like of Lawton. Even three decades later, during the heady days of Brian Clough in residence across the banks of the Trent at the City Ground, the old lace city could not muster the same enthusiasm and instant rapport that Lawton engendered. To reflect that his impact was indeed immense may well be understating the case. Ten buses fully laden with Magpies' fans set off early on the morning of Saturday, November 15 for the County Ground, home of Northampton Town, where Lawton would make his debut later in the afternoon.

Expectations of entry onto the terraces were not high. 330 people were travelling but the County allocation was just 125. The ground was packed to capacity, only the second occasion it had witnessed a 21,000 crowd, with thousands still queueing outside at the turnstiles as kick-off approached. When the gates opened at 1 pm the scene had been the same but the patience of later arrivals would ultimately be in vain. Inside the visitors' dressing room, Lawton was preparing himself and his team mates. Each captive audience was equally entranced by the Lawton's aura.

Having said his farewells to Chelsea after the training session 24 hours earlier, it was the first opportunity for the less vaunted members of the County side to meet their new skipper.

"He was a perfect physical specimen," Sewell recalls of that first encounter in the raw, so to speak. "He stood over six-foot tall in the dressing room, not an inch of fat, like a man mountain he was. He made me smile really, sitting next to me wearing his boots and socks and jock strap, nothing else. Just limbering up. 'Think on now' he said. 'Don't panic if you are under pressure. Play as you have always played and you know where I will be, knocking around. Just look up and you will see me and clear the ball.' Tommy was just so casual about it because he knew what he could do and what he was capable of." By 4.40 pm that day, Notts, who were third from bottom of the Division Three (South), had secured their first away win of the season. Lawton, of course, scored one in a 2-1 triumph, the goal coming early as many still queued to gain entry.

Although Bob Dennison, the Northampton centre-half, earned praise for his performance against the England man, the former Newcastle United, Fulham and Nottingham Forest stopper confessed later: "I just couldn't believe it, I just couldn't believe that anyone could jump that high; not and head it in too!" *The Guardian Journal*, Nottingham's morning paper to the *Evening News* then, enthused about Lawton's debut. "There were many who expected wonders from Tommy Lawton... There were two wonders – a goal after four minutes which only Lawton could have scored and a team inspired by his presence. There was always that masterly Lawton touch which international inside forwards know so well, his precise ball control and his skill in bringing the wing men fully into the game."

One person remained unmoved by the waves Lawton was making in the football world. Rosaleen Lawton stayed at home in Kenton. She seldom watched her husband play and admitted "I'm not at all worried about Tom. I shall just do my shopping as usual."

The following week, his home appearance against Bristol Rovers would add a further 10,000 to the Meadow Lane audience. The thoroughfare of Arkwright Street on Saturday afternoon had seen nothing like it before as Bristol fans making their way from the Midland Station and home supporters combined to make a human tide heading to the game which was watched by 31,450. Extra turnstiles had been ordered by Wilf Fisher, the club secretary, with seating tickets at 3s 6d (18p) available and a limited amount of Main Stand tickets going for 4s 6d (23p).

The era before multi-media coverage and saturation and, more often than not, sycophantic reporting required devotees to attend matches to see the likes of Matthews, Finney, Lofthouse et al. It also required a deal of effort, most working men performing the Saturday morning shift before clocking off for the game. Travelling away meant time off and since Britain's transport system left something to be desired in the '40s and '50s, the journeys for weekend and night games were frequently long and torturous. Yet still they turned out in their thousands. Lawton's attraction, though, ran a little beyond the one-dimensional confines of football. His athletic prowess and sporting talents, described as a player with "dynamite in his boots as well as his head" by a contemporary observer with a more fertile imagination than most, were obvious.

His panache on the pitch was equalled off it. To the outside world, he had a celebrity marriage and all the trappings of wealth that came with it. In short he was a man totally in possession of his own destiny.

If that was a false impression, his reputed brushes with authority in the football corridors of power, were not. His dislike of the accepted order of things and his willingness to speak out when others preferred to be silent, caught the mood of post-war England. Lawton's was a cult status, revered by the working classes but denigrated by the game's ruling bodies which treated his words and deeds with a mixture of circumspection and dread.

That uneasy alliance was no different at Meadow Lane. Although he received only a £10 signing-on fee and £300 from Chelsea for five years' accrued benefit service, his annual income was far in excess of the £12 per week (£10 in summer) that County were obliged to pay him (not forgetting £2 win, £1 draw as incentives).

Apart from his fashion sense, Lawton owned a grey Sunbeam Talbot sports car and wrote regular features and articles for national newspapers as well as making a variety of media-related or public appearances, helping launch or promote business and commercial interests. He was also in receipt of royalties from his book. Such a high profile lifestyle earned Lawton something in the region of £3000 per annum and made him the first surtax-paying professional footballer. He also had the option of employment for a four-figure sum over a period of five years, yet the stability and security he craved and which had been promised by the County board never materialised. "Nottingham became a boom city when I joined, the average gate leapt from 7,500 to 37,500 but while I earned a lot of money for Nottingham as a city, I got nothing more than was I was due," Lawton would recall with just a hint of rancour.

"Actually I didn't even get that, because Stirling Seimig, the typewriter firm owned by one of the directors at which I was promised a job for life, went bust. You could see the directors counting the money in their heads as the gates went up. They were all paying customers. Imagine another 25,000 on the gate, all that extra revenue but not a penny of it went to the players, some of whom were on £10 and £8 winter and summer wages. It wasn't until I suggested to Charlie Barnes, the chairman, that this was a bad policy and would only undermine the team spirit that things changed and all the squad was put on £12 and £10." In fact, the seeds of discontent had been sown at Meadow Lane even before Lawton arrived and on the day of his debut, his detractors at boardroom level would not have been encouraged by developments. "I had heard that all the board were unanimous about my coming to Nottingham but I wasn't so sure. Then when I turned up for the first game away to Northampton I couldn't believe what I was seeing. There were more directors' wives and friends waiting to get on the team coach than there were players. I told the chairman that I wanted them on another coach. If it didn't happen I wasn't going to Northampton."

Lawton, self-assured, handsome and perhaps even arrogant to the dowdy members of the County board, prevailed. As he put it: "Some semblance of discipline was introduced into the club and a male-populated coach left for Northampton." Doubtless the hackles rising and the wellcoiffured feathers ruffling could be visibly seen as the separate omnibuses departed Meadow Lane that day.

Whatever the opinion of the hierarchy or their perceived grievances, there were no such reservations on the terraces. Lawton, who had actually turned out as a guest for Notts in a couple of games nearing the end of the war, did not disappoint either. He scored a couple against Bristol on his home debut on November 22. Sewell, an inside-forward with impressive fleetness of foot and speed of thought that defeated the less mobile centre-halves of the day but whose form had been erratic to say the least that season, was also twice on target to complete a 4-2 scoreline. A formidable partnership had been forged, one which Sewell acknowledges was the catalyst in a career that would see him become the most expensive footballer in Britain when County sold him to Sheffield Wednesday for £34,500 in 1951.

"The point was that he took time to help others and was also an inspiration on the pitch," Sewell said. "His touch was fantastic and when he got up and smacked a header wide to Eric Houghton, the left-winger, it went like a blooming rocket to the touchline. He had this knack of going one way then the other and no one could catch him once he had gone. Then he would float in behind his markers and if you caught him right with a cross, there was nothing on earth to compare. As a target you could always find him, no trouble. But for all his ability and how much better he was that the rest of us, he was never a rollicker. Sometimes he would take training and teach us how to head the ball properly. He'd use a barbell and have us standing around in a circle, representing numbers of the clock, and shout out the time and when it was your turn to head it. You watch the likes of Andy Cole or Alan Shearer and their ability to head a ball comes nowhere near the sort of power and direction Tommy used to get. They seem, in comparison, off-balance. It's as if the finesse of heading has gone out of the game."

From being a team devoid of motivation and seemingly utterly dispirited, County rediscovered a sense of pride and purpose. It was an instant remedy in many respects although promotion would not be achieved until the season of 1949/50, a runaway success that brought the Division Three (South) championship pennant to Meadow Lane.

Frank Broome, Harry Adamson, Bill Baxter, Tommy Deans, Tommy Johnston, Billy Evans and Aubrey Southall provided the nucleus of the title-winning side, the sort of professional stalwarts that are essential to achievement in team games.

However, it was without doubt the cutting edge and star quality imbued upon County by Lawton and the rapidly maturing Sewell that elicited record attendances at such notable venues as Newport, Bournemouth and Torquay. At the close of their first full season in collaboration, Sewell had scored 26 goals to Lawton's 20 – and this, as Sewell explains, despite the best efforts of the England centre-forward to maintain the status quo. "We were playing, actually we were hammering, Newport County. A cross came over from Frankie Broome and I thought this is goal number five for me. Suddenly, the next thing I knew I was being sent flying and then I looked up to see the ball in the corner of the net. Tommy, who had barged me out of the way, then picked me up. 'What the hell is going on then Tom,' I asked him to which he replied that he wasn't going to let me get another and beat him on the day." The final score was 11-1 to the Magpies. Lawton, 4, Sewell 4 and honours even all round! Seduced by his charisma off the pitch, Nottingham was courted on it not only by Lawton's awesome prowess but also the guile of the tall striker. His immaculate control and astute awareness of others on the pitch placed the graceful leader of the line in the same position granted to him by his prodigious leaping powers, that was head and shoulders above his contemporaries, even more so at this lower level of competition.

An appreciative football public acclaimed Lawton on his travels while back in the Midlands, he had given County the edge in terms of potential and crowds over their fierce local rivals Nottingham Forest.

That the balance of power had shifted north of the River Trent to Notts was underlined during the promotion season when County completed a memorable double with a 2-0 victory before 46,000 supporters, Meadow Lane's biggest of the season, a record at the time. Lawton and Sewell shared the goals then but neither strike was as spectacular as the one headed home by Lawton in the first Nottingham derby of the campaign, back in November of 1949 at the City Ground. The distance from which the bullet header that bulged the back of the Forest net that Saturday afternoon may have been embellished over the years. Even today, some observers argue it was scored from outside the penalty area despite photographic evidence suggesting Lawton was closer to the penalty spot. Such varied recollections, however, fail to diminish a goal that has become part of the derby match folklore at both the City Ground and Meadow Lane.

Though everything in the garden appeared green at club level, the colour was more an arid brown and becoming increasingly barren on the England front line. Lawton, ever candid but sometimes to his own detriment, could not disguise his contempt for the establishment at the Football Association or those who paid lip service to its regime and leaders, many of whom were happy to select in splendid isolation without a genuine grasp of what was required (how times don't really change, maybe).

Always one to flaunt convention, his penchant for inhaling a half-time cigarette with his soul mate Frank Swift, the Manchester City and England goalkeeper, was a cause of irritation to those in charge. The aroma of a lit Woodbine that permeated the Wembley dressing room during the interval inspired outrage from the likes of Jimmy Trotter, the England trainer, an ire hardly soothed when Lawton and Swift would then proceed to thrash the opposition without a hint of being caught short of breath.

At least away from the global stage, Lawton flourished in the more parochial setting of Nottingham. Following that home debut in November 1947, the next game at Meadow Lane enticed 45,116 to the old ground with an estimated 10,000 locked out for the visit of Swansea on Boxing Day. The trend continued into the 1948/49 season with attendances way above the 30,000. When Notts ventured forth, accompanied by Lawton, the trip took on the importance of a stage visit. At Millwall, 44,627 stood and sat after queueing to see him; Norwich and Bristol City accounted for over 29,000 each and 26,493 turned up at the Vetch Field, Swansea on January 22. Way out west in Solva, Pembrokeshire, a group of young football enthusiasts decided to hire a bus to see Lawton on only his third appearance ever at the Vetch. The week before, Notts, or Lawton County as some preferred to call the Magpies, had administered that 11-1 hiding to Newport County. South Wales, with Swansea top of the division and primed with six Welsh internationals, eagerly anticipated the free-scoring men from the Midlands.

For several of the group of students, farmers and fishermen it was to be the first time they had watched a league match. Gerald Phillips, then just 17, was the instigator of the voyage into the unknown. "I'd been a Tommy Lawton fan from a small boy. I'd listen to Raymond Glendenning's commentaries on the crackly wireless and the next morning grab the paper and read the back page. I never read any more of the paper – just the back page for sport, especially if Tommy had been playing. Those players were like gods. Matthews, Shackleton and Lawton, we'd never seen them, only heard and read about them. It didn't matter that they were English. Nationality didn't come into it. They were footballers."

A 32-seater bus hired from the Western Welsh depot in St David's carried the gang to Swansea for ten bob apiece (50p). "A trip to Swansea was a big thing for us and with no dual carriageways, the journey was very pedestrian, taking the best part of four hours to travel 70 miles. The chance to see Lawton, though, was too good to miss." They were greeted at Swansea High Street station by a newspaper billboard that read: 'County Without Star At Vetch.' "We all thought the worst but when we had managed to buy a paper, the player in question was not Tommy but Eddie Gannon, a wing half and Irish international. Good player, but not Lawton." Gannon had 'flu and had been replaced by Bill Corkhill.

After queueing for an hour, in a heavy downpour, Phillips and his party paid 1s 6d (8p) to file onto the terrace behind the goal at the Town end. "There was no trouble. The crowd was packed in so tightly it was impossible to have a fight! The pitch was like a paddy field and getting worse by the minute." Swansea won 3-1 but it is the memory of Lawton that lingers in parts of South Wales even today. "In Wales we were told that Stan Richards could head the ball as well as Lawton and he was good but I think Tommy was the better of the two. Denis Law was brilliant, Roy Bentley could head a ball and Frank Stapleton was also good in the air – but Tommy was, I think, the best header I ever saw. When he went up for the ball it was as if he was suspended in mid-air and the timing of his jumps was immaculate."

Moments from that game at the Vetch have stayed with Gerald Phillips ever since. "Close up, his ball control was exceptional. He chased one that looked certain to go out over the goal line. He got there and, in a flash, hooked it back into the centre. It was simply outstanding. Another time, he went up for a centre with the Swansea centre-half Reg Weston, ducked and Weston was hit full in the face. He couldn't get out of the way." Gerald Phillips' story is the epitome of how football was played and perceived by supporters, capturing the quintessential qualities of innocence and expectancy in the provinces when the big names came to town. The esteem in which he was held had no bounds back in Nottinghamshire. Trevor Mitchell was living with his mother and sister in a squatters' camp at Scofton in the north of the county at the time. "I had no interest in football at all. I'd suffered with TB and had always been told by my mother not to play 'that horrible game.' So, at school in Worksop, while the other kids were kicking a ball around in the schoolyard, I was the sickly one, the weakling, standing in the corner with a scarf wrapped round my neck watching the others enjoy themselves." Then Lawton's transfer to Meadow Lane was a pivotal point for young Mitchell. "My brother just wouldn't stop going on about it. Fred, something of a war hero, newly married, was living in Nottingham. After every game he'd be enthusing, 'Tommy did this' and 'Tommy did that.' Eventually, he persuaded me to go to Nottingham and watch a game. Reluctantly, I caught an East Midlands bus from Worksop. It took about an hour down to Huntingdon Street in Nottingham where my brother met me and we walked down to Meadow Lane. The crowd was all over the road, there wasn't much traffic in those days, just a few trolley-buses going down to Trent Bridge. The thing I remember is the noise of the crowd, they were all talking away, everyone was so excited at the prospect of going to a game. There were long queues to get in, no such thing as all-ticket games then. We paid 1/6d (8p) and stood on the cinders and the shingle at the scoreboard end.

"I can still remember the first time I saw Tommy – this great big man with hair slicked back and a centre parting, rubbing his hands together as he went up to the centre circle to toss the coin." An indelible impression had been made on the 13-year-old Trevor. "I thought I'm going to be a centre-forward and play for England. So I'd practise with a tennis ball, wherever I went and I became quite good, I finished up an athlete and I played cricket as well as football. A remarkable transformation for the weedy lad." Mitchell did not discover fame on the international stage for England at football. However... "In 1978, I was chosen for the British team in the World Hairdressing Championships in New York. Not football, but I'd made the team, realised an ambition and represented my country just like Tommy Lawton." The winning style, need it be said, was not slicked back with a centre parting.

Whenever they could scrape together the money, Trevor and Fred followed Notts all over the country, but the special treat was to go to the Empire Cafe, in the shadow of the old Empire theatre of varieties, on Forman Street before matches. "I didn't know why we always had to go there until, one day, Fred says 'That's Tommy's seat you're in.' He'd looked through the window one day and seen Tommy in there with Oscar Old and Billy Baxter. One time I went down to the ground with the idea of getting Tommy's autograph. I waited around for ages before Tommy appeared with Billy Baxter. He signed my book, squeezing his eyes as the smoke from his cigarette drifted up. I said 'Thanks, Tommy' and patted him on the back. When I told my brother, he said, 'You touched him! With which hand?' And grabbed hold of my right hand. That's how much he meant to us. He was like royalty." Rumours that Lawton was a privileged case at Notts, earning more than the maximum wage were rife. "'They said he was getting £20 a week – so what? He was worth it." Trevor Mitchell will not hear a word said against his hero, even now. "When Tommy lost his England place to Jackie Milburn, we immediately hated Milburn because he got our Tommy dropped. All these years on, I suppose Tommy's still a part of my life. When I'm at home in Hampshire and I see a magpie in the garden, I don't salute it, I immediately think of Tommy Lawton." There were those supposedly 'in the know' who whispered that there was a turnstile at Meadow Lane from which Lawton took all the proceeds. In the city today, among those of a certain vintage, opinion is still fiercely divided about whether Lawton took under-the-counter payments from Notts. "I made money for Nottingham and for Notts County but nothing other than wages for Tom Lawton," was the immovable stance taken by the centre-forward.

Naturally, there were exceptions to such rose-tinted scenarios of those genuine football fans of the golden age. Few were more incongruous to the image of rosettes, rattles and jolly good sportsmanship than that conjured up on November 5th, 1949 as County were striding towards their divisional title. Paying a visit to the Den, the home of Millwall, was to become a notoriously dangerous and unwelcome social engagement on the football calendar. Even in 1949, the fathers of the fans who were rightly to become pariahs in sporting circles during the '70s and '80s, were leading by example. Lawton had dealt with abuse from Scottish fans and the taunts of front-line soldiers during the war, but he was quite shocked by the spiteful nature of the venomous remarks directed his way in south east London. Turning to Frank Broome, his pre-war England colleague, he said: "Let's do this lot, Frank, and get out of here." Lawton duly obliged with the first goal and Jackie Sewell added two more to secure the points.

Sadly, the likes of David Beckham are forced to endure such loutish behaviour in today's game but in 1949, it was a rare occurrence. Lawton was upset all the more because he had 'guested' for Millwall during the war years.

"It was different to any sort of barracking that you received in Scotland," Lawton would recall many years later, confirming how the events of that afternoon had touched him. "At Hampden, they'd call you no good with a sense of humour. This was just foul-mouthed filth. Disgusting, but now all you have to do is get on a bus and you hear the same thing." Whatever the level of insult, nothing would deter Lawton and County from being crowned Division Three champions in 1950.

A memorable derby double over Forest was initiated in December with a 2-1 win at the City Ground, Lawton and Frank Broome on target in front of a sell-out 38,000 crowd. Four months later, on April 22, Forest were again defeated, this time 2-0. Once more performing before a capacity audience, the scorers were Lawton and Sewell, naturally, providing the goals that finally secured the title and all but dashed their rivals' hopes of promotion. It didn't get much sweeter for Magpies fans! The only blight was the departure of Arthur Stollery, who was relieved of his managerial duties. Lawton was asked to take over as player-manager but declined, preferring instead to concentrate efforts on the field to furthering the club's climb back to the Division One. "Arthur had been sacked and it was his own fault but his wife blamed me. Arthur was a nice bloke but he was not ruthless enough with the players and his knowledge of football was limited. He was popular, true, and a superb masseur but naïve in the ways of the professional game. In all honesty I did try to help him but he decided to go his own way and when our form dipped during my second season he was sacked."

Little John, a sobriquet for the journalist who penned Notts County's notes in the *Football Post*, the local pink 'un, reflected upon the championship season and wrote about Lawton's capacity to entertain. "We say farewell to a season which has been one of the most successful in the history of the club. Never before has the average attendance been so high and a new ground record for Meadow Lane was established when 46,000 saw County make certain of the championship in the return match against Forest. "Before many weeks are past the club and the players will be in the midst of championship celebrations. The first of this nature was last Sunday [April 30] when the captain, Tommy Lawton, and his wife, invited the whole of the playing staff to their house. It was a grand evening and Tommy expressed his delight that he had had the honour of leading such a fine set of fellows on the field of play. The chief toast was 'Success to another season' for Tommy will not rest until Notts are back in the First Division."

The toast was an ominous one, for after the partying came the hangover, a particularly virulent one which would not abate with the sporadic application of tonic, but ultimately token, victories. County's loss of form was in sharp contrast to the buoyancy that had made them the team to be feared both home and away as they turned the previous season's championship race into a procession.

Perhaps the upward spiral had been too steep, following that rapturous campaign that had been acclaimed by record audiences. Lawton had sensed that the euphoria that brought on the hype was premature and unwarranted.

"As our Division Two life dawned, suddenly the manager was a 'great' manager and the players were 'great' players, most of them internationals. In fact, they were a lot of big-mouths who were inept at playing and had to be carried for much of the time. Promotion only proved emphatically the low quality of our staff." His contacts from the international arena and elsewhere still carried considerable weight within the game. Raich Carter, of Derby County, and Wilf Mannion, of Middlesbrough, were two inside-forwards with the skills to open up a game and Lawton implored the board to buy them, along with Charlie Mitten, the Manchester United winger, who Lawton felt would have provided the kind of service upon which he thrived. On his recommendation the players would have come but even though the turnstiles clicked away in unrelenting fashion, thus bulging attendances and the bank balance, none of the three musketeers in Lawton's vision for County's First Division future came to Nottingham.

Politics and in-fighting were no strangers to Lawton's career. As it was with England, so it proved with Notts County. And even away from Meadow Lane, Lawton could not find sanctuary in his domestic life. Unable to escape the feeling of turmoil and disruption, it was during this period that he finally divorced his first wife. Lawton was granted a decree nisi at Nottingham Divorce Court against Rosaleen May Lawton, of Old Hall Drive, Mapperley Park, on March 14, 1951. The court heard that adultery had been committed with Adrian Van Geffen, described as a company director, of Loughborough Road, West Bridgford. At the time, Lawton gave his own address as Mapperley Hall Drive, where he was staying with Gladys May Rose, later to become Gaye Lawton, the love of his life whom he would eventually marry.

"All of Nottingham knew what was going on," Lawton recalled. "Everywhere I went there were nudges and winks and smirks. Eventually, I couldn't stand it any longer. I hired a private detective. That first marriage was the worst day's work of my life. The second was joining Notts County. I should have stayed at Everton and transferred the wife. Then I should have stayed in Division One for as long as I was able. Notts County was a terrible mistake that dogged me all my life."

The scandal, too, remained with him throughout his days in Nottingham. More than a year after his own separation, Lawton would be cited as co-respondent at the same Nottingham court by wealthy businessman Harry Reginald Rose. Lawton and Mrs Rose, a glamorous lady in the Nottingham social scene, had been staying in a caravan in Mablethorpe and the allegations of adultery were not denied. Both split marriages left a child in limbo, Amanda was his daughter by his first wife while Mrs Rose already had a six-year-old daughter, Carol Ann.

Back at Meadow Lane, the complex duplicity and almost insidious nature of football life compared favourably with Lawton's tangled romantic one. Within the Notts camp, a game of Chinese whispers was being played out. Eric Houghton, the manager, Bill Moore, the trainer, and Leon Leuty, the centre-half, were the chief conspirators who recruited others to their cause of usurping Lawton and his influence from the ranks.

Such behaviour was all the more galling to Lawton who had been instrumental in bringing all three of them to Meadow Lane. Houghton and Moore from Torquay United, Leuty, whose premature death from leukaemia in 1955 would be universally mourned in the game, arriving from Bradford Park Avenue.

Lawton, whose immense stature had been largely responsible for the club's upturn in fortunes, was furious. "I deeply resented implications that were being made. For instance, some people thought that I still harboured hopes of managership despite having earlier turned down the offer. Others were also under the misguided impression that I was receiving favours from directors. Perhaps they had forgotten that it was me who had originally asked for all of us to perform on an equal financial footing.

"Maybe my opinions were voiced with more authority and carried more weight in the boardroom but that was only because I had been proved correct in the past. Besides there were some directors with whom I didn't always see eye to eye, mostly in relation to the playing staff. Quite frankly they were not up to scratch but when I made my feelings known, they were turned against me. That sort of atmosphere breeds contempt and it was almost inevitable that I would move on." The bad feeling spread to the pitch. It was a situation that could not be tolerated for very long although it endured for the first season when Notts, having imperiously swept all before them to gain promotion, struggled to finish sixth from bottom.

"The board announced that my domestic problem was the reason for me being placed on the transfer list. I hadn't asked for a transfer but they felt it was in the best interests of the club that I should go. Make no mistake, I was forced out of Meadow Lane and away from the supporters who I had taken as much to my heart as they had me." Envy or spite, no-one knows for sure, but Lawton's persona as a leading player who could mix it and be one of the boys most certainly bred jealousy. In such an environment, rumours festered. Notts cast aspersions upon his character and contrived, in many ways, to exceed the vitriol of those Millwall louts on November 5, 1949. The denouement and final ignominy came when they stripped Lawton of his No. 9 shirt, handing it to Cec McCormack, a new signing from Barnsley. Lawton was moved to inside- right.

"Not since the days when I was an Everton stripling, when I lined up alongside Dixie Dean, had I played inside forward." Could there be a more fitting epitaph for the final months of Lawton's period of time at County than Iago's lament in Shakespeare's Othello? "Who steals my purse, steals trash; 'tis something, nothing 'Twas mine, 'tis his, and has been slave to thousands; But he that filches from me my good name robs me of that which not enriches him, And makes me poor indeed."

When Lawton left for Brentford in March 1952, his detractors had won the day but County were to be the losers. Apart from the indelible mark he left on the club and city, his friendship and alliance with Sewell, both on and off the park, was to prove an eternal bonding for both men. "From a personal point of view, he took time out to help me but he was also there for the team as well," Sewell recalled. In March 1951, Lawton's partner in goals had been sold to Sheffield Wednesday for the British record fee. If the news aggrieved and shocked County supporters, it also underlined the ambition of the County board. In those more draconian days when directors ruled the game and its players, Sewell was told he would be leaving on Thursday morning before training. At 8 pm that night, he was still at the Victoria Hotel in Nottingham awaiting to be hear confirmation of his transfer, having been kept isolated from the outside world all day.

"I only knew it was a British record the following day when I was awoken by my landlady at the digs, screaming and bellowing at me. 'What have you done, Jack, leaving us like this?' Of course, I hadn't done anything. The buggers at Notts told me it was not going to be a record. On the Friday, I went to say goodbye to the lads. Tommy took me to one side and walked me around the pitch. I think he could see I was on the point of breaking down because in all honesty I didn't want to leave Notts and such a nice set of blokes. On top of that I was bit apprehensive to say the least, this little lad from Whitehaven who hadn't been anywhere or done much in the game to speak about.

"Tommy told me not to be nervous, not to be afraid of the fee. 'Play as you always play, you'll get better,' he said. 'Remember they are paying that money for what you can do. That's why they want you so just keep doing what you have always done. You'll be fine.'" Sewell's horizons were indeed to widen. He won a Division Two championship medal with Wednesday, an FA Cup winners medal while at Aston Villa and six England caps.

"I remember going on the tour of Canada before the 1950 World Cup with an FA side and talking to Stanley Matthews about Tommy. He was a great admirer of Tommy. He said he would just stand there in the six yard box and tell him to plant the ball on his head, which of course was something Matthews wasn't too bad at it, was he? I think the point I always bear in mind when recalling Tommy is that when he came to Notts he wasn't exactly a young man any more. He was 28 and still a great player but I could only imagine what he was like when he was 19 and running about everywhere with Everton." There were others whose opinion of Lawton further cemented the notion that a legend had indeed graced Meadow Lane for several years.

Arthur Milton, the last double international at cricket and football, was conscripted from Arsenal, where had signed virtually straight from school in Bristol in 1946, to do his National Service. Part of his posting led him to Chilwell Army barracks, Nottingham, where he spent much of his time playing for his unit and a local club in the Notts Alliance. He had the opportunity to witness Raich Carter in action at the Baseball Ground with the Derby County side that won the FA Cup that year but when Lawton arrived the following season at Meadow Lane, he was able to see striking perfection in motion at close quarters. "He came out looking like a film star. Jet black hair, parted down the middle, slicked back. It was his heading that amazed me. Not just the power of it, but his ability to get up there before everyone else and then just hang there. He was a classic, absolutely classic. Two wonderful feet, just so mobile and quick."

Lawton's affinity with the Nottingham public remained with him throughout his life, yet strangely his adopted city was a source of discomfort and immense heartache to the man. The breakdown of his first marriage and the demise of his international career ensued as a result although the unrest and disenchantment within his domestic life was already well progressed and beyond redemption by the time he had arrived in the East Midlands.

MATCH OF THE DAY

Italy v England
Stadio Communale, Turin
May 16th 1948
Italy: Bacigalupo, Ballarin (Torino), Eliani (Fiorentina), Anrovazzi (AC Milan), Parola (Juventus), Grezar, Menti, Loik, Gabetto, Mazzola (all Torino, capt), Carpaliese (AC Milan)
England: Swift (Man City Capt), Scott (Arsenal), Howe (Derby Co), Wright (Wolves), Franklin (Stoke), Cockburn (Man Utd), Matthews, Mortensen (Blackpool), Lawton (Notts County), Mannion (Middlesbrough), Finney (Preston)
The headline for the following day in the News Chronicle *summed it up – "Our best ever Soccer display abroad." It probably was and still is, though, unfortunately Tommy Lawton can hardly claim it as one of his most impressive performances – even though he scored one of England's four goals.*

Charles Buchan, the paper's reporter, described it as a "wonderful victory (that) did more towards restoring British (sic) prestige abroad than cartloads of propaganda."

The Italians, World Cup winners in 1938 and therefore still officially the holders, were said to be on a bonus of £60.00 a man to win. They had spent the previous three weeks at a mountain retreat honing their fitness while England's players had seen out the closing stages of the domestic season with rationing still very much in force. Of the squad that travelled to Italy, Henry Cockburn, Stan Pearson and Johnny Aston were part of the Manchester United side that had just won the FA Cup and finished second in the league. Stan Matthews and Stan

Mortensen were both in the Blackpool side beaten at Wembley, Jack Howe had reached the Cup semi-final with Derby, while Bill Nicholson had done so with Spurs and Laurie Scott had won the championship with Arsenal. Eight players whose seasons had meant that there was no chance of taking it easy whatsoever.

On arrival in Italy, the players were immediately aware of the intense interest in the game – the first between England and a former enemy nation since 1945. The Italians tended to disregard England's 10-0 thrashing of Portugal in Lisbon the year before, while concentrating on the defeat by Switzerland on the same tour. Yet, since then, England had been unbeaten. Anticipation heightened hour by hour up to kick-off time.

Crowds queued for up to 18 hours to buy a ticket, which could then be resold on the black-market for 300 times their face value. A previously unheard of number of journalists – no fewer than 600 – arrived from all over the world to cover the most attractive international fixture played since the war.

For three days prior to the game, the England party was based at Stesa, the resort on Lake Maggiore, some two hours from Turin, where nine years before Lawton, Matthews and the rest of the England team had arrived to a tumultuous welcome from the Italians only four months prior to war breaking out. If the players expected a cushy couple of days after the hard season, they were mistaken. According to Stan Mortensen, Walter Winterbottom worked them in training "as never before – I put in two or three days of the hardest work of my football life." Tommy, equally hard worked, was trying desperately to disguise a leg strain, hoping that it would clear up so that he could play. He needed to – in the press there was growing opinion that his move into Division Three (South) was not improving his game. Along with the problems in his domestic life, it added to the stress he was feeling and probably contributed to him telling Winterbottom that his blackboard tactics were not welcomed by players who had forged their careers without his help – "You're going to tell Stan Matthews how to play outside right? And me how to score goals? You've got another think coming" Lawton's international days were numbered from that point, especially as he had again been severely critical of the high handed way the FA dealt with players' expenses for internationals. "Before the Scotland game, I had been in London on business and took the train to Glasgow from Euston. Afterwards I claimed for my ticket as usual and they told me 'You live in Nottingham now, you can't claim from London.'"

Lawton was not best pleased and said so. Another nail in the Lawton international coffin, particularly as the FA had just raised the international match fee to £20.

Only four minutes had gone when Matthews took two Italian defenders out of the game with a deft feint and sent an exquisite 40 yard pass into the path of Mortensen sprinting goalwards at top speed, Parola was across to cover but Mortensen from an acute angle fired into the roof of the net. A phenomenal goal – even some of his colleagues thought it was a fluke, that he had meant to cross. Mortensen always said that he intended to shoot and " as luck would have it, I hit it truly." He reasoned that the goalkeeper was off his line to cover the possible centre to the otherwise unmarked Lawton.

Twenty minutes later, Mortensen was sent clear again by Matthews and this time he centred for Lawton. Although he was tightly marked by Parolo, he created enough space to rifle a shot past Bacigalupo. While most of the reporters at the game saluted Mortensen's first goal, Tom Finney thought that Lawton's effort was more impressive "It was scored at a crucial moment, the Italians were getting on top of us. Tommy took the pass 12 yards out and made it look simple, effortless, yet it flew past the goalkeeper, who was poised to dive, before he could move." In the meantime, Frank Swift, captain of England for the first time, had saved superbly from Gabetto and parried two headers from Carapallese while Menti had twice been on target but ruled offside.

Italy should have been well ahead by half-time, instead they were two down and on arrival in the dressing room were sprayed with ice cold water from a siphon by their team manager Vittorio Pozzo. He had to repeat the exercise from the touchline in the second half when Gabetto's header from Mazzola's cross hit the underside of the bar, bounced down and Swift leapt across to clear, the Spanish referee ignoring Italy's claims that it had crossed the line.

"Pozzo was up and down the touchline, spraying these siphons of water over his players to cool them down. One time, he was just by me, I shouted, 'Hey, is there any whisky in there?' He said, 'No, there is not.' I said 'I don't want any then!' He just looked at me, gone out." Lawton remembered Pozzo, a Piedmontese, as a "great man. Not just for what he did in football with Italy, but because, during the war he'd been in the resistance, guiding British prisoners of war who'd managed to escape, over the mountains to Switzerland." Pozzo was a great admirer of English football. Pre-war he had been a foreign language teacher in England, and became a big fan of the great centre-forward, Steve Bloomer.

Italy's frustration was complete when Tom Finney scored twice, mesmerising their defence after taking passes from Mannion and Mortensen. England were unassailable. Finney himself called it the finest performance by any team that he ever played in. Buchan in the News Chronicle *simply enthused about the display with special mentions for the outstanding contributions of Swift, Mortensen the "match winner," Howe on his debut at left back, Scott, Franklin and Wright.*

Buchan mentioned Lawton twice, no criticism was made, but in the Daily Express, *under the headline 'Mortensen beats Italians, Swift bars the way to everyone' John McAdam wrote: "It would appear that Lawton's day at centre-forward is over." Carlo Parola's display against Lawton was of the highest class, barely allowing the England centre-forward a kick, apart from the vital one in the 24th minute. Said to be the world's highest paid player at the time, he fully justified his reputation to Billy Wright. "One of the best footballers ever produced by his country. Tall, well built and as handsome as any film hero ... he was magnificent." That would have been little consolation to Lawton who discovered that John Graydon, in the* Daily Graphic, *thought that "of the England forwards, Lawton was the least successful, revealing nothing like his old form." In the* Daily Mail, *Roy Peskett thought Parola was "the perfect centre-half, who was two yards faster than Lawton." Mortensen was "atomic," a "Blackpool dynamo" whose 60-yard dribble made the second goal for Lawton. England won through expert defence and because "the forwards knew how to shoot when the opportunity arose." According to an agency report, crowds packing cafes in Rome to listen to the match on the radio went home "gloomily" but full of praise for the England team for producing " tactics never seen before in Italy."*

Charles Buchan agreed: "never have I seen a better display from a British team abroad... perfect teamwork, footwork and co-operation." Later (1950) he was to write that he considered this team to be the finest he ever saw. Having been a part, albeit somewhat subdued, of a great show, Lawton had to wait four months before he would know whether he would be teaming up with England again. Back to the Third Division and Notts against the likes of Torquay, Newport, Exeter and Southend.

A year later the football world was in mourning for the Torino team which perished when their plane bringing them home from a match in Spain crashed into Superga Hill. Of the Italian team that had played against England in 1948 Bacigalupo, Ballarin, Grezar, Menti, Loik, Gabetto and Mazzola were killed.

The match in Turin was played the same weekend as the touring Australian cricket team under Don Bradman plundered Essex for 721 runs in a day at Southend – "deliberate, merciless, brilliant in its execution," wrote Crawford White in the *News Chronicle* on a day when superlatives ruled the back pages.

Advertised in the same editions – 'Charles Butler man-tailored coats' for eighteen coupons and £7.3s.8d (about £7 – 18) and King Six cigars '1/7d (8p) was never better spent in setting aside the cares of the day'. Did Tommy perhaps invest 1/7d, when his expenses came through?

CHAPTER TWENTY-THREE

1948 – NOTTS COUNTY POST LAWTON – ENGLAND'S DILEMMA

Jackie Milburn replaced Lawton in the England team in October 1948. "Denmark in Copenhagen turned out to be my last game for England, my swansong" said Tommy. "I had a stinker. I missed four good chances: Len Shack, well, he must have missed as many again. Afterwards Winterbottom took me on one side and said 'I think we're going to give Jackie Milburn a go next time." I thought 'Well, it's ages before the next game, we'll see.' But Jackie did come in for the next game and I never got a look in again." Tommy had not been at his best in Copenhagen. He was again carrying an injury that he had omitted to tell Winterbottom about and he had already demonstrated his contempt for the man he referred to as "that Manchester United reserve."

With England failing to score against a side that had talent, but which had conceded three goals to England's amateurs not long before, changes were demanded and the scapegoats were Lawton and his inside-right, Jimmy Hagan, who was discarded after winning just one cap.

Charles Buchan was always one of Lawton's sternest critics. A player for more than 25 years in the league, a goal-scoring inside-forward himself, he was steeped in the game but, on this occasion, even he thought the decision to drop Lawton was ill-advised. "It was a match which should have been won comfortably, but many easy scoring chances were thrown away. I suppose Lawton and Hagan were to blame to some extent, but they were not the worst offenders by any means. Both, I thought, played well in midfield and deserved at least another chance for England. But it never came." So Milburn, the popular Geordie, was the first man other than Lawton to wear the England number nine shirt in an official international since 1938 when he was called up for the game with Northern Ireland in Belfast.

Even though Lawton was by now playing lower division football with Notts County, he retained plenty of supporters in the media and on the terraces, insistent he was still the best centre-forward in England. However, in the north east they were clamouring for the inclusion of their man, who had scored a hat-trick for the Football League against the Irish League the previous month. So it was Milburn, as Winterbottom had suggested, who came in and scored on his international debut. Milburn generally impressed with his strong running and powerful shooting but he commented that he was not especially enamoured with the lack of atmosphere in international football.

Milburn held his place for the next three matches but then, surprisingly, opted to accompany Newcastle United on a tour of Canada during the close season rather than join up with England for matches in Scandinavia and against France. For the first international of the following season, against the Macaulay at Goodison Park, England chose to leave him out, even though he was in decent form for Newcastle.

Lawton had watched the situation unravel from a distance. He had scored seven goals in the first seven games of the 1949/50 season, albeit in Division Three (South) against the likes of Bournemouth and Exeter, but he was still being touted to return as England's leader. Eventually, the selectors looked elsewhere. Since Lawton's last cap, Milburn, Roy Bentley of Chelsea and Jack Rowley of Manchester United had all been called up and each had enjoyed significant moments without actually looking the part.

Jesse Pye of Wolves came in for his first (and only) cap against Johnny Carey's Ireland as England went down 2-0, their first home defeat outside of the Home Nations' Championship. Such was the concern at the setback that Lawton was again in contention for a place in the World Cup qualifier against Wales at Ninian Park in October 1949.

England were in a similar situation to that which had cropped up pre-war. No centre-forward was, it appeared, capable of claiming the position on a permanent basis. Pre-Lawton: Drake, Mills, Fenton, Steele and Broome. Post-Lawton: Milburn, Bentley, Mortensen, Rowley and Pye. Waiting in the wings, the up-and-coming Nat Lofthouse, at 24 starting to make a big impression at Bolton but in 1949 regarded as too inexperienced to play for England. So no recent phenomena this.

Until the defeat by the Republic of Ireland, England had been confident of qualifying for their first World Cup Finals in Brazil. Indeed, there had been many boasting that England were still the best team in the world and favourites to win the competition outright. They ignored the fact that filling the centre-forward position was becoming a major problem. As it was the choice for England's number nine, in the press at least, was between Lawton of Third Division Notts County, just turned 30, and Milburn of First Division Newcastle United, five years his junior. Milburn had blotted his copybook by complaining that too many players in the England side played for themselves and that did not endear him to the regulars in the team, but they, of course did not pick the side.

The current England centre-half, Neil Franklin, put in his two pennyworth when he said, after a Newcastle v Stoke match at St James' Park that Milburn, even though he had scored in a 4-2 win, was less than the finished article. Asked about Milburn's attributes, Franklin replied a little curtly: "Well, he's not a Tommy Lawton." If only Lawton had decided to move to Sunderland when he was on the list at Chelsea, or, perhaps, had he been allowed a transfer to Arsenal, then his England future might have been assured right up to the 1950 World Cup, maybe beyond.

In 1949, Stanley Matthews thought that Lawton's move to Notts County had cost him his England place. "But for dropping into a poorer class of football he would still have been England's leader." Willie Thornton, the Rangers centre-forward who won seven caps for Scotland between 1947 and 1952, thought that the England teams he faced had problems that they had not had to deal with for years. "The absence of stars like Carter and Lawton has left them in an anaemic state. Transfusion and new blood is being introduced at every opportunity to restore the 'patient' to his former healthy appearance."

Thornton was also a journalist of some repute. He thought England's best half-back line was Britton, Cullis and Mercer. They had appeared together eight times in war-time internationals but not subsequently. Thornton suggested that England was able to minimise the loss of that half back trio by "obtaining an ideal blend of skill and power in their forward line, which included 'wondermen' Matthews, Carter, Lawton and Mannion... now, compelled to make changes both in defence and attack, they don't possess a compensating department to balance their deficiencies elsewhere."

Tommy, difficult as it was for him, kept his own counsel. He had little choice. He knew that his criticism of Winterbottom had been a major factor in him being dropped from the England team. "There were plenty of things I could have said, but I thought I'd better not. I was scoring goals, in the First Division would have been better, but it wasn't. I think that most of the England boys who knew me wanted me in the team again. Billy Wright told me as much, but it wasn't his choice. It wasn't even Walter Winterbottom's entirely. It was those blighters in blazers sitting around with their gins and tonic." For the World Cup qualifier in Cardiff, Milburn was, eventually, selected. Alongside him, Len Shackleton won the third of his, ridiculously few, five caps. Between them they totally destroyed Wales, 4-1, with Milburn scoring a hat-trick. Even Raymond Glendenning, a friend of Lawton's for years and a great admirer, admitted: "Milburn has come to stay as the England centre-forward. I have put forward the claims of Tommy Lawton... but Milburn was chosen and fully justified his choice." At last, it seemed, a centre-forward had been found who could replace the great Lawton; but so loyal were Tommy's supporters in the media that he was always mentioned when England teams were selected in 1949 and 1950. Right up until the team was picked for the 1950 World Cup in Brazil, it was even being suggested that he should return as captain. (George Hardwick skippered England in all the 13 internationals from the end of the war until a knee injury meant that he lost his place. Goalkeeper Frank Swift took over for two games, but after the Copenhagen debacle, the selectors plumped for Billy Wright, an England regular since the war at half back). Tommy never took the captaincy suggestions seriously, he was always a great believer in Wright – "a great player, a fine captain and a great pal." Tommy did, though, still harbour hopes of reappearing for

England in fairy tale fashion at the World Cup. When Milburn was injured and missed the next three internationals, Lawton thought that games against Northern Ireland and Italy would have provided ideal opportunities to demonstrate that he still had international class – particularly the match against Italy and his old adversary Carlo Parola of Juventus. Lawton did his best to force the selectors to take a final look at him with eight goals in five league games. Eventually it was Jack Rowley, of Manchester United, who was given another chance. He scored four against Northern Ireland, and produced a brilliant effort after 76 minutes against Italy at White Hart Lane. Yet Rowley was only a year younger than Lawton, hardly one for the future either, and the Italy game was, indeed, his international swansong. Bentley was back for the pre-World Cup tour.

The Chelsea man was England's number nine right up until the ill-fated match against the USA in Belo Horizonte. Milburn did not play in that game but he knew perfectly well why England lost – "Shooting used to be the strong part of our game, but in Brazil, even as a forward I must admit this, it was our weakness." England captain Billy Wright conceded that the wrong players were taken to Brazil: "If the forward line of 1946-48, Matthews, Mortensen, Lawton, Mannion and Finney, had been kept together for the World Cup, we would have been fine." Milburn had looked the man most likely to lay permanent claim to the England number nine shirt in succession to Lawton, but injuries and the selectorial system used at the time meant that other players were going to be placed in the frame and given chances. There was no coherent policy in team selection and no obvious planning, until it came, coincidentally, to Brazil.

The Grimsby fish merchant, Arthur Drewry, later to become President of FIFA immediately before Sir Stanley Rous, was the only FA official in Brazil and he picked the team in consultation with Walter Winterbottom. They decided, after beating Chile in Rio de Janeiro in the first match, that the same eleven should play against the USA. Drewry, was aware that Stanley Matthews had been taken to Brazil specifically to break down packed defences but Matthews was left a disappointed spectator on the bench. Tommy mused: "If they weren't going to play Stan, then they weren't going to use a Third Division centre-forward." Lawton's move to Notts County in 1947, fulfilling his long standing promise to Arthur Stollery and to ensure a secure future, had backfired. Stollery quit 16 months later through ill health; Tommy was not set up for life, far from it; England lost their best centre-forward well before he should have retired from international football. Both paid dearly for it.

When the 1950 World Cup took place, Tommy was still only 30. By then he had been playing Third Division football for the best part of three years – but he was still scoring goals. Later, Tommy regretted the decision to drop out of the First Division at such an early age: "I should have played at the top for as long as I was able." He had chances to stay in the First Division, but domestic circumstances and a sense of honour dictated otherwise. So he never did win more substantial honours post-war than the solitary Third Division Championship he achieved with Notts in 1950. And who knows? He might have been won the top honour in the game – a World Cup Winners' medal with England.

Billy Wright, for one, thought it was a possibility. He agreed with Milburn that had England's shooting been better in Brazil then overall victory was within range. "Not since Tommy Lawton at the top of his form have we seen a player able to hit or head a ball accurately from all angles as could the one-time England centre-forward and I will be so bold as to say that, had the Tommy Lawton of a few years ago been leading our forward line at Rio de Janiero, we might have brought back the Jules Rimet trophy." At the time, Tommy never suggested as much, though he was told, frequently, that he had made the wrong decision to move 'downtable.' He was his own man, he made his own decisions. Only in much later years did he acknowledge that he had made a mistake by moving to Notts when he did. About England and the 1950 World Cup he would smile quietly "I don't think that any team I was in would have lost to the Americans."

CHAPTER TWENTY-FOUR
1950 – NOTTS COUNTY
THE WORST DAY'S WORK

The boom in post-war gates had resulted in a near black-market in star players. Wilf Mannion had effectively gone on strike at Middlesbrough after his request for a transfer had been turned down. Mannion and his club mate, the England captain George Hardwick, had both been approached with offers of up to £4,000 cash if they managed to have themselves transfer-listed. The rewards at more fashionable clubs were considerable compared to those on Teesside, but Hardwick, for one, certainly refused.

Lawton wondered whether the inducements were for real. "It was one thing getting onto the list, it was another actually being transferred. Yanto at Everton wanted to go because he didn't like what Cliff Britton, the manager, was doing at the club after I'd gone and they'd sold Joe (Mercer) too. In the end they put him on the list but wouldn't sell him. Matt Busby told him that. Matt wanted him at United to help bring the 'Babes' through.

"Wilf (Mannion) told me that Villa once offered him £3,000 to go on the transfer list and Real Madrid and Juventus five times as much. But Middlesbrough just wouldn't let him go. The club could get rid of you if they wanted. But you couldn't leave them when you wanted. They had it all ways. They only offer you a one-year contract. Then when they knew you were desperate for the money, they'd reduce your wages. It was a bloody slave market." It all begs the question that if Lawton was such a money grabber, as some of the Nottingham public insisted (and still insist) then, surely, he would have been back in the First Division at some stage during the 1948/49 season? Whatever the case, Notts County could hardly argue that they did not get value for money from Lawton. Opposition players certainly thought so. George Edwards, the Welsh international left winger, had moved from Birmingham City to Cardiff City in December 1948 for £6,000. In December 1950, Cardiff visited Meadow Lane. "Tommy would have been in his 30s then when I last played against him. He'd been around a long time, through the war years and he'd started playing at such a young age. So he'd lost half a yard but he was still a very good player. He made up for it by using other tricks, being clever, varying his positional play. He had others to do the running him, like Jackie Sewell. And he would talk to people. He was very fond of that. He'd be passing the time of day with the centre-half, then he'd be off! Oh, Tommy! He had an aura about him. I met good players regularly over the years like Ted Drake, Tom

Finney, Nat Lofthouse. These were big names, but none bigger than Tommy."

Ben Collins grew up in Kislingbury on the outskirts of Northampton in the thirties. As a football-mad youngster , the exploits of the teenage Lawton at Everton were etched in his memory. "When I was a schoolboy, he was my idol. The pictures of him always with that brilliantined hair. Always immaculate." Collins achieved his own ambition when he signed for Northampton Town in March 1949, aged 20. Eventually, he succeeded Bob Dennison at centre-half and over a period of ten years made 224 appearances for 'The Cobblers' in Division Three (South) captaining the side in later years.

He played against Lawton only once – on a Thursday evening in late April 1950 when Northampton travelled to Meadow Lane. Notts promotion to Division Two had been confirmed the previous Saturday. "It was a pleasant Spring evening, we kicked off at about 6.30 as there were no lights in those days." With the Championship shield being presented to Notts' captain Lawton and a big crowd of 31,843 in attendance it turned into a gala occasion. Notts won by two goals to nil, Lawton scoring twice and Collins "enjoyed" an experience he was never to forget. "Tommy was the player I found it most difficult to play against," he said some 48 years later. It was not the Lawton goals that remained in the memory but a near-miss. "I can see it now. We were just outside the penalty area when a cross came in from the left. I went up for it with him, but was amazed that my head was only level with his waist. He was way up above me. He did no more than flick it with his head and the ball went about six inches wide of the post. Our goalie had no chance. The power he got at that height, well!" Lawton's skill was already legendary and Collins knew all about that. What surprised the young man was Lawton's incredible friendliness. "He was chatting to me all the time, about the crowd, our players, theirs, anything at all. He called me by my Christian name and was just lovely to me. I know it sounds naive, I probably was, I was a young 22, but even though I was his opponent, I felt he was looking after me. I was the novice. He'd done everything in the game and he was just so kind, not a trace of unpleasantness. I really had the fullest admiration for him. He was such a friendly man, a lovely chap, a gentleman."

For George Edwards, even in later life, after some grim experiences, Lawton "carried himself with the air that he was still Tommy Lawton, the famous centre-forward. He knew who he was and how good he was. I always got that impression, though it never came through in anyway arrogantly or offensively. He was aware of his brilliance as a player, but it never showed unduly, he was never one of those pompous idiots who strut around like some do. He remained a nice man, a very kind man. I am proud to say that I knew Tommy, always have been. There are times when you want to impress. When I went home, back to my village, Kilgetty in Pembrokeshire, they would ask 'Do you know any of the great names?'

And I would be proud to say 'Oh, yes. I know Tommy Lawton.' It was always a privilege to meet him."

MATCH OF THE DAY

Division Three
Nottingham Forest v Notts County
The City Ground, Nottingham
December 3, 1949
Forest: Walker; Thomas, Hutchinson; Anderson, Gager, Burkitt; Scott, Love, Ardron, Capel, Kaile
County: Smith; Deans, Rigby; Chapman, Baxter, Adamson; Broome, Sewell, Lawton, Evans (W), Johnston
Rain in the morning made for extremely heavy going; a wind blowing towards the Bridgford End (away from the River Trent) which County took advantage of in the first half after Lawton won the toss, a feat acclaimed by deafening cheers from the visiting supporters. When security and policing methods are recalled from football's golden age in Nottingham, it is often remarked, sometimes by the very bobbies on the beat themselves, how just three or four officers would patrol the perimeter of the playing surface with not a hint of trouble. And this despite crowds of almost 40,000 bulging Meadow Lane or the City Ground.

For the city's first derby game since February, 1935, 90 officers and two mounted policeman were employed to supervise. They were never called into action, though, during what was reported to be a good-natured contest both on and off the park. Children, as a generation may recall, were pushed to the front and allowed to see the game from the running track around the pitch.

Notts were top of Division Three's southern section and arrived at the City Ground unbeaten in 16 matches. Forest, one place below but five points adrift, were hoping for a fifth consecutive victory. In the dressing room beforehand, County players, and Lawton in particular, were anticipating the fixture as eagerly as the fans.

The Wimbledon team of the 1980s perhaps thought that they invented the term 'Crazy Gang' and imagined their antics as original and novel. But County's pre-match ritual made them appear rather tame by comparison.

"I made the team go stark naked and perform an Indian war dance in the dressing room," Lawton would recall with a glint in his eye many years later. "It was my antidote for tension. Most of the lads were always uptight before a big game and with a capacity crowd queueing to get in at the turnstiles we needed some sort of relief. The sight of them all whooping and hollering was a sight for sore eyes. But it worked!"

Jackie Sewell recalls Lawton was also prowling around the visitors' dressing room with a tad more apprehension than was usual. "I had never seen him like that, he was like an animal stalking the place. I said 'why don't you relax,' because that was the advice he always gave me but he snapped at me and told me to shut up. 'I've got the mortgage on my house in Mapperley on this,' he said. 'I won't be able to pay it if we lose. Don't go missing any chances today otherwise I'll be kicking you over the top of the stand by your backside.' Now I was only a single lad with no responsibilities like a wife or mortgage. I don't know how much was the truth and how much he was trying to psyche himself up but he went on to score one of the most memorable goals I've ever witnessed."

The headed goal which is still debated in Nottingham today arrived in the 28th minute after a period of sustained pressure. With the wind at their backs, County's impressive attacking flair was to the fore, Frank Broome giving them width and pace on the right wing with Sewell and Lawton darting down the middle to disrupt a shaky Forest defence in which the normally indomitable Horace Gager, the captain, was struggling to cope.

It was from Broome's right wing corner that Lawton climbed to thunder a header beyond Harry Walker, the Forest goalkeeper, who scarcely moved as it entered the net like a tracer bullet.

Gager measured the distance at 30 yards; Crawford White, of the Daily Express, noted that "Lawton rose two feet higher than anyone else... near the line of the penalty box." Contemporary photographs reveal an effort from around 10 yards out. Even so, White reported it was the "the hardest header of his [Lawton's] distinguished career... I have never seen anything like it. He made a spectacular leap, timed the flight of the ball uncannily and nodded his head. The next thing the crowd saw was the ball hurtling past the Forest goalkeeper... soccer sorcery."

The local Football Post recorded that it was a "grand" goal in its running copy. On reflection the following week, Little John penned in his County notes thus: "The County are playing marvellously well together as a team. No wonder on the play of Lawton that his name has come into the headlines again with the query as to why he is still overlooked for international matches. Surely the unanimous opinion of all the leading sports writers of the day present at the City Ground cannot be wrong, Lawton today is as good as ever he was and his play still has that classical touch which cannot be emulated by another leader." Lawton himself recalled the moment years later: "Some folk would have you believe it was my only goal such was the publicity it received. Frank Broome took a corner on the right to the Bridgford End of the ground. He swung it out a bit too far and I met it just right, on the run and in mid-air. They say where there's no sense there's no feeling, so maybe that's why I scored so many with my head!" Sewell has the last word on the goal: "Frank was told to hit the ball at an angle somewhere in the region of the penalty area. In those day, centre-halves marked man-for-man in the area but Lawton began his run outside the 18-yard box so Horace Gager reckoned he could leave him alone and not worry about it. When the cross came in, though, Tommy had made up so much ground and he seemed to take off a mile into the air. He clobbered the ball just right and it flew straight as an arrow past Harry Walker. What with the weight of the sodden ball and the timing of the run, it was simply unstoppable, inches under the cross-bar to the right-hand side of the goal."

In the gathering gloom of the second half, Wally Ardron might have levelled for Forest before Walker distinguished himself twice by denying a cheeky Lawton back-heel and then a blistering 20-yard shot from the County centre-forward.

Nevertheless, he was not to be denied when nine minutes from time, he bore *down the right wing, beat Jack Hutchinson, the left-back, and crossed low for Broome to apply the simplest of finishing touches. Tommy Capel, the Forest inside-left and most expensive player at £14,000, pulled one back in the 86th minute but County duly and deservedly prevailed to maintain the momentum at the top of the table. Such was the balance of power in the city of Nottingham then that County's next home games would encourage crowds of between 32,000 and 44,000. Only 12,000 would see Forest slip to a third successive home defeat, against Brighton, shortly before Christmas, 1949. The scales would tip decisively in Forest's favour when Brian Clough was appointed their manager in January 1975. But for all the Nottingham derby matches before or since, none is talked of in such awe and still with so much controversy as the one that witnessed the full extent of Lawton's sublime and irresistible powers to head a football.*

CHAPTER TWENTY-FIVE
1952 – BRENTFORD
MORE CAPITAL DAYS

"I'd just got on the wrong side of a lot of people at Notts that I'd done a lot of good for. They were the first to turn on me. I thought, 'They think they're great players let them get on with it.' They said the unrest in the dressing room was because of me, but they'd had no complaints when we'd been successful. I'd looked after some of them in more ways than one, done them more good turns than their own mothers." The wheels were put in motion to ship Lawton out of Meadow Lane. "Not a word was men-tioned to me until Wilf Fisher, the secretary, told me that Eric Houghton had gone to Barnsley to sign Cec McCormack. If he got him, I would be out of the side." Tommy was mystified by events. "It had been decided that I had to go. I'd been a hero at Notts, but now they were throwing me onto the scrapheap. Dropping me into the reserves wasn't going to help me make a move or save any money. They'd signed my replacement and now they'd got to pay him and me. It didn't make sense." Fisher informed Tommy that Hull City were interested in signing him. "I met their officials at Bawtry and they put an offer to me. Even though Raich Carter was the player-manager there, it wasn't the move I wanted but I did agree to go Hull the following day to see them play Forest." On November 24th, Tommy Lawton sat in the stand at Boothferry Park as Hull were beaten 4-1. "It was a favour to Raich. It was only to show the supporters that the management were trying to sign someone new."

McCormack arrived in December 1951 and Lawton played alongside him in the first team, not officially transfer-listed but the board put it around that he wanted to go "for domestic reasons. They also said they didn't want me to go, but they had a funny way of showing it. I just let them get on with it. What had annoyed me was the way they handled it. Leaving it all up to the secretary to tell me I wasn't wanted was hardly the proper manner of doing things. They'd given Hull permission to approach me, without telling me. They'd arranged the meeting at Bawtry, without first mentioning it to me. In the end I felt very let down." In January 1952, Lawton heard that Brentford were interested in signing him. "I thought that in London maybe I could hit the jackpot again. Brentford were in with a chance of promotion and I thought that maybe the next season I'd be back in the First Division again." On February 16th, Lawton ably demonstrated that he had lost none of his ability as he inspired Notts to a 5-2 win over Brentford at Meadow Lane. "Afterwards I had a word with a couple of their lads, Jimmy Hill and Ron Greenwood. They'd both asked for a transfer because they didn't get on with the manager Jackie Gibbons. I wondered whether it would be the right move after all."

On March 14th, Tommy Lawton left Meadow Lane, negotiations with Brentford had finally been completed. "I believed I'd given Notts good service. The average gates had gone up six or seven times, we'd won promotion. I'd had a hand in the coaching and development of Jackie Sewell and they'd sold him for a record fee. They bought me for £20,000, sold me for £16,000. That looks like good business to me." Brentford were slipping down the table, having taken just five points from ten games and they had sold Jimmy Hill to Fulham. Lawton's signing gave the club a much needed boost as they looked to him to put their promotion bid back on the rails. As far as the public was concerned he had lost none his charisma. 31,000 turned up at Griffin Park the next day to see his debut against Swansea, 9,000 more than had been there for the previous home game. Brentford won 3-1 and an air of optimism returned.

The championship challenge faded however, though the crowds continued to roll in. Over 100,000 saw Brentford's three games over the Easter holiday, the Griffin Park gates were closed on Good Friday, when Sheffield Wednesday, with Derek Dooley and Jackie Sewell, attracted 38,500. Dooley scored a hat-trick as Brentford's slim remaining chance of promotion vanished when they were beaten 3-2. For the first few weeks, Tommy commuted from Nottingham, catching the early express down from Victoria to Marylebone. If necessary, he stayed overnight at the Carnavon Hotel on the North Circular. Eventually he moved into a bungalow in Twickenham.

Brentford's best times were certainly behind them, but chairman Frank Davies and his brother, Harry, the vice chairman, had dreams of making them formidable again. The club needed crowds of 26,000 to break even. Lawton's signing boosted attendances initially, but they rarely averaged more than 19,000. Just before the start of the 1952/53 season, Gibbons resigned as manager, citing differences with the board. Assistant-manager Jimmy Bain, who had been with the club for some 24 years, was promoted. His first signing was left-winger Les Smith from Aston Villa, Tommy's war-time team-mate returning to his old stamping ground. Brentford made a steady start to the season but struggled from then on. When Ron Greenwood was sold to Chelsea, Brentford looked a side short of talent and long in years. Tommy was not enjoying his football, but life in general had taken a turn for the better. On September 23rd, at Caxton Hall, he married the woman he adored, Gaye Rose. Jackie Sewell was his best man. Despite some turbulent times in their marriage, Gaye remained Tommy's staunchest supporter.

Brentford were in danger of relegation. "Jimmy Bain was not a good manager, he preferred to let things happen rather than make them happen. He wasn't guiding the club in the right direction. I had numerous disagreements with him as did other players." By Christmas, the board had decided that Bain would resume his old position of assistant-manager and Lawton would take over as player-manager. At the end of the season, Brentford avoided the drop by just four points, though their calamitous run of no wins in the last five matches left them with little real hope for the following season.

Tommy Wilson, a Fulham full-back in the '50s, remembers a Second Division match in March 1953. Brentford were coming off a good run, having beaten Notts County 5-0 and, a week later, they had won 3-2 at Filbert Street against Leicester City, but then they lost at West Ham and morale had obviously taken a bit of a dip.

"There were 25,000 spectators at Craven Cottage – mainly to see Lawton of course. By half-time, we were 2-0 up and soon afterwards 5-0 ahead. Tommy Lawton just shrugged his shoulders as he kicked off again and said: "Let's get this over with." There was no fight left. I never thought that I'd see the day when Tommy Lawton gave up." Tommy knew he was up against it. "I'd got myself an 'ulcer' job. Given a free hand, if everything on the field was left up to me, then I thought I could keep Brentford up. But there was no money available for players and the youngsters coming through, like Jimmy Bloomfield, were not ready. The best players, like Hill, Greenwood, Peter Broadbent and Bill Slater had all left. I admired the work done by Matt Busby at Manchester United. He had mixed his youngsters with some good old 'uns – like Allenby Chilton, Jimmy Delaney and Jack Rowley. The trouble was, we didn't have any good old 'uns, so I had to find some."

A year or so earlier, Matt Busby had tried to sign T G Jones from Everton, to bolster his Manchester United defence. Jones, having effectively walked out of Goodison in protest at the way the club was run, was playing for Pwllheli in the Welsh league and running a hotel. Lawton spent two weeks there during the summer trying desperately to persuade his old mate to sign for Brentford. To no avail. In the meantime, three of Tommy's former England colleagues had achieved their ambition, winning the FA Cup for Blackpool at Wembley. "I was delighted for the two Stans and for Harry Johnston. It just showed anything was possible. I suppose it's the best Cup Final ever. I was pleased for them, but it just brought home to me that I was further away from winning the Cup at Wembley than ever."

Player-manager at Griffin Park was a role that Lawton did not find to his liking. He frequently lost patience with the players of lesser ability that he had around him and the whole business of playing and managing was extremely stressful. Tommy admitted that he was not ready for management, especially playing and managing. "I was only 32 or 33 and still a bit of a perfectionist. I set myself the same high standards in managing that I did in playing and just couldn't achieve the two." Having been brought up in the tough schools at Turf Moor and Goodison Park, Lawton had little time for the less capable player who, when things went wrong, turned to him and asked "What do we do now boss?" "Just imagine saying that to

Dixie – you'd get a thick ear!"

He did not think that it was possible to be a successful player-manager in the Football League. His own training had to be limited to the required minimum, there was no time available for scouting or watching the reserves, so no opportunity to build a team apart from one based on the reports and opinions of others. "When I was at Griffin Park, I was worried about our financial state, worried about our form on the field, and worried about the ever present threat of relegation. After ten months of that sort of strain I was well nigh a nervous wreck."

Bill Slater, who made a handful of appearances for Brentford as an amateur in 1952 before he joined Wolves, was not impressed by Lawton's contribution. "He was reserved and introverted most of the time, no longer a dynamic leader." The final straw of Lawton's managerial career at Brentford? "Dear Old Pals." With no money to spend in the transfer market, Lawton had brought in two players from Notts County – Frank Broome and Ian McPherson. He thought they could do a job for him and did not cost much in fees. Broome who had played for England alongside Tommy pre-war was 38. McPherson had the right pedigree, playing for Rangers pre-war and winning a championship medal with Arsenal in 1948. Tom Whittaker had managed McPherson at Highbury. He described him as "an exasperating player. He could be brilliant, at times almost better than Matthews. Yet at others he could be so ineffective." McPherson was 33 by the time he arrived at Griffin Park. During the war he had won the DFC and bar flying Mosquitos as an RAF Squadron Leader. In 1953 it was his football talent which most interested the Brentford fans and they were not too impressed. Griffin Park never saw anything from him to compare him with Matthews. The team's form and confidence slumped and on September 5th 1953, Brentford lost 3-0 at home to Bristol Rovers. Lawton was not in the line-up, but McPherson and Broome both were and from the terraces came the jeers of the crowd and the strains of "Dear Old Pals." Unused to such abuse, Tommy was hurt and upset and determined to resign the manager's job at the board meeting the following Tuesday.

Brentford lost the next match at home to Doncaster Rovers 4-1, Lawton, back in the side, scored the goal. There was a 2-1 defeat at Lincoln and then four days later a 3-0 beating by Doncaster again, this time at Belle Vue.

Tommy could hardly have been more despondent. Even at this early stage of the season, Brentford looked relegation candidates – nine games played, only three points collected and nine goals scored. The club had no cash, crowds were dwindling. There was little chance of recruiting fresh talent and a new manager had yet to be installed. Against Doncaster, Tommy had been "clobbered" and to add insult to the injury received, the referee had failed to notice the foul. To cap it all, Tommy was 200 miles away from home in midweek. He thought he had failed as a manager and was now failing as a player. He suddenly felt every one of his 33 years.

He rang Gaye.

There are several different versions of the next sequence of events. Tommy probably tried to embellish the story when he related it in later years. "Gaye sounded excited when I rang her and told me to call her back from a phone box away from the ground where no one could overhear. When I called again she said 'I've had Tom Whittaker on the phone. He wants you to play for Arsenal.'"

It is a nice story but unlikely to be strictly accurate. *In My Twenty Years of Soccer*, Tommy himself wrote that it was the Brentford chairman Frank Davies that he phoned after the Doncaster game and the chairman informed him of Arsenal's interest. It certainly seems highly doubtful that Whittaker would phone Lawton at home, especially when he only had to look at the fixtures in the paper to know that Brentford were away at Belle Vue.

According to Tommy again, he called Whittaker himself that night from Doncaster and hearing confirmation that Arsenal wanted him, resigned as manager of Brentford. Tommy's memory was definitely playing tricks – at that stage he had already quit the job.

For the correct version of events perhaps we should turn to Tom Whittaker's own *Arsenal Story*. Arsenal, defending league champions, were in the doldrums at the start of the 1953-54 season, without a win in eight games, having lost six matches including a disastrous 7-1 defeat at Sunderland. Whittaker had tried to sign new players – John Charles from Leeds, Ivor Allchurch from Swansea, Fulham's Bedford Jezzard and Bobby Robson, Johnny Morris of Leicester and Jack Froggatt from Portsmouth. For one reason or another he had failed every time.

A 2-0 win at Stamford Bridge on the Tuesday after the Roker Park defeat eased some of the immediate pressure but Whittaker was still desperate for new players, especially with his club captain, Joe Mercer, out with a long term injury.

On Thursday, September 17th, 1953, Whittaker received a telephone call in his office from the Brentford chairman, Mr Davies. He told Whittaker of Brentford's precarious financial position and said that they needed to sell their only major asset – Tommy Lawton. Whittaker replied that he did not think that Arsenal's problems would be solved even if he bought a centre-forward of Tommy's ability. "Later that day, it came to me like a flash – "Why not sign Lawton? He is still a great player and might give our inside-forwards that service they seem to be lacking. He's a colourful personality and good for the box office." He dialled Brentford's number.

Tommy was in the treatment room at Griffin Park for attention to the injury received at Doncaster the previous afternoon. An hour later he was at Highbury, "delighted at the chance of playing for a club he had always wanted to join." Tommy said that he dashed across London – "even Stirling Moss wouldn't have caught me." He also said that he tried to reason with Whittaker – "I didn't want to let him down. He was an old friend who'd been trainer of the England team pre-war. I was 33 and hadn't played in the First Division for donkey's years but he convinced me that Arsenal needed my experience and influence to pull the team together. It was a great opportunity." Tommy joined Arsenal on Friday September 18th, 1953 – six years after Chelsea had refused to let him go to Highbury; nearly eight years since Whittaker had tried to sign him from Everton and almost 17 years since George Allison had rung up Turf Moor inquiring about the availability of young Lawton. When Tommy arrived at Highbury he admitted that not joining Arsenal when he was a teenager at Burnley was "the biggest mistake I ever made in my footballing career." Unfortunately, Tommy was to make several more mistakes in his career that would lead to some extremely dark days for him.

Whittaker called the Arsenal chairman, Sir Bracewell-Smith, to inform him of the signing. The parsimonious chairman was startled, "How much did you pay for him?" he demanded. Whittaker replied "Chicken feed." Actually the fee was £10,000 with James Robertson, Arsenal's reserve right winger, going to Brentford in part exchange.

The Press Association phoned Whittaker just after midday on that Friday for confirmation of the team to play Manchester City at Highbury the following day. Whittaker slowly went through the names: "Kelsey, Wade, Barnes; Shaw, Dodgin, Bowen; Forbes, Logie, Lawton..."

"Lawton?" said the reporter. "Which Lawton?"

"Oh, just a young lad we've taken on." said Whittaker.

He was believed because earlier in the season against Huddersfield he had called on a groundstaff boy, Gerry Ward, to become the youngest player ever to represent Arsenal. However, closer questioning revealed the unlikely true story and, just as Whittaker had predicted, Tommy's name was still box office. 65,869 turned up for the match, an improvement of more than ten thousand on the previous home gate. Most of them were hardly able to believe their eyes. England's great football hero was no longer languishing in Second Division football but was back at the top at the age of 33.

Among the huge crowd were two VIPs. Team captain Joe Mercer was out of the side with injury but he travelled down from his home in Hoylake to see his old Everton team-mate make his debut in Arsenal's colours.

The 81-year-old C B Fry was also there. In his day, the ultimate sporting all rounder, Fry had played football and cricket for England and held the world long jump record for 21 years; he was a classical scholar who stood for parliament and who had turned down the offer of the throne of Albania. In his imperious way, he despatched a telegram to Whittaker saying: "I want to see what's wrong with Arsenal. Please send tickets." Whittaker obliged and, on the Monday after the 2-2 draw with City, received another telegram from Fry which read "Can't see anything wrong. Looks alright to me."

Whittaker was a big, squarely-built man with thinning hair swept back revealing a large, broad forehead and an open honest face. For up to 18 hours a day, he could usually be found at Highbury, behind his desk in his office, jacket off, sleeves rolled up, winter and summer. Tales of his immense strength were common – how he could lift up a player under each arm and carry them off the field; how one player tried to pick up Whittaker's bag containing his kit and training equipment but could only stagger half a dozen paces with it.

Born into a military family in Aldershot, he was brought up in his father's native Newcastle. He was in the Army and Navy in World War One before he joined Arsenal as a professional in 1920. Injured and forced out of playing the game at the age of 28, he took up training and physiotherapy and became manager at Highbury when he succeeded George Allison in 1947. Tommy liked and respected him and the feeling was mutual. Whittaker said after Lawton's Arsenal debut: "Lishman got both goals, the first from a pass by Tommy who became a great favourite with the crowd from the kick-off. When I saw that pass I knew the gamble of bringing back a 33-year-old centre-forward to the First Division was a success."

The game produced only the fifth point in ten games for Arsenal as they began the defence of their championship and probably proved to Tommy himself that he was not as far up the hill towards retirement as he had imagined. "I felt out of place, the difference in standard was obvious but there was no doubt, I knew then that I'd wasted my time in Divisions Two and Three. I should have stayed where I belonged, not footled about down there." Unfortunately, there was no "Welcome back, Tommy" from the Manchester City centre-half David Ewing, a tough Scot with a reputation for no nonsense football. The injury Lawton had picked up at Doncaster was still not fully cleared up and so when "Ewing clobbered me," as Tommy insisted, "I had a severe ankle injury and was out of the game for about six weeks." It was not an entirely wasted six weeks, though, for Tommy could view Whittaker close up at work as secretary-manager and physiotherapist when he tended to the injury. He was encouraged to spend as much time as possible with the rest of the team. Whittaker thought his presence would be good for morale and it did bring results as Arsenal began to climb away from the foot of the table.

Tommy also took the opportunity to visit Eamonn Andrews at Broadcasting House when he was presenting *Sports Report* on the old Light Programme. Tommy had been one of the programme's first guests in 1948, now he was renewing old acquaintances. The producer, Angus MacKay, persuaded Tommy to broadcast – even to the extent of reading the classified results. The programme was one of the first at the BBC where regional accents were acceptable – Andrews being from Ireland – but Tommy's broad Lancashire was a little too much of a cultural shock, even though he tried to flatten out the vowels. "I was OK I suppose, for a novice,' said Tommy, "but I couldn't pronounce Alloa correctly – at least not in Angus' view. It would come out as All-OA. Angus would really let rip – 'You've done it again!' he'd shout. The harder I tried to get it right, the more I would dread it as I saw the name looming up and when it came to it – out it would come again – All-OA. But it was a wonderful experience and I think, if I'd have stayed in London, then I would have probably kept on with it."

Tommy always thought that he had an aptitude to be a commentator or a sports reporter on a newspaper. His old England pal Frank Swift was a success as a columnist on the *News Of the World,* Charles Buchan was on the *News Chronicle.* Tommy reckoned he could do the job as well as many of the press men around "After all, I knew more about it than most of them did!"

In his experience he regarded the best sports journalists to be found in the provinces. His judgement may have been coloured by a national newspaper reporter making excuses for him when he had played poorly. "He blamed my teammates, said I was badly supported, when he knew that I'd had an absolute stinker and it was his job to say so." Later, Lawton discovered that the journalist wanted to ingratiate himself with him to glean some information. "I never spoke to him again." It was not until much later in life – in 1984 – that he did have a chance to prove that he would be an asset in any branch of the sporting media when the *Evening Post* in Nottingham recruited him to write a weekly column. With a mix of insight, analysis and nostalgia they were always eminently readable.

One of the players already on the Highbury staff when Lawton joined was right-winger Arthur Milton. Capped by England as replacement for the injured Tom Finney in 1951, Milton was now to play with Tommy after watching him from the terraces at Meadow Lane when he was on National Service. "It was a great experience to play with him. He was past his best when he came to Arsenal but he was still a brilliant player. Joe Mercer was already there, of course, so we had two elder statesmen from the same era and the same area – Liverpool way. They were grand characters. I was more friendly with the likes of Jimmy Logie, Don Roper and Dougie Lishman, but we all looked up to Joe and Tommy."

Milton, now retired and living in his home city of Bristol, not far from Clifton Downs, recalls his years at Highbury with great affection. "There were great days at Highbury, I really enjoyed them. I was fortunate, really lucky in fact to get a cap in the days of Matthews and Finney, but to have the chance to play with good players, well, it just made you play better."

He liked the attitude of Mercer and Lawton to the game. "On Saturdays, if we were at home, we'd go down to the Great Northern Hotel at King's Cross for lunch. Something light, a bit of chicken maybe. We'd have this team talk from Tom Whittaker and we'd all listen and then get on the coach for the ground. When we'd changed and were in the tunnel waiting to go out, Joe and Tommy would be up front and Joe would turn to us and say 'Forget all that at the hotel, let's go out and enjoy ourselves!' Tommy was more serious than Joe. He'd hold up a ball and say 'Just make sure you give this to a red shirt and you'll be alright.' They were good players and they made everyone else play that much better."

Milton suggests that the reason Arsenal signed Lawton at such a veteran stage was to try and repeat the success they had when they brought in Ronnie Rooke from Fulham. Signed at the age of 35, Rooke came into the side which won the championship in 1948, proving so effective in combination with Mercer. Rooke's success with Arsenal was also one reason for the club deciding that they did not need Lawton when he was available from Chelsea. Not that Chelsea had any intention of allowing him to move to Highbury.

CHAPTER TWENTY-SIX
1953 – ARSENAL
HALCYON DAYS

A week after the Lawton signing, Whittaker took his revitalised Arsenal side to Ninian Park for a league game against Cardiff City. Before kick-off, in the corridor outside the dressing rooms he met an old friend, Dr William Hughes, the medical officer of the Welsh FA, who was also involved with Barry Town. The pair exchanged brief pleasantries before Hughes asked: "Are you only interested in signing old fellows these days, Tom, or are you after good youngsters too?" Whittaker confirmed that he had no plans for turning Highbury into an old folks home. "In that case you should take a look at this boy we've got at Barry – a real jack-in-the box." Whittaker took Hughes' advice and had Barry watched twice in a weekend, as they beat Stonehouse of Gloucestershire in an FA Cup tie and then walloped Hastings United in the Southern League. The star of both matches was a live wire, a real bundle of energy, recently demobbed after National Service with the Royal Engineers at Aldershot. On October 1st 1953, accompanied by the Barry manager, Bill Jones, Derek Tapscott walked into Highbury for the first time, "I'd come all the way up from Cardiff on the train with Bill," said Tapscott, "never once had he mentioned where we were going. It wasn't until he bought the tube tickets at Paddington that I had any inkling we were going to Highbury." Late that afternoon, Tapscott signed for Arsenal for a fee of £2,750.

Whittaker commented that he would "forget about Tapscott for two years, while he learns his trade the 'Arsenal Way.'" The older Arsenal players, especially Tommy, took a liking to the young Welshman. "Tommy was such a help to me in training, he used to guide all the youngsters, telling us what to do and also what not to do. He taught us how to head by hanging a ball at the end of the tunnel and as we came out for training we'd have to jump and head it properly. No flick ons. He'd shout 'Head it properly, with your forehead, then it won't hurt.' Tommy, Doug Lishman, Joe Mercer, Jimmy Logie, they would all try to put right anything that was wrong with our game. When I went to the Arsenal I had a weak left foot. In no time I could shoot equally well with either foot. They'd spend hours on extra training, they didn't have to do it but they saw us as part of the team. Tommy said 'We'll help you – as long as you listen.' It was the way they'd learned from the generation before them."

The way Tommy had learned from the likes of Dixie Dean at Everton and before that at Burnley from Bob Brocklebank, Dusty Miller and Alick

Robinson. The Lawton tuition paid off. Far from being two years before Tapscott was ready for the first team, he was there in six months, having scored 13 goals in 15 Combination games and building up a great rapport with the fans of Arsenal's reserve team. On April 10th 1954, Tapscott was picked at inside-right for Arsenal against Liverpool at Highbury in place of the injured Jimmy Logie.

At five feet nine and weighing only 10st 7lbs, Tapscott appeared younger than his 21 years, but there was no doubting his enthusiasm or energy and he was still listening. "Tommy said 'I'll tell you where to go and when, where to run, where to be.' And he did! As the ball came to him, he would be going up to head it and he'd call out 'Near post, far post, flick on,' whatever. Nine out of ten times he was right. All I had to do was the running, but I didn't mind doing that for him, because he let me bang them in!"

Three precise Lawton passes in four minutes each gave Tapscott a chance to shoot. From the first he was offside. The second, he fired over the bar. From the third, his shot clipped the boot of Liverpool goalkeeper Dave Underwood but still had enough pace to cross the line. Arsenal one up after 20 minutes, Tapscott had scored on his first team debut.

Six minutes later, tragedy struck for Arsenal in an already troubled season. Skipper Joe Mercer went for a ball at the same time as full-back Joe Wade. The teammates collided with an audible, sickening crack. Mercer stayed down, his right leg fractured in two places. Mercer had pestered Whittaker all week to play against Liverpool, most of whom were friends of his as he did most of his training at their ground. Whittaker had wanted Joe to "fade out quietly" but reluctantly agreed to pick him for the match. It was the last game he ever played.

Just before half-time Don Roper made it 2-0 to the ten men and soon after the break, Lawton was prompting Tapscott again. The youngster missed a sitter, then thumped another into the side netting, before a beautifully judged through pass left him clear for his second goal. Lawton directing operations had brought the best out of Tapscott. One reporter noted "Lawton was unselfishly spoon-feeding Tapscott in the closing stages in the hope of giving the youngster a hat-trick in his first league game. Liverpool's defence was wide open to the brilliant through passes laid on by Lawton."

"My two goals against Liverpool were so simple," said Tapscott, "I just had to sidefoot them in. Tommy made it so easy for me. Afterwards he said to me 'That's the start of a good career.'" The following Monday, Wales' selectors, impressed by Tapscott's "speed, vigour and enthusiasm," picked him for his first full international – against Austria in Vienna on May 9th. Yet no Welsh official had actually seen his Arsenal debut! The selectors were tipped off by a journalist about his performance. One of them rang Whittaker who had no qualms about recommending Tapscott for a cap. The press wanted quotes. Tapscott responded modestly "I want to thank everyone at Arsenal, but especially Tommy Lawton for giving me all those goalscoring passes on Saturday." More than 40 years on, Derek Tapscott still enjoys the memory of that hectic, glorious week. "You just couldn't dream of a start to a professional career like that. First team debut, scoring two goals, then picked for Wales. Nobody's ever done that. Then on the Friday, Good Friday, we were at Portsmouth. Jimmy Dickinson, an England regular was marking me. Tommy said 'Look, we'll do just do what we did last week and they're in the bag for you.' And, with a bit of luck and Tom's knowledge, I got two more. What a start! Six days, two matches for Arsenal, four goals and a cap for Wales!"

In Tapscott, Lawton perhaps saw something of Jackie Sewell, maybe even the young Tommy. He liked the way Tapscott with that curious, skipping run would dart over to slap a seasoned pro on the back after a good move. Tommy encouraged him, tried to smooth his way and, unselfishly, set up goal scoring opportunities for him. "I only wish that I'd played with Tom ten years earlier," says Tapscott now. "I played with him at the end of his career, yet he was still quick, still had a tremendous shot with either foot and his heading ability was out of this world. I might have been a better player if I could have met him earlier, I'd have scored more goals." As it was, Tapscott scored 68 for Arsenal in 132 league and cup appearances, then another 79 in 194 league appearances for Cardiff.

In 1999, the coach of Spartak Moscow and the Russian national team, Oleg Romantsev, was outlining his belief in the flow of football psychology from one generation to the next. Lawton would have agreed that the ideas he learned from the likes of George Brown and Dixie Dean were passed on through Jackie Sewell and Derek Tapscott and, later, onto Tony Hateley and Jeff Astle in a natural footballing progression. Romantsev declared "Players never get tired of winning games and that's why every victory is special. We have players at Spartak who've won six league championships and we have some who've yet to win a thing. The psychology of the winner is that it is passed on from generation to generation. Their predecessors helped them to win. Now it is their turn to help the new generation succeed."

There is nothing new about the way that footballing knowledge is passed on from generation to generation and despite the advent of modern multi-media aids, simple demonstration and word of mouth remain the best ways.

At the start of the 1954/55 season, Lawton was laid low with a bad cold. Whittaker decided against picking Tapscott for the first match at home to Newcastle United, preferring Cliff Holton at centre-forward and Jimmy Logie at inside-right. Tapscott came in for the next game at Everton, Lawton returned for the third of the season at West Bromwich Albion, but Arsenal lost all three – shades of the previous season looming. Then one home victory against Everton was followed by another – against Tottenham and the clouds were lifting – though one newspaper thought Tottenham should have been soundly thrashed by much more than 2-0

"Lawton was a model for any young centre-forward with his head flicks, generalship and positioning" but when it came to converting chances, he was, it was suggested, now "far too slow." When Sheffield United visited Highbury on September 11th, the Arsenal machine was running smoothly. Lawton was up for a header in the first minute that was palmed away off the line by full-back Graham Shaw. Alex Forbes scored the penalty. In the 66th minute, a neat Lawton back-heel sent Tapscott away to score Arsenal's third of the match and his first of the season. Arsenal won 4-0 but Lawton had yet to get off the mark. Again he was a target of criticism in the press – "he had quite a number of chances of the sort he would have snatched in his earlier days." Lawton usually dismissed criticism from the press. However, it often stimulated him to put on a show. Sure enough, he scored two in a 4-0 home win over Burnley, and, next game, two more in a 3-3 draw at Leicester City. As early as the second minute, no doubt inspired by a record league crowd of 42,486, Lawton was away from the defence like a young colt and fired in a shot that brought an excellent save out of the Scottish international goalkeeper John Anderson. After 33 minutes, Lawton stabbed one goal in from a Tapscott pass, then produced a typical header in the 77th minute to salvage a point. *The Leicester Mercury* was impressed "His ease and grace in making the quickest of headway certainly gave the home defence some trying moments." The most remarkable moment of all came just after half-time when a fierce shot from Roper caught Lawton full in the face. In an instant he spun onto the still dropping ball and volleyed it a fraction over the bar. Finished? Not yet, but he definitely felt it after Arsenal's next excursion.

After Arsenal's irregular start to the season, Tom Whittaker was in two minds about the club's proposed midweek trip to Moscow for an exhibition game against Dynamo. The Soviets had specifically requested that Arsenal make the trip, which made the invitation difficult to turn down. Arsenal would be the first foreign club side to play behind the Iron Curtain. Yet no help was forthcoming from The Football League who refused to postpone either the Leicester game or the next match away to Sheffield Wednesday the following weekend. So Arsenal were forced to play three away games in a week while travelling over 3,500 miles when transportation systems were not as sophisticated as nowadays. The Arsenal team caught the London express from Leicester Central to Marylebone. Tommy recalled: "We had a meal on the train. If we'd have known what was coming, we'd have had everything on the menu! Before we got into Marylebone, Billy Milne, our trainer, came round and told us that we had time to go home and pack a few 'extras' but that we had to be at the Cobourg Court Hotel in Bayswater by midnight. Well, it was gone nine o'clock by the time we got off the train. Walley Barnes and I lived close to each other in North London – in Palmer's Green – so we jumped in a taxi. By the time it reached my place it a quarter past ten. So we arranged for the driver to take Walley on to his house then come straight back for me. In the meantime I'd had chance to say hello and goodbye to Gaye, pack a bag with some clean clothes before heading back to pick up Walley again. He'd picked up his bag, said hello to his wife Joan and dashed out of the door. It was just the start of a hectic week, a never-to-be-forgotten trip."

The Arsenal party was up before dawn and shepherded onto the team coach for the journey to Northolt Airport near Uxbridge. As they boarded the coach, the players were handed their passports, stamped with newly acquired visas, granted, at the last possible moment by the Soviet Embassy. "It was then that we realised that it was not going to be a straight-forward trip – fly there, play the game, fly back. Oh no! Left on the pavement outside the hotel were about 50 of our fans from the Arsenal Supporters' Club who'd forked out about £200 each to come with us. Really, they were subsidising the players. And there were three or four press men including Peter Wilson and Roy Peskett. They'd all been refused visas and couldn't come. So they got a bit of a ribbing from the rest of us. You know 'found out about your criminal record have they?' that sort of thing. We were all a bit giddy, very excited. Even me, at, what 35, I was thrilled at the chance to go behind the Iron Curtain." It was an historic trip. The Soviet Union was effectively closed to westerners because of the Cold War. It was a journey into, if not quite the unknown, certainly the most mysterious.

Two BEA Vickers Viscounts had been laid on to take the party on the first leg of the journey to Prague. For Tommy, this was an eye opener. Previous journeys by air had been in the likes of war-time Dakotas. A Viscount, with its four prop jets and comfortable cabin, was comparative luxury. "I'd never seen anything like it. No noise, no bumps it was like a flying hotel." There were surprises all the way. The sensitive nature of East-West politics at the time meant that the Viscounts were under strict orders to arrive in Czechoslovakian airspace between 3.59 pm and 4.01 pm. These were the first British airliners to arrive in Prague for five years. Eight Russian MIG fighters escorted them until they were safely on the ground. The BEA planes were given half-an-hour to off load, refuel and take off again. As they disappeared into the clouds, the team was pointed in the direction of two Aeroflot planes that were to take them on the next leg of the journey. "Well, you wouldn't believe it. They looked like something out of the war, the first one. No luxury this time. It was freezing cold and didn't even have seat belts. We had been travelling about 11 hours and all we'd had was a cup of coffee. We were told that lunch would be served on the plane but saw no sign of it. About an hour into the flight we weren't cold anymore but boiling hot! It was a most uncomfortable journey and all they gave us was a cup of cold tea and some hard tasteless biscuits." After about three hours flying, Walley Barnes spotted lights on the ground and asked the stewardess whether they coming into Moscow. "Niet' she replied. When they disembarked, Arsenal found they were in Warsaw. The planes were refuelled and the players went in search of something to eat in the airport building. They were disappointed. "There were shops, of a sort, but there was nothing to buy. No cafe or restaurant or even a canteen. So we just sat around. Raymond Glendenning was the only one with any cigarettes left, so we smoked his and trooped back onto the plane regretting setting off in the first place."

Having been unbearably hot before landing at Warsaw, the plane was now freezing cold again. After take off, food again failed to make an appearance. Tom Whittaker was sitting across from Tommy alongside the secretary of the Football Association, Sir Stanley Rous. Whittaker told him "We will never do this again." Two hours after Warsaw, Jack Kelsey spotted lights below. "Moscow!" he exclaimed. Once again the answer was a stern "Niet." This time it was Minsk. The other aircraft had been waiting for more than an hour at Minsk for the main party to arrive. When it eventually touched down, Lawton entertained them and mystified the Russian interpreters and guides by telling them "We've been in five countries since Prague. We've been round Everest and I don't know how Tensing climbed it! We've been to Moscow twice but couldn't get across the river! And we were in the salt mines! They gave us swords. You slice the salt into blocks, then you pick up a block, hold it above your head and stagger up a ladder." With the appropriate actions, it was a funny routine and buoyed up the spirits of a very depressed and weary set of footballers. "There were three Russians who were with us all the time from Prague. Sitting together, glum-faced. They never spoke to us through the whole trip. We called them the 'Three Stooges.' I suppose they were KGB or whatever. Anyway, while the rest of us were laughing and joking, their expressions never changed. Not a flicker."

Food was eventually provided – but not to the satisfaction of the team. Tom Whittaker took one look at the chicken soup "with bits of long dead chicken floating about" and decided to stick to tea with lemon. Most of the players followed suit when Lawton ladled out a chicken leg that was covered in "big, black pores. And there was some other meat that was so rubbery none of us could get it down." They stayed at Minsk airfield until 1 am, expecting at any moment to be called back to the planes for the onward journey to Moscow. Instead, they were hustled into an ancient bus as an interpreter explained that the weather was now too bad for them to continue. Lawton's group was taken to a ten-storey building and shown into a dimly lit dormitory. In the one room there were 25 single beds. Whittaker noted that "a number of shadowy figures were already fast asleep and snoring." Two hours later they were woken up for the bus ride back to the airport. There were only two "rather grubby" lavatories and two wash basins for each floor so the mighty Arsenal were, as Lawton described, "a collection of unwashed, unshaven, tired, hungry and dispirited fellows" who boarded the planes for the two hour flight to Moscow.

Mikhail Semichastny, captain of the Dynamo team that had played Chelsea in 1945, welcomed Tommy on arrival at Moscow. There were speeches, bouquets of flowers, but still no food. In fact nothing until the party arrived at the Hotel Mockba in Red Square at 12.30 pm.

"The lads really tucked in – we were starving! Then we were supposed to rest for a couple of hours, but most of us spent the time checking for hidden microphones. We looked everywhere, under the beds, behind pictures, in flower vases. We inspected the walls for spy holes. You see, we believed what we'd read in the papers and in spy stories, that everyone from the capitalist west would be watched night and day. Well, we weren't! At least, I don't think we were! They treated us like VIPs, the hospitality was just overwhelming."

Seemingly to his own surprise, Tommy enjoyed Moscow. "I thought it was magnificent – all those beautiful buildings, the Kremlin, Lenin's tomb, the University. It was like something out of the Arabian nights. And the people were far from the cold, secretive lot that was the general impression at the time." Training at the Dynamo stadium on that first afternoon in Moscow was also an event. "We were used to the spacious Highbury dressing rooms with the underfloor heating and so on, but in Moscow, they had lounges with couches and easy chairs. Carpets and tapestries. The only problem was when we went out on the pitch. The ground was heavy, the grass long and tough. But the stadium itself was a magnificent sight."

He was a star in Russia. Crowds that gathered to watch Arsenal training in the Dynamo stadium pointed him out to each other, while whispering his name – "Lowton." The match kicked off in the evening of Tuesday October the 15th. Arsenal, took a while to find their bearings, then settled down to play well against a fast moving Dynamo side who led 1-0 at half-time after a goal from their inside-forward Ilyin. In the second half, Arsenal had nothing left to give, conceded four more goals and Dynamo also missed a penalty. Whittaker described it as "a depressing defeat" while Lawton thought that "no club side in the world could have won there after the experience we'd endured." The following day, October 6th, Tommy was delighted by a surprise 35th birthday lunch, arranged by the Dynamo club at the hotel. Caviar, steaks, a huge ice cream birthday cake, drinks and a special gift – a Russian-made camera. Semichastny was, of course, in attendance as was Kovic, who had played in goal on the Dynamo Tour of '45. Later that day, a reception at the British Embassy ensured that most of the players were partying to the early hours. On arrival back at the hotel, they were surprised to find Tom Whittaker waiting in the lobby. "I thought, oh Lord, that's torn it!' said Lawton. " But he didn't seem to be bothered at all because he was obviously worried about something else. In fact he was waiting for our passports with the exit visas to come back from the Kremlin. There was only about an hour to go before we had to leave for the airport." The passports duly arrived and Arsenal were able to leave for home, once again via Prague, but this time through a series of violent snowstorms.

On arrival back at Northolt, Lawton, Barnes and Kelsey were met by the BBC to be interviewed for that evening's *Sportsview*. "It's a good job they got hold of us that night," said Tommy. "Because if we'd have found out what the press were saying about us on that trip, then we'd have been taken off the air! The papers had panned us and the public was sneering at us, but nobody had mentioned that the journey there was so difficult and uncomfortable. That we'd had no food and hardly any sleep. All the public knew was that we'd been hammered in Moscow and it wasn't a good performance. Kenneth Wolstenholme was about the only one who gave us any credit."

Tommy was overlooking the fact that English football was at a low ebb. Earlier in the year, Hungary had beaten England 7-1 in Budapest, the second such drubbing in six months. In the World Cup in Switzerland that summer, England were knocked out in the quarter finals by the holders Uruguay, although there were signs that with the likes of Tommy's former teammates, Wright, Finney and Matthews, some respectability was returning to English football. Even so, it was no surprise that the press saw the defeat in Moscow as yet another illustration of the ills of the English game.

Lawton admitted that it was disappointing defeat, especially as he was firmly of the opinion that the 1954 Dynamo side was not as good as the 1945 version – "not in the same street! The '45 side would have beaten us by ten goals. They had better ball players, they were more solid all round, they were faster and they shot better and more accurately." He also preferred to accentuate the positive. "Sporting links and especially the interchange of football teams between countries leads to better understanding. We found out things about the Russians. They discovered things about us. The wider knowledge of other lives and customs can only be good. Not at a political level perhaps, but just at a level akin to the general public."

CHAPTER TWENTY-SEVEN

1954 – ARSENAL
FINAL LAST CHANCE

Tom Whittaker later questioned the wisdom of travelling to Moscow, "but we accepted the match because Dynamo specially invited Arsenal. I suppose you can't turn down an invitation as pressing as this." As a diplomatic exercise, it was probably a success. In footballing terms, it was a shambles. "Maybe the journey had something to do with it," said Whittaker, "but that is, of course, not an excuse." Tommy was quietly sarcastic even against the boss he respected. "We'd missed two night's sleep. That had it's effect. Of course, it was no excuse!"

The day after the return from Moscow, Arsenal were away again – against Sheffield Wednesday at Hillsborough. With Logie and Lishman unfit, Tapscott and Lawton had to play. Alongside them was Jimmy Bloomfield, making only his second appearance for Arsenal. After such a draining midweek journey, little was expected, but they secured their first away win of the season, 2-1, Bloomfield scoring the winner, his first goal for the club, after Tapscott had played a major part. Tommy was fit to appear in only two of the next ten league games plus the annual friendly against Racing Club de Paris. Arsenal went into a slump, winning only once during that period. Whittaker was after new blood, putting in a bid for Aston Villa's influential wing half, Danny Blanchflower. As Tottenham were also in for him, Villa could name their price. Eventually they decided to ask £40,000, the Arsenal selectors baulked at this, leaving Spurs to get their man and future captain of their famous double winning side of 1961. Arsenal's policy of refusing to pay what they regarded as inflated fees for players was to cost them any chance of a return to their former prom-inence. Patching up the team with veterans like Lawton and hoping bargain-priced youngsters like Tapscott would reach full potential was becoming an old-fashioned option.

Lawton was back in the first team on Christmas Day 1954. Arsenal beat Chelsea at home before 47,178 and Lawton scored the goal. It was Ron Greenwood's last game for Chelsea. "I lost my place to Stan Wicks for the Boxing Day return at Stamford Bridge. Tommy heard that I'd been dropped before the second game and he said to me 'Don't worry, I'm going to murder Wicks and then you'll get your place back.' But Wicks was young and did well. The match was drawn and he kept his place." In fact, Chelsea were to lose only three more league games that season as, under former Arsenal star Ted Drake, they won the championship for the first time in their history.

Lawton – now 35 – realised 1955 would most likely be his last chance of achieving his sole remaining playing ambition – appearing at Wembley in an FA Cup final. It would have been a grand way to conclude his illustrious career, having been disappointed in the Cup "my bogey competition' so often in the past.

On January 8th 1955, Cardiff City came to town in the FA Cup third round. With Welsh international Trevor Ford at centre-forward, Cardiff, then in the First Division, were a dangerous side and were only beaten when Lawton scored in the closing stages. He had been closely marked throughout by Stan Montgomery, the Cardiff centre-half, who had played against Lawton before – in Division 3 (South) and Division Two so knew what to expect or so he thought. After the game, Derek Tapscott caught the train home to Wales from Paddington and met up with the Cardiff players in the Buffet car. He was cornered by Montgomery. "He only had one bloody kick all match and he scored!" he exclaimed. "It's bloody disgusting!" Tapscott just smiled. "One kick's enough, Stan. What a goal though!"

Now 68, Tapscott remains at his fighting weight – ten-and-a-half-stone – living close to Whitchurch Golf Club. "I occasionally see Stan around the village where I live. He always comes up and says 'I know what you're going to say – one touch is enough!' He's never forgotten it!" Montgomery is among the centre-halves who regarded Tommy as their most difficult opponent. "He was definitely the best player I ever had to mark. He had everything. Just think about it, he would have been worth a fortune today. We used to get to know our opponents during matches – quite often we would be chatting away as it really was man-to-man marking in those days. Tommy liked a chat, so did Stan Mortensen, but then, whoosh! They'd be off!"

The result should have kick-started Arsenal's season and given renewed impetus to Lawton's ambition. In round four, Arsenal drew the champions Wolves – away. Whittaker was bold enough to state "A win here and we're favourites." January 29th 1955; the tie of the round. 52,857 at Molineux. Arsenal were in form with Doug Lishman and Don Roper scoring goals, Derek Tapscott had replaced Jimmy Logie in the side and was convinced Arsenal would beat Wolves. "I can see Tommy now, head way up above Bert Williams' hands. Bert was a great goalkeeper, but Tommy was well above him and seemed to be heading it down but it went just over the bar. If he'd have scored then, we'd have won. I'm certain of that." Arsenal lost to a 60th minute Roy Swinbourne goal. According to Whittaker "some of our players lost their concentration for the vital split second which means defeat." Dennis Wilshaw had swept in a cross from the left that beat goalkeeper Jack Kelsey. Dennis Evans cleared, spectacularly, from underneath the bar. As Les Smith placed the ball for the corner-kick, Arsenal were still congratulating Evans on his acrobatics. Swinbourne rose unchallenged to head in. Tommy was right – he never did have another chance in the FA Cup though he said at the time that "even now, I am hoping against hope that I might pull off my dearest ambition." Perhaps saddest of all, two weeks after the Molineux defeat, Tommy returned with Arsenal to Burnley, where it all started for him almost 20 years earlier. He was determined to prove to his old fans that he could still play. Arsenal were outplayed and lost 3-0, "Nothing went right for me or the team and my old Burnley pals went away convinced that Tommy Lawton, the young lad who started his career amongst them, was a has-been." It was his last appearance at Turf Moor. According to Derek Tapscott, "I was fortunate, very fortunate to play with two great centre-forwards in my early days. The first was Stan Richards at Barry Town." Richards was small for a centre-forward (5'10") and entered the professional game late, at 28 with Cardiff City." In 57 appearances he scored 40 goals and was called up for his one cap for Wales, when Trevor Ford was injured for the match with England at Maine Road in 1946. Wales lost 3-0, Lawton scored one and made two for Wilf Mannion. Richards later played for Swansea before joining Barry.

By the time Tapscott came on the scene, Richards was 35. "Yes, Stan was at the end of his career, but what a centre-forward. A great header of a ball. And there were a few around – Lofthouse, Milburn, Mortensen, Ford, John Charles – but Tommy was the best of the lot. He was just the greatest and always will be. I was a fan of Tommy's before I went to the Arsenal. As a forward myself, I always admired him. There was something different about him, an aura about him. The height he used to get and he used to hang in the air for so long. You just wondered how he did it – did he have wings? Nobody could head a ball as hard as Tommy. Lofthouse, John Charles, Nobody. John Toshack? Well, I don't think that Tosh headed a ball properly, he never got behind it. He was fortunate because he was tall and at flick ons he was brilliant, but heading a ball properly? No! Not after you'd seen Tommy Lawton!"

Arthur Milton after he left Highbury, played in the Bristol City that won the Third Division South title in 1955. His centre-forward was John Atyeo – "a great goalscorer, a very strong, big lad, good in the air. But he was entirely different to Tommy Lawton. The mark of a good player is that he makes other players play well. Tommy did that. So did Jimmy Logie at Highbury, but Atyeo couldn't do that. He relied on other people to make the goals for him." Atyeo was one of Lawton's successors as centre-forward of England, playing six times between 1955 and 1957, scoring five goals and never appearing on the losing side. Competition was tough though coming from the likes of Tommy Taylor, Derek Kevan, even the versatile Tom Finney and Atyeo was never an established member of the side despite a brilliant record 314 goals in 596 league games) with Bristol City.

CHAPTER TWENTY-EIGHT

1956 – KETTERING HIGHBURY TO ROCKINGHAM ROAD

There has never been any doubt that Tommy enjoyed his two years at Highbury, even though, through injury mainly, he did not play as frequently as he would have liked and, certainly, he would have wanted a higher goal tally. Yet, while at Arsenal, he was projected back onto the main stage – the First Division – with a top class club and he revelled in the limelight. "If a player wants a transfer from this club, you can take it from me – there's something wrong with the player." Unfortunately, at Highbury in the '50s, there was something radically wrong with a club that was living on past glories and showing a marked reluctance to spend in the transfer market at the going rate.

Tommy became a near regular on BBC Radio's sports programmes, he appeared on television game shows such as *What's My Line?* with Gilbert Harding and Lady Isobel Barnett and he received numerous invitations to fashionable openings and parties, first nights and exhibitions. He made friends with the stars. One in particular was Jimmy Young, then a singer, a friendship which had begun in Lawton's Chelsea days and continued while he was at Arsenal. Doors were open to Tommy. Everyone it seemed wanted to know Tommy Lawton. Colin Cowdrey, the great England batsman recalled Tommy and Stanley Matthews appearing in the England dressing room at Lord's during a rain delay in a Test match. "They recounted the great days – and I was fired by their enthusiasm for the game and their dedication to natural fitness. Just imagine my excitement. As a youngster I watched football every Saturday, seeing Tommy leap to head a Matthews centre is an abiding memory." In later years, Lord Cowdrey called on Lawton in Nottingham. "It was sad. He was obviously not very well." Eventually, the constant attention made Tommy uncomfortable. "I was barely able to go anywhere without attracting attention. I couldn't just go for a quiet drink like any normal chap and sit in the corner with the paper doing the crossword; there was always someone who'd come over and try to start a conversation, always the same old conversation – 'What about that goal...' or 'When you came to play at...

"Basically I'm a loner," he admitted. "I have always preferred my own company." Even though he made it clear that he did not want to be approached, too many would refuse to be put off. 'I suppose it was so they could lord it with their cronies saying 'When I was having a drink with Tommy Lawton the other day...' It made them feel good, but it did nothing for me." Yet, sometimes, it was difficult to resist performing the role the public expected. "Because I was famous, people thought I was a playboy! Those who really know me, know that was just untrue. We did not go to a nightclub in London – we couldn't afford it. I'll admit, though, that, occasionally, I did put on a front and played up to the image the public had of me." Eventually, rather than court trouble, he decided never to be seen alone in a pub or a bar. A decision provoked when in 1953, his inside-forward and sometime captain at Highbury, Jimmy Logie, had been the subject of an orchestrated campaign by supporters, disgruntled by Arsenal's abject start in defence of their championship. It was alleged that Logie had been seen drunk late at night before matches. Tom Whittaker knew the allegations to be untrue and spoke out in defence of Logie while impressing on the rest of the team the importance of not providing trouble makers with the slightest ammunition. For the remainder of his playing days, Tommy took the advice.

Derek Tapscott remembers Tommy at Arsenal as "being always immaculately dressed. But then he had to be because you weren't allowed to walk up the steps at Highbury without wearing a jacket and tie. For away matches it was always blazers or suits." Arsenal was a brilliantly well organised club by the standards of the 1950s. Under Whittaker they employed 11 paid scouts, operating all over Britain and Ireland, plus several other contacts abroad, all passing on information about clubs, players and methods. The drawback was, that for all their fine organisation, Arsenal were always likely to be outbid in the transfer market because of their reluctance to pay, as the board saw it, inflated fees. Unfortunately for the club, the youngsters were not training on as quickly or in as great a number as had been hoped and the reliance on experienced veterans was pronounced. They also had a tendency to look back to their great days of a generation earlier and insist on doing things the renowned 'Arsenal Way.' It was a way that had its merits but which was rapidly becoming outmoded, though few other clubs could boast having made over £300,000 profit since the war ten years before. It was some turn around. The boom in gates ensured that Arsenal, who had emerged from the war years more than £160,000 in debt, were now the "Bank of England" club but wary of bargaining for players they wanted through transfers for fear of jeopardising that wealth. Arthur Milton blames Tom Whittaker for the decline in Arsenal's fortunes. "Looking back, Whittaker only won things with the players that had been left him by George Allison. When it came to replacing people, I don't think he was that good a judge. I mean, I thought Jimmy Logie was 50 per cent of the side, yet he got rid of him after the Spartak game and replaced him with Derek Tapscott. Well, I found with Tapscott that when I used to go down the wing it was never there and when I didn't go, it was! I don't think that Tom Whittaker helped the club or himself and, in the end, the worry of it all killed him." Milton is highly qualified to speak of the "Spartak Incident." On November 9th 1954, Arsenal entertained Spartak Moscow at Highbury and ten minutes into the second half were losing 2-1. Milton, according to Tom Whittaker "hared downfield and roared into the Spartak penalty at top speed, only to be hurled to the ground by a Russian defender." Referee Latychev gave Arsenal an indirect free-kick. He was immediately surrounded by protesting Arsenal players. With club captain Logie in the forefront of the protests, certainly not part of the "Arsenal Way," it was inevitable that he would be reprimanded. He never appeared again in Arsenal's first team and in February 1955, departed to be player-manager at Gravesend. In many ways it was inevitable that two of football's "grandees" – the institution, Arsenal, and the individual, Lawton, eventually should have come together.

For Tommy it was a most satisfying time in his life. His home life was at last settled with Gaye, he enjoyed being in the capital and, though circumstances later forced him to sell much of his football memorabilia, one item he never parted with was his Arsenal player's tie. Lawton was not at Highbury for long, but it was sweet while it lasted and might have been even sweeter.

In 1955, he was offered the chance by Guinness to play a major part in their advertising campaigns. Denis Compton had long been "The Brylcreem Boy' on all their posters, now Lawton was about to be the face of Guinness. His fee was a small fortune – £10,000 – but Arsenal told him to turn it down. No Arsenal player was allowed to be associated with alcohol.

The 1955/56 season had started well for Tommy. In his first game of the season against Cardiff City at Highbury he had rattled in a hat-trick in a 3-1 win, taking advantage of an inexperienced Cardiff defence. His old adversary Stan Montgomery had left Cardiff for Worcester City at the end of the previous season and his place was taken by John Frowen, still trying to make his way in the game. Lawton scored in the next three matches too, six goals in four games, while, of the other Arsenal forwards, only Tapscott and Roper were off the mark. Then the goals dried up. Arsenal, after eight games, had only that one win against Cardiff to their credit and as they stumbled to a third successive 3-1 defeat, this time away at Sunderland, Lawton had to take a hard look at himself and his prospects as a first team player. Whittaker had just paid £20,000, plus Brian Walsh, to Cardiff for wingers Gordon Nutt and Mike Tiddy. According to Arthur Milton this was another illustration that Whittaker and Arsenal were losing the plot – "He'd signed two right-wingers, without knowing it! He thought one was an outside-left and the fellow who went in part-exchange, Walsh, well, he was a better player than either of them!" Even so, suddenly, Arsenal had a surfeit of forwards in their 20's. David Herd had been signed from Stockport and Vic Groves was soon to join them from Leyton Orient; Tommy could no longer be certain of a place. On September 24th 1955, a rainy autumn day at Roker Park, Sunderland were winning easily, Len Shackleton was running the show. Arsenal were sinking to the bottom of the First Division and looked a poor side, even with the injection of new blood on the wings – Tiddy and Nutt were making their debuts. There were over 55,000 in the ground. Tommy sensed it was the end for him. He had missed one decent chance and could not get into the game. "I looked around. I thought it would be my last competitive game as a player with Arsenal, my last at that level." There was a sense of acute depression and loss. "There's no more of this for me I thought. It's the scrapheap now."

Derek Tapscott recalled: "He seemed very happy at Highbury for the short time he was there, he seemed to get on with everyone, we all looked up to him and so did the manager and the trainers, everyone had respect for Tommy. That's why I'm surprised that he never went on to a better job than he did. Once he'd left Highbury, that seemed to be it."

In October 1955, Lawton turned 36 and, although he was earning the best money of his career, £17 a week, he was playing reserve team football and so missing out on the first team bonuses. "If only I'd been born 15 or 20 years later," he would sigh in his latter years. Those of us who never had the pleasure of watching him in his prime sighed along with him. Tommy realised he had to make a decision on whether to play on, as some of his friends were content to do (indeed Stanley Matthews continued for the best part of a decade). On the other hand he could begin to prepare for, in the jargon of the times, "hanging up his boots."

He thought he would be good enough for another four or five years, slower naturally, but craftier and still with that remarkable finishing power, especially in the air. A Second or Third Division club would have benefited from signing him but Tommy, having already experienced more than enough of life as a player in the lower divisions decided to look further ahead. He again flirted with the idea of working in the media, but instead decided to stay in the game, hopefully, as a manager. At Highbury, he studied the methods of Tom Whittaker as he dealt with the players and the coaches, the office staff and the public. He began to see where he had gone wrong at Brentford and, most of all, according to Tommy, he had learned from Tom Whittaker the value of a good scouting system. Whittaker and Lawton talked about the future and it was Whittaker himself who told Tommy that if he wanted to become a manager, then he should start at the bottom and learn the trade as he worked his way up. He was insistent that Tommy should "Do the lot. Organise your own office, find your own players; in fact do all the jobs that are handled by a staff of dozens at Highbury." Eventually, Tommy agreed to follow Whittaker's advice and Arsenal officials promised to find a suitable position for him. Tommy's last senior appearance for Arsenal was in a friendly on November 21st 1955 at Ibrox, a 2-0 defeat by Rangers. There were over 35,000 in the ground. His last game ever for Arsenal was, coincidentally, against his previous club, Brentford, in a Football Combination game on

December 26th 1955. There was nothing nostalgic about it. Whittaker was concerned that the intense Christmas programme could result in a few injuries and he wanted Lawton to be as near match-fit as possible, in case he had to call on him after the holiday period. It did not happen. Tapscott, Groves and Bloomfield remained fit. They seemed to be the future. Doug Lishman, also out of the side, was attracting the interest of Nottingham Forest and it was also time for Tommy to leave the main stage. The position Arsenal suggested for him was not quite what Tommy had anticipated. When he had said that he wanted to learn the trade, he thought that a job somewhere within Highbury would have been most acceptable. In the meantime, one of Arsenal's directors had links elsewhere and the best offer came from Southern League Kettering Town. So on February 1st 1956, Tommy found himself signing for Southern League Kettering as player-manager. Another £1,000 had been added to the £61,000 in transfer fees that were paid to acquire his skills over his 20-year league career. For Tommy, it was a good deal – financially. At Highbury, he had earned a maximum of £17 a week; at Kettering he was on £1,500 a year, plus expenses, plus ten per cent of the gate receipts when the attendance was over 3,000. Yet, on reflection, some years later, Tommy thought he might have jumped ship too early.

At Arsenal, Whittaker was the secretary-manager, common at the time: he had spent over 30-years of his career as player, then trainer (really the first of the physiotherapists) and had assumed the top job, knowing that, at a club like Arsenal, the day was approaching when the two positions, secretary and manager, would have to be divided. Tommy himself never suggested that Arsenal might have made a mistake by letting him go, he would never say a word against Whittaker, but his own bleak future and, perhaps, Arsenal's lean years, might have been utterly different had he been retained on the staff at Highbury for another twelve months. Before the start of the 1955/56 season, the Arsenal chairman, Sir Bracewell-Smith, told Whittaker that it was time to look around for a young manager to take over some of the responsibilities and eventually assume the reins when Whittaker, then 57, retired. Two names were mentioned, Ted Drake and Alec Stock. Drake, the former Arsenal player, appeared five times at centre-forward for England between 1934 and 1938, but was eventually discarded at the age of 25, eclipsed by the teenage Lawton.

Drake had been a real Arsenal favourite. In his first season at Highbury, he scored 42 league goals, the club record; the following season, he scored seven goals in one match, away at Villa Park. Stock was in charge at Third Division Leyton Orient, but he had enjoyed his finest hour-and-a-half when as player-manager of Yeovil of the Southern League, he scored one of the goals that beat First Division Sunderland 2-1 in the FA Cup Fourth Round of 1949.

Meanwhile, Drake was managing Chelsea with great success, having won the championship in 1955. Bracewell-Smith and Whittaker decided that it would be neither fair nor appropriate to approach him to move to Highbury. So they settled on Stock. As Lawton started work at Kettering, Stock resigned from the manager's post at Brisbane Road and joined Arsenal on February 13th 1956 as Whittaker's assistant. It was a bold step by the normally conservative Arsenal to appoint the bright, ambitious, articulate Stock. As assistant-manager, he saw his job at Highbury as being mainly concerned with the coaching of players. Whittaker had outlined that when he said Stock's duties would be "working with the players under my direction."

Stock wanted to sweep away the old Arsenal ways that were rapidly becoming an encumbrance and instil organisation and direction. The club's resistance to change was strong, though, and the senior players reacted particularly unfavourably to Stock and his new methods. They reverted to training for only their statutory two hours each morning, something which would have been unheard of had Lawton and Mercer still been around. Stock's idea that he was there to "knock the team into shape" was not welcomed by the players and, faced with a mini-revolt, Stock found that what he said, very rarely went. On one occasion he sent an inside-forward who refused to play on the wing during a training session to Whittaker's office with instructions to wait for him there. (Derek Tapscott would not admit to being the player concerned, but did not say that he was not).

Stock entered the office a few minutes later with the intention of demanding stern action against the forward, only to find him relaxing with Whittaker over a dry sherry! The atmosphere around the old marble halls was not good. On March 24th 1956, Arsenal were away at Sheffield United. Stock was told to stay at Highbury and watch the reserves against Aldershot. While in Sheffield, the senior players held a meeting and decided: "There can be only one boss here." The youngsters, Tapscott and Haverty and Stock's ex-Orient men, Clapton and Groves were not involved, but were told of the outcome. As a result, Stock spent only 53 days at Arsenal before the Leyton Orient chairman prematurely announced that Stock was on his way back to Brisbane Road. Stock had no choice but to resign, informing Whittaker that he wanted to go back to Leyton Orient to help them win promotion from the Third Division. This was undoubtedly true, but his position at Arsenal had also become untenable. Arsenal began the search for another manager-in-waiting but the man they were looking for, perhaps, they might just have let go – to Kettering.

Derek Tapscott is most disparaging about Stock – "Tommy would have done a better job in 30 days than Stock would ever have done had he stayed longer than 53 days. Alec did not go down well at all. I would much sooner have had Lawton as coach than Stock. In the short time I was with Tommy he taught me such a lot, as he taught a lot of good players like Jimmy Bloomfield and Danny Clapton. To be honest, we learned nothing from Alec Stock." Politics perhaps played a part in Lawton's move to Kettering. Tapscott thought it was "disappointing for everyone at

Highbury when he left, we lost all that experience. Kettering wasn't big enough for Tom. He should have gone to a Division One club, then I'm sure he would have gone a long way. Perhaps his name was too big for some directors? It was such a shame, he was a great loss to the game."

It has never been satisfactorily explained why Lawton did not stay at Arsenal and integrate into their system. Whittaker thought the world of him, the players respected him. Joe Mercer, at the end of his career, had been offered a coaching post, the board apparently anxious to retain his experience but seemingly content to lose the services of Lawton. Was it because he was not "of the Arsenal" in the fashion of George Allison, Tom Whittaker and Jack Crayston? Yet the greatest of them all, Herbert Chapman was an "outsider" and Stock had no Arsenal connections. Arsenal might have helped themselves and Tommy if they had given him a post at that time instead of shuttling him off to Kettering. Tommy's son, Tom Lawton, remembers his father suggesting that Whittaker did intend him to return to Highbury in some capacity after he had served his apprenticeship at Kettering. The circumstances, though, precluded that happening.

Involved with the things he understood, football, not money, Lawton would have done a good job at a major club. Derek Tapscott says "I'm surprised that he never made it as a manager, I thought he had the capability to go a long way. I'm sure that if he had been given the chance with a top club, like the Arsenal, he would have made it."

George Edwards agrees – up to a point. "There was no system in football that helped players once they'd got to 35. It's different these days, there's fortunes around for players, but then, when you finished playing it was the scrapheap. Top players became managers of public houses, or, if they did stay in the game, they were just given a sponge and told "You're the trainer now!" George Blackburn was our trainer at Birmingham City and he couldn't stand the sight of blood, yet he was the man who was dealing with us when we were injured." It was similar even at Arsenal. Joe Mercer frequently told the story of how when he broke his leg in his last game, he dreaded the Arsenal trainer Billy Milne being the first to treat him, "otherwise I might not have had any leg left. Once when Tommy Wright of Sunderland broke his leg on a goalpost against us, he screamed 'Don't let our trainer on!' only for one of our lads to tell him 'Ours is worse than yours, Tommy.'"

"That was the kind of inadequacy that existed then," says Edwards. "What was needed was a system which looked at a player like Tommy, say, and discover that his best role would be as a PRO, representing somebody, somewhere. A system which could differentiate qualities and train them for the next stage. That is professional football as it should be. But it wasn't in those days. Players didn't even get paid properly. Today, Tommy Lawton would make a million a year and more."

CHAPTER TWENTY-NINE
1956 – KETTERING
BIG NAME – SMALL CLUB

Kettering's modest outlay on his transfer fee was immediately recouped by the publicity value of his signing which was covered by television, unheard of for a non-league club, but another illustration of Lawton's celebrity status, even as late as 1956.

Kettering were not one of the stronger sides in the Southern League. Even on Tommy's debut they lost 2-1 at home to Yeovil on a snow-covered pitch at Rockingham Road. The gate was a healthy 4,000, double the average. The locals had never seen such a crowd at their ground. A fortnight or so into the job, Tommy realised that the club had little to offer unless he made dramatic alterations to the staff. By the end of the season he had decided who he wanted to discard and who to retain and had started to cast around for characters who would improve the playing strength.

Whittaker's philosophy on scouting had been absorbed and, inevitably, Tommy turned first to his former boss for help. Kettering needed a good goalkeeper and Arsenal had four on their books, including a 20-year-old named Jim Standen.

Standen was being wasted at Highbury. At times, he was even second choice for the 'A' team, but Tommy reckoned that he might make the grade. "He looked the part but lacked confidence. The only way to cure that is by experience." Tommy made a deal, his first as manager of Kettering, "It was a gentleman's agreement with Tom Whittaker, no money changed hands." Kettering had Standen on permanent loan but in emergency he would have to return to Highbury if Arsenal found themselves short in the goal-keeping department.

Standen improved as a goalkeeper, while at the same time helping Kettering's defence. Later, he kept goal for West Ham in the days of Bobby Moore, Martin Peters and Geoff Hurst, when the Hammers won the FA Cup and the European Cup Winners' Cup at Wembley in successive years, 1964 and 1965. He was no mean cricketer either, on the Worcestershire staff from 1959 to 1970. He topped the First Class bowling averages when Worcestershire won the 1964 County Championship with 64 wickets at a cost of 13 each. Tommy was undoubtedly pleased that, ultimately, Standen reached the top. "I think that without his time at Kettering he wouldn't have gone so far."

Tommy made a good fist of that initial spell as manager at Kettering.

Training was reorganised for the part-time staff and he approached the task of rebuilding the team with enthusiasm. The players had lost the habit of winning – Lawton changed that. And he decided that he had to find his own talent. He put an advert in the *Kettering Evening Telegraph* offering young players a week's free coaching, under the guidance of "ex- England international Tommy Lawton," on the club's ground. In later years, Lawton was not highly regarded as a coach, but in 1956, it was generally thought that he had the excellent coaching attributes. As Tom Whittaker put it: "His name attracts thousands of all types and classes to the game. He has a magnetic quality. He earned this reputation by his own efforts and ability. He has a great reputation as a player and he only enhances that by the splendid work he's doing coaching youngsters in his own fine style." Tommy, however, did not rate himself as a coach – he disliked formal coaching anyway.

"I didn't have the temperament for it, I was too impatient, a per-fectionist. Players who could think for themselves I liked, the others were never going to make it." Tommy had a point. The old style secretary-manager was disappearing, replaced by the more energetic, 'track suit' type. Lawton did not fit comfortably into either category. The politically correct thinking of the time was that professional sport being a short and precarious career, one should always have a trade to fall back on. Lawton thought not. "A player can't do two jobs at the same time. If you've decided to be a professional footballer then go out and be a full time one. You have to be full time to stand up to the pace of football." He did accept, under pressure, that the 'Preston Plumber' – Tom Finney – was an exception! It is also worth noting that for two seasons, 1955-56 and 1956-57, he was officially player-manager making 34 appearances and scoring 20 goals.

By the end of the first season of Lawton at Kettering, he had managed to keep them in the First Division of the Southern League and tenth position, 17 points behind champions Guildford City, was even better than the board could have hoped for when they brought Lawton in. Effectively, in six months, he had transformed the club.

Tommy himself, meanwhile, was musing over what might have been at Highbury as he scanned a Kettering fixture list which read more like a club cricket programme than the sort of thing that he had been used to: Tonbridge, Hastings, Lovell's Athletic (the toffee makers from Newport) and Exeter City... Reserves! Meanwhile, the strain of running Arsenal and Highbury had finally taken its toll on Tom Whittaker, as it had on one of his predecessors, Herbert Chapman. Whittaker died after a heart attack on October 24th 1956. Football lost a fine man and Tommy one of his greatest admirers and supporters at a crucial time.

Shocked and saddened by the death of his managerial mentor, it became apparent to Tommy that there were few characters he could turn to for advice and, given the competition in the football world, fewer still who would offer any. But then "I thought I knew the game. I was ambitious."

By Christmas 1956 in Tommy's first full season, Kettering were ten points clear at the top of the Southern League. He had dabbled in the transfer market to good effect, signing Geoff Toseland (Kettering-born, he had spent an unsuccessful couple of seasons at Sunderland) and Jack Goodwin (Tommy knew him at Brentford). They were the wingers who supplied the ammunition for Bob Thomas (ex-Fulham and Crystal Palace) and Tommy himself. He needed time while the youngsters came through and the best way of buying that time, he thought, was to copy Whittaker at Arsenal and employ experienced players at the end of their league careers. He had enough recent knowledge of all three divisions to be aware of players who would be assets for Kettering.

In defence, experience was certainly the key. Amos Moss was secured on a free transfer from Aston Villa at the age of 34 and made captain. full-back Harry McDonald came in from Crystal Palace. Jack Wheeler was bought from Huddersfield to keep goal when Standen went back to Arsenal and Norman Plummer, a big, win-at-all-costs centre-half, was signed from Mansfield to replace Larry Canning. (Canning, a bright, intelligent Scot, was sold to Northampton in June 1956 and subsequently made a career as a football reporter for BBC Radio in the Midlands and for local newspapers).

Tommy, himself, had only one complete season at Rockingham Road with the 'Poppies." At the end of the 1956-57 season they were champions by a clear eight points having won 28 of their 42 games and lost only four. Tommy was distinctly annoyed that one of the four defeats was against "that bunch of amateurs" – 2-1 at Lovell's Athletic! In all they scored 106 goals (Tommy, for him, a mere 15 in 30 games). It was a remarkably entertaining season. Chelmsford were beaten 6-4 at home and Gravesend, who eventually finished fifth in the league that season, were thrashed 7-0. Revenge was also taken on Lovell's, when they went to Rockingham Road they were beaten 5-0.

For the local newspaper reporters, Tommy's short stay at Kettering was a godsend – a personality manager with a gift for PR and a success as well. Ian Davies recalls Lawton holding centre stage in the lounge bar of the Royal Hotel. "He would stand there, with his back to the fire answering questions about the Poppies. Somehow he would always manage to turn it into a castigation of Walter Winterbottom, the England manager, for whom Tommy had the utmost contempt. It was the only subject that I can recall him using bad language about. He was usually very mild in language." At Kettering, Tommy had done the job he had been asked to do and he thought that he could now confidently expect offers from the rest of the football world to come in. Unfortunately, the timing was not right for him to return to Highbury. Arsenal had reverted to type and appointed from within to replace Whittaker in the shape of Jack Crayston, very much in the Highbury mould, "that elegant gentleman of the football field" as Whittaker himself described him. Crayston was in charge as manager with

Bob Wall as secretary. Arsenal finished fifth in the First Division for the second year running and there were high hopes for the following season. Crayston had been a good player, eight England caps, and one of Whittaker's assistants at Highbury since 1947, dealing with some of the book keeping and scouting duties. Yet when the idea of grooming Whittaker's successor was broached first in 1955, Crayston had not been in the frame. By the end of the 1957/58 season, Arsenal were in mid-table and had been knocked out of the FA Cup ignominiously – beaten in the third round by Northampton Town of Division Three (South). Crayston resigned, frustrated by the Arsenal board's continued reluctance to part with money for transfers, in particular to spend a record fee on Cliff Jones of Swansea. Subsequently, Crayston's judgement was proved correct as Jones became a central figure in Tottenham's double winning side of 1961, alongside Danny Blanchflower who, when at Villa in October 1954, had been a target for Whittaker until the board ruled that £40,000 was too expensive a price to pay.

As Arsenal looked around again for a new manager, Lawton was not even a name that came under consideration. Joe Mercer was the favourite since he had been doing sterling work for a couple of seasons as manager of Sheffield United. After much speculation and some deliberation, he turned it down and the job went instead to George Swindin, the former Arsenal goalkeeper who had managed Peterborough United, then of the Midland League, to some giant-killing performances in the FA Cup. Lawton's record bore comparison with Swindin's, but Swindin of course had spent 17 years at Highbury and, in any case, by then Lawton had taken the decision that was to lead to some grim, miserable times for the former hero.

CHAPTER THIRTY
1957 – NOTTS COUNTY FAST DOWNHILL SLIDE

The second coming at Meadow Lane didn't quite live up to expectations. Since he described the day he put pen to contract as one of the "worst day's work of his life" when he joined Notts County originally, Lawton's first encounter should perhaps have been sufficient to sway him against ever returning. Yet even the fateful nature of that November transfer of 1947 was transcended by his decision to take charge of the Magpies. The truth was that ten years since his arrival in Nottingham, the city had moved on. A slightly more fickle and sophisticated audience awaited him now, one which was far more critical than the one that embraced with open arms as a player. A decade of social and economic change had also witnessed Nottingham Forest's slick and crowd-pleasing side emerge as top dogs on the south bank of the Trent. A far cry from Lawton's halcyon period with the Magpies.

"It sent my life on a fast, downhill slide," Lawton would recall of his return, an uncontrollable vortex that ultimately led to awful degradation, although much of it self-induced.

And yet there had been such calm in his life before the storm which began brewing in January 1957 when initial overtures were made to Lawton by Notts County. By then, even the twilight years of his playing career were effectively over, his prodigious athleticism diminished considerably, but he was making a name for himself as a manager. One of his best signings was Jack Wheeler, the former Birmingham City goalkeeper, whose reputation for consistency at the highest level was second to none. In his prime, Wheeler established a record that will never be bettered. While at Leeds Road – he and the entire Huddersfield defence, Laurie Kelly, Bill McGarry, Don McEvoy, Ron Staniforth and Len Quested – appeared in all 42 matches of Town's Division Two season of 1952-53 when they gained promotion behind Yorkshire rivals Sheffield United.

"Kettering may have been a part-time club yet it was run along the lines of a full-time one," Wheeler recalled. "He was the sort of manager who looked after his players – if you did it for him, he would make sure you were rewarded. He insisted that if the team were playing a distance away, we would travel on Friday and stay overnight. If there was a game in or near London, Tommy would usually be the centre of attraction. Everyone made a fuss of him down there, he was a celebrity." From his own playing days, Wheeler was no stranger to being on the sharp end of a Lawton foray.

"I remember when I was playing at Birmingham, we came up against County in the FA Cup with Tommy playing at centre-forward. There was a full house of 52,000 at St Andrews. We were in the First Division and they were in the third and before the game Harry Storer, our manager, told Ted Duckhouse, the centre-half, to 'let the big fella know you are there, as quickly as possible.'

"Ted was a real Black Country hard man, solid, reliable and honest but that day Tommy played deep, well behind the front two strikers. We had never encountered anything like it. He just ran the game. At half-time, Harry was fuming. 'I thought I told you to get close and stay tight on Lawton,' he said to Ted. 'But I can't go that far and follow him, boss,' Ted protested. Poor old Ted didn't know what he was supposed to do and he went back out, still muttering in his Black Country accent that he hadn't a clue what the manager wanted him to do.

"That was the beauty of Tommy's game. He had the ability to drop off and go deep like an inside-forward and go and get the ball and in those days centre-halves seldom crossed the half-way line looking for their man. We were well beaten 2-0 in the end. Tommy was outstanding. He had two good feet, timed his heading to perfection and was the easiest of front players to find. Was he the best centre-forward of all time. I'd have to say yes." With such advantages in their team, some might deduce that it was no surprise that Kettering ran away with the Southern League title in 1957. Yet the semi-professional game then was just as competitive, if not more so, than in the more modern era of football. Lawton employed himself sparingly as a player. As a manager it was his astute purchases and use of tactics that helped transform the side beyond recognition from the previous season's also-rans. It was this achievement that spurred on the Notts board to intensify their efforts to persuade Lawton to return to Meadow Lane.

George Poyser, who had been in charge since Eric Houghton's departure in 1953, had been dismissed and Len Machin, the chairman, was adamant that Lawton would replace him. "Against my better judgement, I accepted his offer. The financial rewards and a return to the League were factors that influenced me in believing it was a risk worth taking. How wrong could I be." The intrigue and subterfuge that were prevalent at Meadow Lane and so undermined the final weeks of Lawton's first spell in Nottingham were still rampant and powerful forces at the old club. Poyser had been removed as County toiled in the nether regions of Division Two and it was his successor, Frank Broome, Lawton's former England and Magpie colleague, who had inspired a sustained and successful effort to avoid relegation. Yet as early as January, 1957, news had leaked that Machin was interviewing Lawton with a view to him becoming the next manager. "The news is a big blow to me," Broome said at the time. "Following the backing I received from the players, I was called into the chairman's office and told to 'carry on'. I thought that if things went well I would have a good chance of getting the vacancy in view of the encouragement I had received. I am very disappointed and disheartened. I was told one thing and another has happened." It emerged that Lawton had been summoned to the home on Wilford Road of Machin, who was unwell with a chill. A meeting with the board and Chic Heath, the secretary, took place at the chairman's bedside. Kettering, for their part, insisted upon compensation and a game against Notts at Meadow Lane from which they would be entitled to 50 per cent of the gate money. In the event, Notts decided to bide their time. In the interim period, in the corridors of power, on the terraces and on the pitch, there was a growing feeling that Broome's position of caretaker-manager should be extended to a more permanent one and that he was the right choice to be given the opportunity of leading the team back into the First Division next season. Since the board was virtually identical to the one that sanctioned Lawton's departure five years earlier, Broome appeared to be on safe ground. His supporters, though, had not counted on the single-minded determination of Machin.

On May 10, 1957, he finally got his man when Lawton was afforded an official welcome at Meadow Lane. He took over as the highest paid manager in the League [£2,500 per annum], with unlimited expenses and a club house at his disposal. A fortnight later, Richmond House in Mapperley Park, his former matrimonial home which doubtless represented many heartbreaking and unhappy memories for Lawton, was sold at auction for £6,100. The timing was most certainly coincidence but also the kind of kismet that was ominous. A symbol of his more turbulent experiences in Nottingham during a bleak chapter of his life may have been relinquished but it was also a reminder that he had a past in the city – one which certain factions still held against him.

Among those who were resentful of Lawton's appointment was Alf Hubbard, a Notts director. He had held reservations following the initial approach in January and made them known then. He once more went public in the wake of the latest developments and told the local *Evening News* that he was amazed at the job offer to Lawton. "I was not invited to the meeting nor was Mr Linnell. They [Machin and fellow directors Frank Sherwood and Bertram Edwards] have done this off their own bat. Frank Broome told me that he had to go to see Mr Machin. Naturally I thought he would be offered the managership, as we arranged last Thursday. Since that meeting I have heard nothing. I can't understand how it can be done without a full board of directors." Len Linnell also concurred with his board-room colleague about the decision-making process. Such confrontation hardly eased the path into Meadow Lane and although Broome did eventually accept the job as assistant, (Lawton was against this but agreed to the Machin appointment to keep the peace), the seeds of discontent had already been sowed. A *vox populi* on the streets of Nottingham conducted by the *Guardian Journal* revealed a groundswell of support for Broome. "He should have been given the job," declared one Cyril Malin, a taxi driver, while Harry Walker, of Bulwell and 35 years a follower of County's fortunes, announced upon hearing the news of Lawton's appointment: "If that's the case, I've finished with Meadow Lane." Despite the rather mixed reception, Lawton expressed confidence in himself and his players having talked to Syd Dickinson, the chief scout, and Ron Wylie, the club captain. The formalities out of the way, he dashed back to Kettering in the evening to collect his Southern League championship medal at the club's celebration dinner. After that it was a month's holiday at Sutton-on-Sea with his family before preparing for pre-season training.

Wheeler was also anticipating a fresh start in his life, having been asked to join Lawton at County as first-team trainer. Having just bought a new home with his wife Olga in Kettering for £995, Wheeler was at first uncertain about the move but the offer of a club-house in Wollaton, a fashionable suburb of Nottingham, helped sway his acceptance. It was indeed a momentous decision. Lawton and a plethora of managers and players were to come and go at Meadow Lane, but Wheeler would remain an integral part of the fixtures and fittings for a further 26 years, fulfilling his duties at one stage or another, or more frequently simultaneously, as physiotherapist, team manager, kit and boot-man and painter and decorator of the gradually dilapidating wooden stands and ground. He still lives in the old club house at Wollaton, with Olga, today.

"We were playing away to Hastings and sharing a bedroom when Tommy asked me to go with him to Notts. He knew then he would be on his way during the close season. Tommy was very much a high profile figure and generous to a fault. He made sure I had a good contract but you could sense the hostility against him. And that was despite the fact that he'd sort the lads out, get them fitted for wool suits and waistcoats, nothing but the best for them really.

"Looking back, he didn't really have a chance. The board was split and the players were not all behind him. He inherited a playing staff of 33 professionals from the previous regime, an incredibly high number for what was a mediocre Second Division side. Many of them were simply not good enough. Tommy knew that and he wanted to shed ten of them at least but they were all on cast-iron contracts and few wanted to move on. Life had become a bit too comfortable."

Rather than a harmonious campaign where each individual was pulling his weight for the benefit of the club, the ensuing nine months presented only toil and struggle for Lawton and Notts County. In such an atmosphere of hostility and conflicting emotions, success was never an issue. "I don't think managerial greats such as Tom Whittaker or Herbert Chapman could have turned a club like that around given less than a year to find the answer," Lawton would reflect with justified indignation. "There was no money to strengthen the side and having seen the first team players in action at close quarters, we were desperately short for that level and it wasn't only ability. Some of the attitudes of senior professionals was quite appalling." Burdened with mediocrity, Lawton was swiftly deprived of the genuine quality in his team during the most inauspicious of beginnings. Wylie, a dependable inside-forward, suffered a severe ankle injury in the second game of the season, a 5-1 drubbing by Fulham at Meadow Lane. At first it was feared he would never play again such was the extent of the damage. He would return – but not for several months. Then worse still Gerry Carver, a play-making wing-half, picked up an long-term injury three games later. Both players had been earmarked for the future in Lawton's five year plan to rebuild Notts and take them back to the top but now he was deprived of inspiration on the pitch and loyalty, in varying quantities, off it. Tommy Asher was a young professional at Meadow Lane, 20-years-old, having served his statutory two years National Service. "There was nothing he didn't know about the game," Asher recalls. "He was the first to protect the players from the directors and their whims but some of the older players, John McGrath, Jimmy Jackson and a few others who were not in the first team, were against him. It was only natural.

"I remember playing for the reserves at Millwall and we stayed overnight in London, with all the trimmings and the lot. That was very unusual, especially for a Second Division side in those days. Without doubt he was my mentor and a great inspiration, not only to me but the team. We travelled down to Swansea just a week after I'd made my debut and we had been hammered at home in September. He walked into the dressing room, hung up his coat and said this was where he had scored his three goals for Notts in his playing days. We went out and won 3-1.

"His tactics could not be faulted but it was a body blow to me personally when he left. I lost my way totally and couldn't relate to Frank Hill, the new manager. I think I was most likely in awe of Tommy but I know when I saw him many, many years later he was very bitter about his time at County,." In fact Lawton's only significant venture into the transfer market was to purchase Stan Newsham, a highly regarded centre-forward, from Bournemouth. Despite his reputation, Newsham seldom performed for Notts. In fact, it was mooted that Lawton, aged 38, would return in an amateur capacity and be eligible to play in FA Cup and friendly games. Kettering, who still held his registration, required a fee of £1,000 while the Football Association raised no objections to his registration as an amateur providing Kettering were reimbursed appropriately.

Desperate measures in dire straits but the fact that the deadline to sign Lawton came and went without incident merely indicated the financial paucity of the board matched only by its lack of ambition, a legacy which first came to the fore with the departure of Jackie Sewell to Sheffield Wednesday in 1951 and one which has afflicted successive hierarchies at the oldest football league club in the world ever since. As well as injury, discipline, or a lack of it, in the pro ranks, scarcely nourished hopes. Lawton had been no angel during his playing days but when he encountered the likes of Peter Russell at Notts his heart must have sunk. Russell was a cult figure at the Lane, a talented centre-half who was considered, in some quarters, worthy of an England place. Unfortunately, his excessive antics and extremes served him badly as both a defender and ambassador of the game. Without application and dedication, he was a liability. "Typical of Peter, he was serving a one-match suspension when we played away to Cardiff City," Wheeler recalls. "In those days, you were not supposed to be at the ground, home or away, if you were suspended.

"In the first half of the game, Don Roby took a fearful knock and needed a stretcher to get him off the pitch. We were all in the dugout shouting instructions when suddenly we looked over at the stretcher bearers. One of them was Russell! He'd caught a lift down there with the supporters coach and then jumped over the terraces and barriers to help carry the stretcher. Well, Tommy went berserk. He could have had all of us banned and fined if anybody had noticed he was at Ninian Park! But that was the sort of thing Tommy was up against." The side's fate was sealed over a dismal Christmas campaign that began with a 3-2 home defeat inflicted by Barnsley on December 25. Thus began an eight match sequence that failed to yield a victory, a run that included three successive 3-0 defeats. By February, Lawton was assessing his squad for the summer upheavals and preparing a blueprint for the club's resurgence for the chairman's scrutiny. He could be satisfied that Tony Hateley and Jeff Astle had begun their apprenticeships at the club and point to such as those young centre-forwards to carry the Magpies back to Division Two and then higher still.

"Len Machin didn't know a football from a rugby ball," Lawton said, typically bluntly. "What he did have was personality and I believed in him. In fact, so implicitly did I have faith in him and the club that I went for six months without wages. I was asked to take a £20 drop in salary but refused. It would have meant I was earning less than I was at Kettering and believe me the people and the players were far nicer and open folk than they were at Notts." During Lawton's playing days at Meadow Lane, the club had been the beneficiary of an unprecedented increase in support and therefore gate receipts. The profit margin had become healthier overnight to the tune of £34,500 with Sewell's sale to Yorkshire. And yet just a few years on, Lawton was forced to sell Gordon Wills to Leicester for just a few thousand pounds that were necessary to sustain cash flow. Four straight losses during March was certainly the stuff of relegation form. Yet although County's destiny was indeed demotion, they might have escaped had it not been for a quite incredible escape act performed by Lincoln City. They appeared certainties to go down with Doncaster Rovers but then an abandoned game against Cardiff City in March was to be a turning point. On the same day, at home to Bristol City in the driving snow that besieged Nottingham, County lost 1-0. Lincoln, 3-1 down to Cardiff, were relieved when the game was abandoned. Duly inspired, Lincoln prevailed in their last six remaining games, taking a maximum 12 points. Notts beat Rotherham United on the final day but it was too little, far too late and they finished second from bottom, one point behind the rejuvenated Imps who had accumulated 31 points. In his first full season in a managerial capacity, the fates had seemingly conspired against Lawton from the bickering beginning to the most bitter of ends. If he was seeking solace from his superiors, inferiors or peers, he was once more out of luck. There was to be no reprieve. Lawton was summoned to Meadow Lane on a Tuesday evening and told in no uncertain terms that the board had unanimously voted to dispense with his services. Apart from the indignity of it all, there was also the question of a three-year contract which had been agreed by a gentleman's handshake between Lawton had Machin. The former player should have known better given his disappointment and the broken promises perpetrated by the previous regime. Lawton was given short shrift and three months' wages. His house in the affluent area of West Bridgford on Musters Road was, Lawton maintained, a gift from the club when he became manager. Perhaps there was confusion in its ownership. Frank Hill, the manager-elect, had expressed a desire to take up residence there and his wish was granted.

Lawton told Gaye he would never again turn to football to provide a living. His bitter resentment was perfectly understandable but his eternal reticence, he later acknowledged, was ill-advised. Lawton had much to offer the game but just as in his England days, he discovered that those who remained silent and sycophantic to those in authority often gained preference in consideration of jobs for the boys. "To be honest I was on holiday in Blackpool when the news broke," was how Wheeler remembers the news that came as such a surprise. "I think I read it in the *Daily Express*. There was no way he deserved that. He had been so unlucky in many respects but Tommy was a gentleman to the end. People accused him of so many things, especially in terms of debt and taking advantage. But the record should be put straight. People tended to take advantage of Tommy. He was a very likeable fellow and as a player, I looked up to him for his quality and class. You had to respect that and it's the kind of genuine quality you don't see in the modern game, that's for sure. Yes, he had his failings like most of us. But he brought a touch of something different to Meadow Lane. The television cameras followed him, he still dressed imm-aculately and drove a Jaguar car."

Small wonder the narrow-minded and more limited horizons of the County board and their cronies found Lawton insufferable. Some of those would well remember the swagger with which Lawton delivered his opening gambit at the club back in 1947 – laying down an edict that their good ladies were not permitted to travel on the team coach to North-ampton for his debut game or thereafter while he was captain of the team. How they must have gloated upon his departure, the news of which was announced officially on July 2, 1958. Mr H Hill, a member of the supporters' club executive, described it as a "bombshell. I have no idea what it is all about. I'm stunned."

Clearly, there was ecomomical expediency as well as political point-scoring to be considered. A new board had been reconstituted after an application to the courts. It was Machin, as chairman, and his two fellow directors Frank Sherwood and Ernest Hobson who informed Lawton of his impending dismissal. They cited Lawton's salary of £2,500 per year as the reason, say-ing it would reduce the financial strain the club was currently suffering under. "I am packing up straight away but will continue to live in Nottingham until I have made plans," Lawton told Albert Stapleton, a reporter on the *Evening News* sports desk. "This was a real shock to me especially after the board had gone to so much trouble to get me here." Significantly, the board also announced that Wylie, a considerable asset, would be put on the transfer-list. Lawton had outlined that measure and the sale of Palmer to raise much-needed funds in his five-year plan. Throughout his tenure, Lawton had tried to engender an *esprit de corps* amongst his troops, kitting them out in suits and generally treating them to a lavish lifestyle that only First Division players might have expected.

He tried to call in a favour by inviting the entire playing and coaching staff around to his West Bridgford home, seeking assurances that they would back him to the hilt despite the board's decision. Player power in the face of boardroom bluster had yet to reach its embryonic stage in football. Few assurances were forthcoming, nor could they be in such a climate of uncertainty. Wheeler was one of those who simply could not afford to have the courage of his convictions. "He asked me to resign with him but at the time I had two young kids who had just started school and I'd already given up one life in Kettering to join him in Nottingham. There was no other option. "

As he was booted out of his home, Lawton may even have sensed the irony in the situation. Throughout his playing career he had moved with the grace of ballet dancer and force of an express train on the pitch. Off it, he had careered through the corridors of power like a bull in a china shop, cracking precious egos and irritating furiously the proprietors of the game. Having gained his trust in management capacity, the board at Notts County had struck a blow for the "blazers with gin and tonics" brigade everywhere. Almost like Brian Clough two decades later, Lawton had been sucked into a situation where players and directors neither trusted nor wanted his presence. Like Clough, he was rather too opinionated for some, rather too good a player in his own right for others. The "green eyed monster" lurking inside surfaced to force Clough from office at Leeds United after 44 days as manager. He, at least, was spared the slow torture of decline and fall that Lawton endured during his eleven months at Meadow Lane. The downward spiral was locked in automatic. Destination: rock bottom and beyond.

CHAPTER THIRTY-ONE
THE FALLEN HERO
DAVID McVAY

It was around noon on a sunny September day during 1975. Following the exertions of morning training session at Meadow Lane, a few Notts County professionals headed towards the city. In an era when most players utilised their spare time with commendable prudence, the attractions of a billiard room near the city centre beckoned for afternoon entertainment. First, though, a greater magnet intervened. The Lion public house on Clumber Street. In the corner, a slightly seedy-looking gentleman of middle age. Before him on the bar was a pint of beer and a whisky chaser. The figure, buoyed by alcohol, was holding court with a selection of the male population who were unlikely to deter their host from further drinking and conversation. If they could be called friends that day, it was far from certain that he would be able to rely upon that friendship tomorrow. One of the crowd called me across. I was introduced to Tommy Lawton. "Take care of your body son and listen to what others have to say about your game," was the gist of his sermon in between finishing off a pint of Home Ales best beer in impressive style and time.

Almost inevitably one concluded that this rather shabby man in the pub, dispensing advice from beneath the optics, was a serial bore, past his sell-by date and above all, lamentably bitter about his time in football. The rashness and arrogance of youth that inspired me on that day were all but gone when some ten years later I met Lawton once again, this time not in my capacity as a naive professional footballer but a slightly more frayed-at-the-edges journalist for the Evening Post. *By then, an appreciation of the rigours of life and the outrageous fortune it can muster upon an individual had taken root, one that allowed a greater perception of Lawton's plight. Already he had captured the depths to which he had succumbed in words. "I would leave home of a morning pretending I had a job just like any other working man and I would sit all day in the old Market Square or the library till it was time to go home again. More than once it crossed my mind to walk into the Trent and just end it all." What drives a person so close to the edge of extinction is often an unfathomable riddle. Lawton's demise was no exception except that the chasm between his zenith and nadir was far bigger than most. Initially the step downwards had been an acceptable one, the time-honoured traditional calling to the public bar that awaited most ex-professional footballers in those days. On October 28, 1958, just a few months after being ousted as manager at Meadow Lane, the transfer of the licence to him as licensee at the Magna Carta in Lowdham was approved at the Nottinghamshire Shire Hall by Chief Inspector J A Pearson. The pub, owned by Hardy Hanson, the family brewery chain which dispensed Kimberley Ales, had been recommended to Lawton by a friend of the* family. His name alone would attract customers. Lowdham, a tranquil village located deep in green belt territory several miles to the east of the city, offered Lawton respite and peace of mind from the rat race.

He declared: "I am looking forward to it and plan to settle down. Football is a little precarious and we have got to look to the future." He recalled that they were probably some of the happiest times of his post-football life yet, true to form, he made a decision which ultimately was an irretrievable step in the wrong direction. He said at the time it was for the sake of his children. Tommy, his son by Gaye, had just left the toddler stage behind while Carol, his step-daughter, was running a hotel in the North West. Consequently, he left the Magna Carta in 1962, almost four years to the day that the licence was first approved. He and Gaye had experienced happiness in the interim but, nevertheless, they began their new life with little capital behind them because of the seasonal fluctuations in the pub trade. The Evening Post reported that Lawton would be seeking employment as an "outside representative" an awful euphemism for a door-to-door salesman. Armed with his sales book and awesome reputation, though, Lawton applied himself to the task in hand, calling on a few old friends and publicans and selling them life assurance. In return for their custom, often negotiated over the bar, he would buy drinks. "It started to get worse and although I was not hooked by any means, my home life, so peaceful before, began to suffer." That first year he earned £3,500, a good wage in 1963 but a gradual decline had set in. When he had departed the Magna Carta he stated categorically that he would not return to football management, "not for a £1,000 per week in wages" yet in 1965 he was tempted to take over at Kettering Town, scene of his triumphs in 1957, in a caretaker capacity. Once again he was asked to stay on but the travelling and work and family commitments precluded him from accepting the offer. A year later he was out of work because he hadn't reached his sales quota for the insurance company. There followed a succession of doomed jobs or business enterprises. One of his employers went into liquidation while Tommy Lawton Sports Goods, on Derby Road, shop premises financed by a friend, was forced to close down after just two months because its overheads became unsustainable. That Southern League championship winning side he had constructed at Kettering in 1957 was significant. Pride before a fall springs to mind but what a descent, ten unrelenting years of struggle with the one last abiding memory of the professional game he had served so well being his dismissal, with almost indecent haste and certainly conspiratorial undertones, from Notts County. His old striking partner at Notts, Jackie Sewell, had emigrated to Africa in 1960 and went on to coach national sides on the continent until returning permanently in 1973. Infrequently, he would return for fleeting visits. One such came in 1966, with Lawton nearing his lowest ebb. "I was staying at the old County Hotel, near Theatre Square, and Tommy had given me a ring to say could we meet up. There was no problem. We were mates at Notts and remained so afterwards.

"Before I first went to Africa I visited Tommy at the Magna Carta. He told me you'll need some strong cases to take all your stuff in and he produced a set of trunks for me. Never asked for them back. So there we were in the County when

Tommy says he needs a big favour. He wanted to borrow £250, which was quite a lot of money in those days. There was always the promise that he would pay it back. I had done it before, not nearly as much as that, and never seen a penny but that didn't matter. I'm a big believer if you lend people money you should be prepared not to get it back.

"I told Tommy I would have to have a word with my wife Barbara because it was a lot of money. She was in the hotel, so we had a chat and she just said you must decide. Well, I was in a reasonable financial state and I could see Tommy, now married and with a child, was struggling. So I gave him it without any strings attached.

"After I came back for good I heard a lot of people bad-mouthing Tommy and saying how much he was scrounging and so forth. Those rumours persist even today. But I won't have a word said against him. I remember in our playing days we'd nip to Tom's cafe on Trent Bridge for a cup of tea and a bacon sandwich after training. There was always an old tramp in there who was down on his luck and Tommy would buy him a mug of tea. One day, it was freezing cold with a wind blowing down Arkwright Street and he was in there. Tommy, who dressed like a tailor's dummy in immaculate clothing, took off his Crombie coat and put it round the old boy's shoulders. 'There you go grandad, this will keep you warm for a while.' It wouldn't be long before somebody had pinched the coat because it was so expensive but that was the way Tommy was with his possessions and money.

"If he did borrow cash from anyone it wasn't anything he hadn't paid out before to them. Let me tell you when we were going out on the town or for a meal when Tommy was playing at the club, he was always the first in somewhere to organise things and then the last out, usually picking up the tab. There are certain people who forget that and what he did for them, and how much he paid for this and that." There was a brief lightening of the gloom, even if was preceded by the humiliation of signing on at the dole office. "The shame I felt was unbelievable," Lawton recalled. "The social security staff were extremely kind and understanding but it was heartbreaking standing in the queue and having to sign on.

"At the time, as a family, we were reduced to sneaking behind the settee and pulling the curtains tight shut whenever someone knocked on the door. We reasoned it must be a debt collector and because we didn't have a penny to our names, I was frightened to open the door. Imagine that. Gaye and my entire family stood by me all the way even though the mess we were in was all of my own doing."

It's impossible to imagine the feeling of helplessness and impotency in the Lawton household as the family sat in darkness because the electricity supply had been cut off. The gas was similarly threatened and when the bailiffs entered one morning at 7 o'clock valuing furniture and other household goods, the abject despair must have been unbearable. "My pride and confidence had carried me to the top in the world of football. Outside the game, in trying to make a living, it was a severe handicap," he recollected. It was Vernon's Pools who offered relief from the gloom, taking Lawton on as a regional manager, appointing collectors in various neighbourhoods. After four months of relative calm, Bill Hopcroft, the vice-chairman at Notts County, rang Lawton. The phone call came on a Sunday night and out of the blue. During 1968/69 season, County, who were rock bottom of the old Fourth Division, had just relieved Billy Gray of his managerial duties and Jack Wheeler, Lawton's old team-mate and colleague with Kettering and Notts, was given temporary charge of the team. Hopcroft wanted Lawton's experience and knowledge to assist Wheeler put the Meadow Lane house in order.

For a third time of asking, the black and white hole that had twice before sucked Lawton into a false sense of security was exerting its gravitational pull. For a while, Lawton resisted marginally, keeping his busy schedule with the pools' company going while spending an increasing amount of energy and time at the Lane. Another crossroads appeared on the horizon. Inevitably Lawton, whose next birthday would be his 50th, chose the wrong turning and accepted the position of chief scout and part-time coach that had been offered by Hopcroft.

Less than a year later, a new broom swept through Meadow Lane. Jimmy Sirrel, a tough Glaswegian manager of the old school, was installed as manager at the start of the 1969 season, moving from Brentford along with Jack Dunnett, a London-based Labour MP with a safe constituency seat in The Meadows area of Nottingham, who took control of the club. Within the framework of that regime there was no room for Lawton. In January, 1970, he was effectively booted out of Notts County for the third time in his life. This last occasion was more straightforward and certainly without malice but unlike the previous departures, they were scarcely queueing up for his services outside the ground.

"I didn't even have enough to feed the family, that's how bad it was," Lawton recalled. He became dependant on hand-outs from friends, a tenner here and a fiver there, in the full knowledge that he would never be able to pay them back. His pride was severely dented even more when a newspaper published a photograph of him signing on the dole although it sparked interest in a furnishing company in Colwyn Bay who offered him a job on a reasonable salary with commission and a company car. It was to be the first of several similar ventures which were destined for catastrophe – and a visit from the constabulary. During 1969 and this most depressing chapter of Lawton's life there were eerie echoes of his past, portending to his own future, taking place in London. Amanda Lawton, his 22-year-old daughter from his first marriage whom he had virtually disowned, was appearing in Bow Street Court on charges of stealing money from George Axelrod, an American film producer. Her probation officer said she was "a pleasant girl but lived a life of fantasy." In total she had stolen almost £3,000, all of which would be recouped from her step-father, a Jamaican doctor practising on the Caribbean island. It was Amanda Lawton's mother's fourth husband.

When Lawton read the reports in the newspapers, how he must have reflected upon his words "I should have stayed at Everton and transferred the wife" with renewed sorrow. Predictably, the Welsh connection didn't last. The company was displeased with his order book and wanted their company car returned to Colwyn Bay. As his work prospects deteriorated, so did Lawton's health and while on a holiday on the East Coast, at Sutton-on-Sea, he suffered a suspected thrombosis and was taken to Louth hospital. He was discharged with the warning to take things a little easier. Several days later, at their Patterdale Road home in

Woodthorpe, two police constables paid a house call, acting upon information that Lawton was driving a stolen vehicle. In fact, it was the company car from Wales belonging to Biddulph Industries Ltd. Lawton was still awaiting a severance payment from the firm, which had not been forthcoming, and felt quite rightly that the company should at least travel to Nottingham to reclaim their own car. Eventually they did, without further payment, but not before Lawton and his family had suffered the distress of him being held in a police cell until nearly midnight and then being told to make a formal statement.

Incredibly, more national exposure at his plight led to opportunity knocking once more. The medium this time was television when Lawton was a guest of an old showbusiness friend, Eamonn Andrews, on the Today programme. Again it was a furniture concern, located in London's Tottenham Court Road, that approached the former England centre-forward, hopeful that his name would entice new clientele. The capital firm set up a business in his name, gave him a company car, £2,500 per annum plus an expenses account and a share issue for Lawton's son, Tommy junior. Compared with the £19.50 he had been receiving on the dole, Lawton suddenly had acquired instant wealth. It would not endure. Despite Lawton's best intent and genuine efforts, the firm began to distance itself from his financial affairs. Deposits in his bank account ceased but Lawton believed this to be only a temporary measure, safe in the knowledge that this was an old established company which would honour its debts. Whatever the truth of the matter, Lawton displayed a cavalier attitude all too reminiscent of his daughter Amanda's three years previously. It led to another police presence in the Lawton household, a much more serious visitation with two CID officers hauling him off to Arnold police station to make formal charges. By June, 1972, he too like his daughter was standing in the dock, of the Shire Hall court, accused of obtaining money by deception.

"There were warning signs but I realise how stupid and naive I was in failing to recognise them," Lawton conceded in retrospect. Lawton had obtained a car, colour television, wines and spirits and other luxury goods by passing dud cheques and many of those that had bounced were to friends. David Ritchie, prosecuting, asserted that dishonesty had ruined Lawton's good character and added to his misery. He added that his drinking had become a serious problem and did not help him come to terms with the reality that the glamour of his football days was over. In mitigation, it was shown that the London company, Catesbys, had employed him in good faith but that their parent company Donosbru Furnishings, had gone into liquidation last October. Lawton should have been paid £960 severance upon being made unemployed but in fact he received just £460. At the Nottingham Guildhall, on July 26, 1972, Lawton, aged 52, was put on probation for three years. He owed over £2,500 and was told to pay costs and compensation of £304.50 at £1 per week. "The people I felt most ashamed for were my family. Gaye had no idea I was cashing cheques with friends just to keep food in the fridge. She was devastated when the police called. When the case made national headlines, everyone must have thought I was a professional swindler. I was degraded, labelled a criminal yet I genuinely felt I had done nothing wrong other than being rather too trusting and naive. For months after, I didn't go out, afraid to look anyone in the face straight on."

An old acquaintance, John Mabbutt, was managing director of Floor Maintenance Services in the city, and he immediately took Lawton on his staff. A chance to "regain your self respect" was how he termed it. Lawton grasped it willingly while elsewhere there were moves afoot to come to the great man's assistance. The insularity of the game of football borders on an incestuous nature but the totally acceptable side of those in the sport came to light when Joe Mercer, a former colleague at Everton, Arsenal and during their army days together, was the instigator of a fund that raised something in the region of £10,000 for a friend in need. A testimonial game at Goodison Park was the highlight, with over 12,000 supporters turning out on a bitterly cold November evening in 1972 to show their appreciation of a man who helped bring the League championship home in 1939.

"He was a model on the field, a Bobby Charlton if you like and he brought glamour to the game. He's fallen on rough times and his old colleagues thought they would rally round and help,"said Mercer. A Great Britain XI, valued at £2m, around a year's wages for Roy Keane these days, drew 2-2 with an Everton side while Mercer, Ted Sagar, Tommy Jones, Dixie Dean and Gordon Watson, team-mates from that class of '39, welcomed him onto the pitch before kick-off. "I would have loved to have got out there among them but age had taken its toll." There were other commendable efforts in Lawton's cause, including a game at Meadow Lane, several celebrity dinners around the country and a cheque for £100 donated by George Best. But the compassion of Mercer set him aside, the last of a generation of gentlemen footballers whose generosity and kindness of spirit is anathema to most of today's pros who appear to know the price of everything but the value of nothing.

Seven days after that game, Lawton was lunching in the Savoy Hotel, London, during a Silver Wedding Anniversary celebration. Billy Wright and he represented 1947, the year of the Queen's wedding. The Pathe newsreel flickered away, images of Lawton lining up for England to play Sweden and pictures of his surprise transfer to Notts County. It had been a tumultuous week but reality would intrude sooner rather than later. The expectations of his latest job did not materialise and despite the cash donations and abundant goodwill from around the nation, Lawton strayed again. In August, 1974 he was back at the Guildhall Magistrates Court, this time charged with deception after obtaining £10 from a "trusted friend', one Roland De'Ath, the licensee of the Horse and Jockey public house in Bulwell. It was a seedy, sad affair.

During the proceedings, Mercer was called to give evidence and it emerged that the money raised for Lawton from testimonials and benefit dinners had just about paid his debts. Sir Matt Busby and Andy Beattie had been appointed to supervise a trust fund for Lawton but Mercer explained that: "By the time we had paid his creditors it was not worth setting one up."Lawton had asked De'Ath for £10 in June 1973, saying he needed to cover petrol and expenses to travel to Coventry. "I did tell Ron a lie but I had to have money. We had no food in the house. I was desperate," he told police when questioned. In breach of his probation order two years previously, Lawton was sentenced to 200 hours community service. The *following April, he was reported as being "comfortable" as he recovered in the Nottingham City Hospital from a stomach ulcer operation. The degradation and dismantling of self-esteem was complete several months later. As Christmas of 1975 approached, it was the season of goodwill but there was precious little reason to rejoice in the Lawton home. Since being admitted to hospital he had failed to pay his rates and, with efficiency unique to civil servants, Gedling Borough Council issued a distress warrant for Lawton which resulted in his arrest on November 15 and imprisonment on December 12. For non-payment of £92.56 Lawton was behind bars – but only briefly. Just hours after being taken down to the Shire Hall cells, a friend, who preferred to remain anonymous, intervened and paid his rates. Without being named, the friend told the press with befitting eloquence: "You just have to help a man like Tommy Lawton who has been left high and dry by an unkind world. People have short memories – it breaks your heart to see the people who once clung to his coat tails now forgetting him."*

CHAPTER THIRTY-TWO

1984 – NOTTINGHAM THE FINAL YEARS

Tommy Lawton was perhaps more truly at peace when he died on November 6, 1996 than less tortured souls. Weak and frail in his last days, his spirit remained as tough as the old leather boots in which he plied his trade so gracefully. A week later, a motorised hearse departed a funeral parlour in the back streets of Sneinton and weaved its processional way towards the River Trent and Meadow Lane. The route would have been familiar to Lawton even if the surrounding vista was not, demolished and re-developed by decades of social and economic change. Indiscriminate plundering in the name of progress, some might call it. At the Lane, the home of Notts County and scene of such disparate emotions and achievements for Lawton, the cortege paused before the iron gates of the famous old ground that had witnessed, like The Meadows area whose support it attracted, a mixture of destruction and renovation without quite recovering its character and mystique. County supporters, young and old, or just admirers of the truly great athletes of sport comprised a small crowd, mourning the passing of a legend and an era that would never again be repeated. They watched and reminisced about Lawton's halcyon days as the vehicles set out on the concluding leg of their journey to Bramcote Crematorium, on the outskirts of the city.

That Wednesday had been bestowed with a crisp, sunny morning, the ground underfoot moist with just enough give to take a long stud. Ideal conditions for Lawton in his prime, stalking defenders and menacing goalkeepers as he bore down relentlessly towards his target. His coffin, with a solitary England cap laid on top, was brought down the packed aisles of the chapel. His contemporaries came, Matthews, Finney *et al*, colleagues from England or like Jackie Sewell and Jack Wheeler, from Notts County.

Outside, more of the congregation unable to gain entry, listened to the service being broadcast as they paid their respects. Amid the inevitable sadness and regret, those who had known Lawton, either as a player or in his latter-day existence, also felt a certain serenity. In spite of everything, the great man had not been at odds with the world when he retired to take his place in the celestial Hall of Fame.

That, in itself, is a fitting epitaph, one from which Barrie Williams would have derived immense satisfaction. He rendered an emotive soliloquy at the funeral, one that drew inspiration from the relationship the two men forged when he was editor of the *Nottingham Evening Post*.

In 1984 Williams, whose inherent pursuit of a good story is matched only by his desire to scoop a decent football match, was driving to the City Ground to see Brian Clough's Nottingham Forest play. "I was listening to Radio Nottingham at the time and Tommy was a guest in the studio," Williams, now the editor of the *Western Morning News* based in Plymouth, recalls. "They were talking generally about football and Tommy sounded so bitter and so low. I'm sure it wasn't meant to be so but I found the whole thing very moving. I was determined then to track this bloke down."

'This bloke' might not have captured the imagination of less football-orientated editors of a leading provincial newspaper. Even those with a perfectly good grounding in the national game might not have grasped the significance in the doleful voice that emanated from the car radio that day. Williams, though, had his relations and instincts to thank for spotting what was potentially a feature laced with tragedy and laden with just about every element of human interest that coursed through its paragraphs. "Half my family were scousers, Evertonians and totally committed and devoted to the cause. The stories that my grandad and dad used to tell me about Tommy Lawton were etched on my mind. I grew up in Oswestry, a small market town, and went to school with Alan Ball, later to become an England international himself.

"We'd spend hours throwing the ball to one another using a target we painted on a shed wall for heading practice. My dad, Stan, would come home from work and every time we got near it he'd be saying it was just like Tommy Lawton. He was a legend in our house."

The 'legend' other than Robin Hood that Williams discovered in Nottinghamshire had deteriorated beyond even his own worst fears. Around then, I (David McVay) had occasion to meet Lawton again, this time as a journalist who was to either ghost his weekly column or construct articles about his life and times in present day Nottingham. In the ten years since I had first encountered him, my perception and understanding of the man had changed immensely. Also, with age had come respect and acknowledgement for his status. On first sight, his detached house in Arnold, a middle class suburb to the north of Nottingham, hardly inspired confidence. Put quite simply, the entire property needed several dollops of paint. The interior was dank, deprived of regular care. On the mantelpiece above a grimy gas fire, stood one medal, its inscription impossible to decipher. Here was the home of the most complete centre-forward English football had ever possessed. Those who pale into insignificance to such claims in the modern game will never suffer such a fate nor experience the need to burn a paltry single gas ring when the weather is inclement, merely in order to conserve supplies and money. Anyone with a sense of justice and historic relevance could not help but despair at the jaundiced fate that had befallen him. My brief was to chauffeur Lawton to a nearby sports ground where Tommy jnr, his son, would be playing rugby for Henry Mellish, a local amateur union side. There were shades of that first meeting a decade previously. We talked mainly in the club house bar, Lawton drank pints (but not whisky chasers) and proffered a good deal about the game of football. The vital difference was that here was a much more lucid man but one who was not draconian in his condemnation of contemporary professionals. It was irrelevant as to what they were earning but his frank and vivid recollections merely confirmed that he had re-discovered a certain *joie de vivre* that was to be derived from his own memories. That he was there at all conversing about such as "la-de-da" Alf Ramsey, who he claimed had taken special elocution lessons to better his standing at international level, and with such refreshing candour about himself was in no small way due to the persuasive powers of Williams.

He takes up the story of Lawton's revival thus: "Eventually we tracked him down but he was utterly reticent. I put it to him that we would like to do his life history and he just didn't want to know. He had come into my office on Forman Street in Nottingham with his mind made up, that much was obvious. He was 63 or 64 then but looked much older, stooped and totally hacked off with anything to do with football. Let's face it, the poor man was on his uppers at the time and plenty of people in life had done him a disservice. He was not about to trust anyone, especially a newspaper editor for God's sake. But what he had never lost was his pride and dignity and self respect.

"We sat and talked for about 90 minutes by which time he had finally agreed to let us have a crack at it. Let there be no doubt about, my interest was purely and unashamedly journalistic. I felt this was a cracking story and one that deserved to be told and make the Nottingham public aware of it." What Williams had secured was even greater than he had dared to imagine. A series of quality articles that took Lawton from his childhood during the Depression of the 1930s when as a 14-year-old boy he was hawked around football clubs in the north west by his grandad to the desperate depths of despair and imprisonment that he endured as the classic fallen idol in the late 1960s. "There was a tremendous bond between Tommy and his grandfather, who was far worse than any of the modern agents, turning down several offers from clubs because he didn't think they were good enough for his lad. Some of the other things that emerged I had no idea about such as the time he and Frank Swift had an audience with the Pope.

"He described in hilarious terms how Swifty stood in front of the Pope and said that he wasn't going to kiss his bloody ring no matter what. I'll never forget how Tommy said the two of them just broke up laughing but then they were two very young men then. There were other things that came out too, how he made films with Diana Dors. I didn't realise that he was a Brylcreem sex symbol of his age, driving flash sports cars similar to the George Best image two decades. He told me it was while he was sitting low down in one of his sports cars in Nottingham when this incredible pair of legs walked by. Tommy said that he made up his mind there and then that he would marry the owner – who turned out to be Gaye. That's how they met." It was Gaye who walked arm-in-arm with her husband on October 7, 1984 after Lawton had been lured to a social club at Meadow Lane under the pretext that he would be discussing the forthcoming series of features about his life with Williams and Pauline, his wife. "We had arranged a This Is Your Life evening for Tommy, to help launch the series. Apart from Wilf Mannion, who was unable to attend, the entire England side that Tommy played with were there. The lights were all off as he made his entrance then I looked at him as he walked in. He was absolutely gobsmacked.

"There were over 300 guests on their feet. Charlie Williams, the former Doncaster Rovers footballer cum-comedian did the Eamonn Andrews bit. It was a most wonderful night for Tommy and everyone who was present that evening." As a consequence of Lawton's story being printed in the *Evening Post*, he became a *cause celebre* in London. His tale ignited something in the national conscience and Fleet Street publications were stirred to, for them, unprecedented heights of fervour and interest in a feature North of Watford. "Suddenly he was in demand. Nationals ran abridged versions of our series and he appeared on chat shows and television," Williams recalls. "But the culmination of it for me was when a guy at Brentford got in touch. He remembered Tommy well but he actually thought that he was dead. When he read that he was still alive, he decided to organise a testimonial for him." It took the form of an International XI against a Brentford side, which was then a decent team in the old Third Division.

Tommy stayed in London and on the night of the game, Thames TV had him on their chat show to preview it. Gerry Francis, the former England captain, had put together a team of all stars that included Stan Bowles, all skilful players who could play a bit." Both teams formed a guard of honour that night, and when Tommy walked out, over 7,000 supporters got on their feet and applauded him every inch of the way through that tunnel and onto the pitch.

It had been less than a year since Lawton had stooped disillusioned with life into the office of the editor of the *Evening Post* determined that he would not cast off the ghosts of his past. Williams remembers that balmy evening vividly. "I don't mind telling you that I cried my bloody eyes out. The stature of the man had changed considerably and the man that came into my office twelve months previously had shed 20 years in age as he stood on that pitch. His shoulders were back, wearing a smart blazer and the lot. Let's be honest, he had been re-infected with the game. He'd got the bug back again. The ovation was quite incredible." That was just the start of a friendship that spanned Williams's period in Nottingham. A weekly column, *Lawton's Law,* became an integral part of the newspaper. Williams, who frequented both grounds either side of the River Trent, recalls that Brian Clough, also writing a regular column, had enormous respect for Lawton.

"There aren't many men in the game that you can say that about when it comes to Cloughie. He fitted the criteria of being a centre-forward and from working-class stock. Above all, though, he was a rebel and Cloughie felt a natural affinity towards him." Symbols of the bond between Williams and Lawton and the esteem in which the former player held the newspaper editor are in evidence at his Saltash home. A stunning set of porcelain figures depicting Britain's finest XI in their club colours – Matthews, Lawton, Finney and more – hold pride of place in the study along with engraved crystal glass goblets. "They were all mementoes presented to Tommy once he had re-emerged back into the limelight. On a Monday morning he would sneak into my office when I wasn't there and leave them on my desk. He knew I would refuse them if I was in. 'For Christ's sake Tommy, take them back,' I would tell him. He felt he owed me something but I said to him it was a two-way thing. He was more important to my newspaper than the paper was to him. But he wouldn't hear of it."

Lawton's public persona was greater now than it had been for many years. He was once more feted by organisations and decorated charity events, locally and nationally. One less publicised appearance took place on the Welsh borders when Williams's brother Les asked if Lawton would attend an annual game in aid of a young lad who had died of leukaemia. "It was the most dreadful of days but Tommy must have put a couple of hundred on the gate. We stood in the hut that was changing rooms, bar and shelter. I kept apologising to Tommy for subjecting him to all this but he was brilliant. People, young and old, would come up to him some saying that they remembered him from his Everton days and wanting his autograph. He had time for a chat with all of them. Then every so often he would wipe the condensation off the windows and look out at the match. Because the game was so important to the youngsters on the pitch he made sure that it was important to him. He wanted to show that he was absorbed."

Despite the uplifting nature of the trip to North Wales, it was to be the last one that Gaye, the love of Lawton's life, would attend. She died shortly after in 1988 from a rapidly developing cancer. Her grieving husband would never fully recover from the loss. Williams went to the funeral, a Roman Catholic one, which recognised Gaye as a lapsed Catholic who had been married twice. "The whole thing was so sad. I remember the priest being far less than fulsome in his soliloquy about Gaye. There was such an atmosphere in the church. Someone pointed out that Gaye's first husband was standing at the back, a figure in the shadows. Gaye had been a considerable beauty in Nottingham circles and it was that fabulous pair of legs that Tommy spotted that turned out to belong to his future wife.

"It was a huge scandal in the city at the time. Gaye had left a very rich businessman to marry a superstar, then had stood by Tommy even when he was in the gutter, there was no money coming in and people who owed

Tommy great sums of money turned their back on him. It tended to give an abrasive edge to her personality and on first meeting most people would think: 'Hey, I don't really like this woman'. But it was merely a defence mechanism built up over the years. On further acquaintance, you realised it was just a facade. She had developed this armour to protect her and Tommy from the rigours of what might come against them. Beneath it all was a fiercely loyal wife and on that last trip to North Wales the Gaye we dropped off back in Nottingham after dinner and a long journey was totally different to the one we picked up earlier in the day. I felt she deserved far better at her funeral "

Lawton was devastated. He became more reclusive even though his column dominated the sports pages of the *Evening Post* each Tuesday night. He broke his hip in a fall and Williams recollects driving to the Queen's Medical Centre with his wife Pauline to visit, only to discover that staff could not locate him. "There was a sense of irony which we couldn't help but see the funny side of. How could they possibly lose arguably England's greatest centre-forward on one of their wards." Lawton's son, Tommy junior, organised the final move of his father's life, to sheltered accommodation at Bakersfield, a suburb of Nottingham that once more brought him within a close distance of Meadow Lane. "Irene who ran the place was terrific. She loved Tommy and at his funeral she was there right on the front row. He got back into the swing of things although he was never quite in the same robust health.

"My paper ran a series called *Old and Cold* events which was designed to raise money for pensioners because the government was being so bloody parsimonious when old people were dying of hypothermia all over the place. One night we had a function at a working man's club with a group, comics, pies and pints sort of thing. But the weather was dire, it was blowing a gale, there were blizzards and the temperature was way below zero. Nottingham folk being Nottingham folk turned out to pack the place but I was sincerely hoping that Tommy, being one of the *Post's* team, would not attempt to come. Sure enough, he turned up and I said to him 'what the hell are you doing out on a night like this.'

"After a short time, he was starting to sign autographs and talking to those who wanted to meet him. 'Look,' he said. 'I'm old, cold and I'm here so for Christ's sake get me a pint and stop whingeing.' Bearing in mind he had a walking stick by then, he sat and talked for over three hours as queues formed to have a chat. The lovely thing for Tommy was that he had come full circle. He held no jealously or envy for modern day players and their earnings. His attitude was totally different from when I first met him. He had few regrets and just said good luck to them. He had recognised that the game was much faster and rarely criticised players, who he knew had become more like athletes.

"It was a far cry from his days having a fag with Swifty in the England dressing rooms when the pair didn't give a sod for Walter Winterbottom, some posh prat who signed the expenses and organised the transport. The daft thing was, out of the whole generation of his players, Tommy, with his athletic prowess and ability to head a ball, would have been the most likely to be a leading light in the modern era. I once asked him who he thought England's best centre-forward was at that time and instead of Alan Shearer or Gary Lineker, he picked Les Ferdinand. He felt he was vastly underrated and I suppose he was as near to the modern day equivalent of Tommy as you could get."

Upon his death, Williams penned a personal tribute in his West Country newspaper. He led off with one of the many anecdotes that Lawton shared with him and others who listened, with an all-consuming passion and intensity, to his tales about his life and times. He wrote: *"The schoolteacher in charge of a kids' match was sprinting up and down the line like a demented greyhound. "Run, run, run,' he was bellowing to his young charges. "Move, move, move'. An elderly man watching this pantomine could stand it no longer. He walked up the teacher: "Look mate,' he said, "Never mind all this run, run, run. Get them to play the ball, dwell on it and love the ball and to think'. " Oh, yeah. And who the bloody hell are you?" Nobody son. Nobody at all. "*

LAWTON – THE FIGURES

Burnley
Signed 10th Feb 1935 (amateur) 9th Oct 1936 (professional)
Debut 28th Mar 1936 v Doncaster Turf Moor D1-1
Debut (pro) 10th Oct 1936 v Tottenham Turf Moor W3-1 (Lawton 3, youngest ever to score
league hat trick)

1935/36   7 league appearances 5 goals
1936/37   18 league appearances 11 goals
Total   25 games   16 goals

Everton
Signed 31st Dec 1936 Fee £6,500 (under 21 record)
Debut 13th Feb 1937 v Wolves Molineux L2-7 (Lawton 1)
1936/37   10 league appearances 3 goals
1937/38   39 league appearances 28 goals
1938/39   38 league appearances 34 goals
Total   87 games   65 goals
(nb in the abandoned 1939-40 season Lawton made three appearances and scored four goals)
FA Cup
1936/37
22nd Feb R5r- Tottenham White Hart Lane L3-4 (Lawton 1)
1937/38
8th Jan R3 – Chelsea Stamford Bridge W1-0
22nd Jan R4 – Sunderland Goodison Park L0-1

Chelsea
Signed 7th Nov 1945 Fee £11,500 (club record)
Debut 10th Nov 1945 v Birmingham City (Stamford Bridge) L2-3 (Lawton 2)
Debut (Lge) 31st Aug 1946 v Bolton Wanderers Stamford Bridge W4-3 (Lawton 2)
1946/47   34 league appearances 26 goals
1947/48   8 league appearances 4 goals
Total   42 games   30 goals
FA Cup
1945/46
5th Jan R3-i Leicester City Stamford Br D1-1 (Lawton 1)
10th Jan R3-ii Leicester City Filbert St W2-0
26th Jan R4-i West Ham Utd Stamford Br W2-0
30th Jan R4-ii West Ham Utd Upton Park W1-0
9th Feb R5-i Aston Villa Stamford Br L0-1
12th Feb R5-ii Aston Villa Villa Park L0-1
1946/47
11th Jan R3- Arsenal Stamford Br D1-1
5th Jan R3r- Arsenal Highbury D1-1 (Lawton 1)
20th Jan R3r- Arsenal Tottenham W2-0 (Lawton 2)
25th Jan R4- Derby County Stamford Br D2-2 (Lawton 1)
29th Jan R4r- Derby County Baseball Grd L0-1

Notts County
Signed 13th Nov 1947 fee £20,000 (British record)
Debut 15th Nov 1947 at Northampton W2-1 (Lawton 1)
1947/48   19 league appearances 18 goals
1948/49   36 league appearances 20 goals
1949/50   37 league appearances 31 goals 1950/51 30 league appearances 9 goals
1951/52   29 league appearances 12 goals
Total   151 games   90 goals
FA Cup
1947/48
29th Nov R1- Horsham Meadow Lane W 9-1 (Lawton 3)
13th Dec R2- Stockton Meadow Lane D 1-1
20th Dec R2r- Stockton Ayresome Pk W 4-1 (Lawton 3)
10th Jan R3- Birmingham C St Andrews W 2-0

24th Jan R4- Swindon County Ground L 0-1
1948/49
27th Nov R1- Port Vale Meadow Lane W 2-1 (Lawton 2)
11th Dec R2- Barrow Meadow Lane W 3-2 (Lawton 1)
8th Jan R3- Plymouth Argyle Home Park W 1-0
29th Jan R4- Liverpool Anfield L 0-1
1949/50
26th Nov R1- Tilbury Meadow Lane W 4-0 (Lawton 1)
10th Dec R2- Rochdale Spotland W 2-1 (Lawton 1)
7th Jan R3- Burnley Turf Moor L 1-4
1950/51
6th Jan R3- Southampton The Dell L 3-4
1951/52
12th Jan R3- Stockton Meadow Lane W 4-0 (Lawton 1)
2nd Feb R4- Portsmouth Meadow Lane L 1-3 (Lawton 1)

Brentford
Signed 14th Mar 1952 Fee £11,500 (club record)
Debut 15th Mar 1952 v Swansea Town (Griffin Park) W 3-1
1951-52   10 league appearances 2 goals
1952-53   34 league appearances 13 goals
1953-54   6 league appearances 2 goals
Total   50 games   17 goals
FA Cup
1952/53
10th Jan R3- Leeds Utd Griffin Pk W2-1 (Lawton 1)
31st Jan R4- Aston Villa Villa Park D0-0
4th Feb R4r- Aston Villa Griffin PK L1-2 (Lawton 1)

Arsenal
Signed 18th Sep 1953 Fee £10,000
Debut 19th Sep 1953 v Manchester City (Highbury) D2-2
1953-54   9 league appearances 1 goal
1954-55   18 league appearances 6 goals
1955-56   8 league appearances 6 goals
Total   35 games   13 goals
FA Cup
1954/55 8th Jan R3- Cardiff City Highbury W1-0 (Lawton 1)
29th Jan R4- Wolverhampton Molineux L0-1

England
22nd Oct 1938	Wales Ninian Pk W 4-2 (Lawton 1 pen)
26th Oct 1938	FIFA XI Highbury W 3-0 (Lawton 1)
9th Nov 1938	Norway Newcastle W 4-0 (Lawton 1)
16th Nov 1938	Ireland Old Trafford W 7-0 (Lawton 1)
15th Apr 1939	Scotland Hampden Pk W 2-1 (Lawton 1)
13th May 1939	Italy Milan D 2-2 (Lawton 1)
18th May 1939	Yugoslavia Belgrade L 1-2
24th May 1939	Romania Bucharest W 2-0
28th Sep 1946	Northern Ireland Belfast W 7-2 (Lawton 1)
30th Sep 1946	Republic of Ireland Dublin W 1-0
18th Nov 1946	Wales Maine Road W 3-0 (Lawton 1)
27th Nov 1946	Holland Huddersfield W 8-2 (Lawton 4)
12th Apr 1947	Scotland Wembley D 1-1
3rd May 1947	France Highbury W 3-0
18th May 1947	Switzerland Zurich L 0-1
25th May 1947	Portugal Lisbon W10-0 (Lawton 4)
21st Sep 1947	Belgium Brussels W 5-2 (Lawton 2)
18th Oct 1947	Wales Ninian Pk W 3-0 (Lawton 1)
5th Nov 1947	Northern Ireland Goodison Pk D 2-2 (Lawton 1)
19th Nov 1947	Sweden Highbury W 4-2 (Lawton 1 pen)
10th Apr 1948	Scotland Hampden Pk W 2-0

16th May 1948	Italy Turin W 4-0 (Lawton 1)
26th Sep 1948	Denmark Copenhagen D 0-0
Full England	Caps:23 Goals 22

Great Britain
| 10th May 1947 | Rest Europe Hampden Pk W 6-1 (Lawton 2) |

England (War-time)
18th Nov 1939	Wales Wrexham W 3-2
2nd Dec 1939	Scotland Newcastle W 2-1 (Lawton 1) 8
th Feb 1941	Scotland Newcastle L 2-3 (Lawton 1)
17th Jan 1942	Scotland Wembley W 3-0 (Lawton 2)
18th Apr 1942	Scotland Hampden Pk L 4-5 (Lawton 3)
9th May 1942	Wales Ninian Pk L 0-1
10th Oct 1942	Scotland Wembley D 0-0
24th Oct 1942	Wales Molineux L 1-2 (Lawton 1)
16th Oct 1943	Scotland Maine Road W 8-0 (Lawton 4)
19th Feb 1944	Scotland Wembley W 6-2 (Lawton 1)
22nd Apr 1944	Scotland Hampden Pk W 3-2 (Lawton 2)
6th May 1944	Wales Ninian Pk W 2-0 (Lawton 1)
16th Sep 1944	Wales Anfield D 2-2 (Lawton 1)
14th Oct 1944	Scotland Wembley W 6-2 (Lawton 3)
3rd Feb 1945	Scotland Villa Park W 3-2
14th Apr 1945	Scotland Hampden Pk W 6-1 (Lawton 2)
5th May 1945	Wales Ninian Pk W 3-2
26th May 1945	France Wembley D 2-2 (Lawton 1)
14th Sep 1945	Northern Ireland Belfast W 1-0
19th Jan 1946	Belgium Wembley W 2-0
13th Apr 1946	Scotland Hampden L 0-1
11th May 1946	Switzerland Stamford Br W 4-1 (Lawton 1)
19th May 1946	France Stade Colombes L 1-2
Total War-time	Caps 23 Goals 24

England 'Extras'
| 21st Jul 1945 | Switzerland Berne L 1-3 |
| 24th Jul 1945 | Switzerland Zurich W 3-0 |

(nb- these matches, regarded as 'victory internationals' at the time, have subsequently been downgraded to Combined Services games – even though the England party comprised only 'Full' or 'War-time' International players).

Football League
21st Sep 1938	Northern Ireland Belfast W 8-2 (Lawton 4)
2nd Nov 1938	Scotland Molineux W 3-1
19th Feb 1947	Northern Ireland Goodison W 4-2 (Lawton 2)

Old England
| 30th Apr 1954 | 'Young England Highbury W 2-1 (Lawton 1) |
| 6th May 1955 | 'Young England Highbury W 5-0 (Lawton 2) |

War-time League
1939-40:- Everton 17 apps (16 goals); Aldershot 2 (4); Charlton 2.
1940-41:- Everton 21 (22); Aldershot 8 (13)
1941-42:- Everton 11 (6), Aldershot 16 (16); Millwall 1(1).
1942-43:- Everton 12 (4); Aldershot 15 (25); Notts Co 1.
1943-44:- Everton 25 (18); Aldershot 2 (8).
1944-45:- Everton 17 (16); Millwall 1.
1945-46:- Everton 5 (3); Chelsea 20 (19).

Grand Total
1938-55 International/Representative 104 apps (125 goals)
1936-57 Clubs League & Cup 627 apps (510 goals)
Total   731 games 635 goals

INDEX

132, 133, 134, 136, 140, 141, 153, 156, 162, 170.
Carver, Gerry 205.
Casey, George 60, 80.
Caskie, Jimmy 57, 58, 73, 96, 105, 106, 108.
Celtic 56, 94, 105.
Chapman, Herbert 29, 196, 198, 204.
Charles, John 174, 189.
Charlton Athletic 31, 65, 66, 71, 82, 84, 89, 99, 112, 117, 118, 125, 126, 130, 131.
Charlton, Bobby 214.
Chelmsford 199.
Chelsea 15, 16, 46, 47, 50, 52, 53, 55, 56, 65, 70, 77, 82, 84, 92, 120, 121, 122, 124, 125, 126, 129, 130, 131, 134, 135, 136, 137, 142, 144, 146, 161, 163, 171, 174, 175, 178, 184, 187, 190, 194.
Chester 47, 93.
Chilton, Allenby 172.
Clapton, Danny 195.
Clark, Albert 107.
Clayton, J G T 41.
Clegg, Tom 29, 35, 38.
Clough, Brian 16, 144, 169, 208, 217, 219.
Clyde 112.
Cochrane, Davie 107.
Cockburn, Henry 126, 128, 156.
Cole, Andy 147.
Collins, Ben 166.
Compton, Denis 9, 10, 90, 95, 97, 100, 101, 104, 192.
Compton, Leslie 105, 106.
Constantine, Learie 33.
Copping, Wilf 50, 58, 60, 61, 65, 67, 82, 92.
Cook, Billy 34, 39, 41, 43, 47, 60, 61, 64, 68, 69, 70, 71, 72, 73, 89, 90, 92.
Cooke, Harry 46, 47, 53, 59, 73, 110.
Cooper, Tom 50, 93, 107.
Coulter, Jackie 39, 41, 42, 47, 52.
Coventry City 66, 98.
Cowdrey, Colin (Lord) 190.
Crayston, Jack 58, 60, 61, 196, 199, 200.
Crewe 93, 94.
Crompton, Bob 103.
Crooks, Sammy 70.
Crozier, Joe 101, 102, 105.
Crum, Jimmy 56.
Crystal Palace 199.
Cullis, Stan 41, 50, 64, 67,

68, 73, 74, 75, 77, 78, 80, 82, 84, 90, 91, 94, 95, 97, 99, 101, 102, 104, 105, 106, 108, 115, 140, 162.
Cummings, George 77, 78, 79, 108, 109.
Cumner, Horace 65, 100.
Cunliffe, Jimmy 41, 47, 54, 56, 100, 104.
Czechoslovakia 132.
The Daily Dispatch 32.
Daily Express 61, 79, 158, 168, 207.
Daily Graphic 156.
Daily Mail 104, 158.
Daily Record 133.
Daily Sketch 72, 111.
The Daily Telegraph 69.
Darlington 108, 109.
Davies, Bob 106.
Davies, Frank 171, 172.
Davies, Harry 171.
Davies, Ian 199.
Davies, Jack 47.
Dawson, Johnny 56, 77, 78, 79.
Dean, Bill (Dixie) 8, 9, 12, 13, 14, 16, 21, 22, 29, 40, 41, 42, 43, 44, 47, 48, 49, 50, 52, 54, 55, 57, 58, 64, 73,104, 110, 120, 125, 154, 173, 179, 181, 214.
Deans, Tommy 147, 167.
Dearson, Don 108.
Delaney, Jimmy 105, 123, 172.
Delaney, Terence 8, 12, 13.
Denmark 44, 47, 132, 140, 160.
Dennison, Bob 11, 145, 166.
Derby County 16, 25, 63, 65, 66, 70, 73, 119, 126, 132, 133, 135, 138, 139, 153, 156, 157.
de Valera, Eamon 126.
Dickinson, Jimmy 181.
Dickinson, Syd 204.
Dickson, Bill 137.
di Stefano, Alfredo 9, 140.
Dodds, Jock 98, 105, 106.
Dodgin, Bill 122, 175.
Doherty, Peter 10, 88, 107, 119, 126, 133, 137, 141.
Doncaster Rovers 30, 73, 173, 174, 176, 206, 219.
Dooley, Derek 171.
Dors, Diana 218.
Dorsett, Dickie 64, 76, 95.
Dougal, Jimmy 77.
Dougal, Peter 47.
Dougall, Billy 31, 38. 51.

Drake, Ted 9, 13, 15, 55, 58, 60, 67, 68, 78, 161, 165, 188, 194.
Drewry, Arthur 163.
Duckhouse, Ted 202.
Duncan, Dally 70.
Dykes, Jimmy 107, 108.
Edelston, Maurice 8, 11, 12, 13, 100.
Edrich, Bill 41.
Edwards, Bertram 203.
Edwards, Ernest 104,
Edwards, George 104, 114, 127, 128, 165, 166, 196.
Eglington, Tommy 137.
Elliott, Jack 46.
England 6, 9, 11, 13, 14, 15, 17, 19, 20, 21, 22, 23, 24, 26, 29, 32, 35, 37, 44, 45, 47, 48, 50, 51, 53, 54, 55, 57, 60, 63, 64, 65, 66, 67, 68, 69, 71, 73, 74, 75, 76, 77, 78, 79, 80, 81, 82, 83, 84, 85, 86, 89, 92, 93, 94, 95, 96, 97, 98, 99, 100, 101, 102, 103, 104, 105, 106, 107, 108, 109, 110, 112, 113, 114, 116, 117, 118, 119, 120, 123, 124, 125, 126, 127, 128, 130, 132, 133, 134, 135, 137, 138, 139, 140, 141, 143, 145, 147, 148, 150, 151, 153, 155, 156, 157, 158, 159, 160, 161, 162, 163, 164, 165, 172, 173, 174, 175, 177, 181, 186, 189, 194, 198, 199, 200, 202, 206, 207, 213, 214, 216, 217, 219. 221, 222.
England Schools 24,
Evans, Billy , 11, 147, 167.
Evans, Dennis 188, 189.
Evans Willie 35.
The Evening Express 47.
Evening News (Nottingham) 145, 203, 208.
Evening Post (Nottingham) 177, 209, 210, 216, 219, 221.
Evening Post (South Wales) 30.
Evening Standard (London) 61.
Everton 8, 9, 10, 12, 13, 21, 24, 25, 30, 38, 39, 40, 41, 42, 43, 44, 46, 47, 48, 49, 50, 51, 52, 53, 54, 55, 56, 57, 58, 59, 60, 61, 62, 63, 64, 65, 67, 68, 69, 70, 71, 72, 73, 74, 75, 76, 77, 78, 80, 82, 84, 85, 86, 87, 88, 89, 90, 93, 94, 96, 99, 101, 105, 107, 108, 109, 110, 112, 117, 118, 120, 127, 130, 153, 154, 155, 165, 166, 172,

Bibliography

Tommy Lawton	Football Is my Business	Sporting Handbooks	1946
Tommy Lawton	Soccer The Lawton Way	Nicholas Kay	1954
Tommy Lawton	My Twenty Years of Soccer	Heirloom	1954
Tommy Lawton	When The Cheering Stopped	Golden Eagle	1973
Matt Busby	My Story	Souvenir	1958
Walley Barnes	Captain of Wales	Stanley Paul	1953
Ton Whittaker	Arsenal Story	Sporting Handbooks	1958
Nick Walsh	Dixie Dean	Macdonald & Jane's	1977
Raich Carter	Footballer's Progress	Sporting Handbooks	1950
Frank Swift	Football from the Goalmouth	Sporting Handbooks	1948
Charles Buchan	A Lifetime in Football	Phoenix House	1955
Jimmy Seed	The Jimmy Seed Story	Phoenix House	1957
Bryon Butler &			
Ron Greenwood	Soccer Choice	Pelham Books	1979
Alec Stock	A Little Thing Called Pride	Pelham Books	198
Alec Stock	Football Club Manager	Routledge & Kegan Paul	1967
Billy Wright	Captain of England	Stanley Paul	1950
Peter Doherty	Spotlight On Football	Art & Educational	1947
Stan Mortensen	Football Is My Game	Samson Low, Marston & Co	1949
David Miller	Stanley Matthews	Pavilion	1989
Stanley Matthews	The Way It Was	Headline	2000
David Ball	Dell Diamond	Hagiology	1998
George Hardwick	Gentleman George	Juniper	1998
Nick Varley	Golden Boy	Aurum	1997
Torn Finney	Football Round The World	Museum	1953
Paul Agnew	Finney - A Football Legend	Carnegie	1989
Gary James	Joe Mercer, Football With A Smile	ACL & Polar	1993
Neil Franklin	Soccer At Home And Abroad	Stanley Paul	1956
Jimmy Guthrie	Soccer Rebel	Davis Foster	1976
Jack Cox	Don Davies 'An Old International'	Stanley Paul	1962
Paul Joannou	The Hughie Gallacher Story	Breedon	1989
David Prole	Football in London	Robert Hale	1964
David Downing	Passovctchka	Bloomsbury	1999
Jack Rollin	Soccer At War	Willow Books	1985
Bryan Horsnell &			
Douglas Lamming	Forgotten Caps	Yore	1995
Peter Jeffs	The Golden Age of Football	Breedon	1991
Ed. Brian Glanville	The Footballer's Companion	Eyre & Spottiswoode	1962
LaurieMumford	Centre Forwards: The Great Ones	Pelham	1971
Maurice Edelston &			
Terence Delaney	Masters of Soccer	Naldrett Press	1960
Ian Ross &			
Gordon Smailes	Everton A Complete Record	Breedon	1988
Ken Rogers	Goodison Glory	Breedon	1998
Ron Hockings	Ninety years of the Blues	Hockings	1995
David McVay	Notts County Football Club	Archive	1988
Keith Warsop	The Magpies	Sporting And Leisure	1984
Tony Brown	The Official History of Notts County	Yore	1996
Ed. Eric White	100 Years of Brentford	Brentford FC	1989
Dan Jackson	Positively Brentford	Dan Jackson & Polar	1997
Phil Soar &			
Martin Tyler	Arsenal The Official Illustrated History	Hamlyn	1986
Jeff Harris	Arsenal Who's Who	Independent	
		UK Sports Publications	1996
Fred Ollier	Arsenal A Record	Breedon	1995
Gareth M Davies &			
Ian Garland	Welsh International Soccer Players	Bridge Books	1991
Nick Gibbs	England The Football Facts	Facer Books	1988
Mike Payne	England The Complete Post-War Record	Breedon	1993
Barry J Hugman	Football League Player's Records	Arena	1988
Ed. Tony Brown	The AFS Football Annual 1935/36	Tony Brown	1997
Ed. Tony Brown	The AFS Football Annual 1936/37	Tony Brown	1997
Ed. Tony Brown	The AFS Football Annual 1937/38	Tony Brown	1997
Ed. Tony Brown	The AFS Football Annual 1938/39	Tony Brown	1997
Tony Brown &			
Keith Warsop	Tommy Lawton	Tony Brown	1999
Eds. Glenda &			
Jack Rollin	Rothmans Football Year Books	Headline/Queen Anne Press from 1971